Vocal Traditions

Vocal Traditions: Training in the Performing Arts explores the 18 most influential voice training techniques and methodologies of the past 100 years. This extensive international collection highlights historically important voice teachers, contemporary leaders in the field, and rising schools of thought. Each vocal tradition showcases its instructional perspective, offering backgrounds on the founder(s), key concepts, example exercises, and further resources. The text's systematic approach allows a unique pedagogical evaluation of the vast voice training field, which not only includes university and conservatory training but also private session and workshop coaching.

Covering a global range of voice training systems, this book will be of interest to those studying voice, singing, speech, and accents, as well as researchers from the fields of communication, music education, and performance. This book was originally published as a series in the *Voice and Speech Review* journal.

Rockford Sansom, PhD, is a voice coach in theater and a voice trainer in business and politics. He is Editor of the *Voice and Speech Review* and has published *The History of Voice Pedagogy: Multidisciplinary Reflections on Training*.

Vocal Traditions
Training in the Performing Arts

Edited by
Rockford Sansom

LONDON AND NEW YORK

First published 2023
by Routledge
4 Park Square, Milton Park, Abingdon, Oxon, OX14 4RN

and by Routledge
605 Third Avenue, New York, NY 10158

Routledge is an imprint of the Taylor & Francis Group, an informa business

Introduction, Chapters 1, 2 and 4–18 © 2023 Voice and Speech Trainers Association
Chapter 3 © 2019 Amy Leavitt. Originally published as Open Access.

With the exception of Chapter 3, no part of this book may be reprinted or reproduced or utilised in any form or by any electronic, mechanical, or other means, now known or hereafter invented, including photocopying and recording, or in any information storage or retrieval system, without permission in writing from the publishers. For details on the rights for Chapter 3, please see the chapter's Open Access footnote.

Trademark notice: Product or corporate names may be trademarks or registered trademarks, and are used only for identification and explanation without intent to infringe.

British Library Cataloguing-in-Publication Data
A catalogue record for this book is available from the British Library

ISBN13: 978-1-032-40832-3 (hbk)
ISBN13: 978-1-032-40837-8 (pbk)
ISBN13: 978-1-003-35491-8 (ebk)

DOI: 10.4324/9781003354918

Typeset in Minion Pro
by codeMantra

Publisher's Note
The publisher accepts responsibility for any inconsistencies that may have arisen during the conversion of this book from journal articles to book chapters, namely the inclusion of journal terminology.

Disclaimer
Every effort has been made to contact copyright holders for their permission to reprint material in this book. The publishers would be grateful to hear from any copyright holder who is not here acknowledged and will undertake to rectify any errors or omissions in future editions of this book.

Contents

Citation Information		vii
Notes on Contributors		x
	Introduction: Framing the "Vocal Traditions" Series *Rockford Sansom*	1
1	Cicely Berry and the Central School Tradition *David Carey*	4
2	Linklater Voice Method *Kristin Linklater*	13
3	Rodenburg Voice and Speech *Amy Leavitt*	22
4	Fitzmaurice Voicework *Jeff Morrison, Saul Kotzubei and Tyler Seiple*	34
5	Lessac Kinesensics *Marth Munro, Deborah Kinghorn, Barry Kur, Robin Aronson, Nancy Krebs and Sean Turner*	42
6	Knight-Thompson Speechwork *Philip Thompson, Andrea Caban and Erik Singer*	54
7	Estill Voice Training® *Kimberly M. Steinhauer and Mary McDonald Klimek*	64
8	The Roy Hart Tradition *Kevin Crawford and Noah Pikes*	70
9	The Sharpe/Haydn Method *Edda Sharpe and Jan Haydn Rowles*	82
10	Miller Voice Method *Scott Miller, John Patrick, Liam Joynt and Kristi Dana*	88

CONTENTS

11	A Voice Pedagogy Based in Middendorf Breathwork *Jeff Crockett*	97
12	Vocal Combat Technique *D'Arcy Smith and Chaslee Schweitzer*	106
13	Somatic Voicework™ The LoVetri Method *Andrew R. White*	114
14	Breathwork Africa *Marj Murray and Ela Manga*	123
15	Steiner Speech *Geoffrey Norris*	132
16	Seven Pillars Acting Technique *Sonya Cooke, Tiffany Gilly-Forrer, Cynthia Bassham, Victoria Myssik, Adam Thatcher and Thomas Varga*	138
17	Vibrant Voice Technique *Pamela Prather*	148
18	Acting and Singing with Archetypes *Bill J. Adams and Christine Morris*	157
	Index	163

Citation Information

The chapters in this book were originally published in various volumes and issues of the journal *Voice and Speech Review*. When citing this material, please use the original page numbering for each article, as follows:

Introduction
Framing the "Vocal Traditions" Series
Rockford Sansom
Voice and Speech Review, volume 16, issue 2 (2022) pp. 220–222

Chapter 1
Vocal Traditions: Cicely Berry and the Central School Tradition
David Carey
Voice and Speech Review, volume 14, issue 1 (2020) pp. 86–95

Chapter 2
Vocal Traditions: Linklater Voice Method
Kristin Linklater
Voice and Speech Review, volume 12, issue 2 (2018) pp. 211–220

Chapter 3
Vocal Traditions: Rodenburg Voice and Speech
Amy Leavitt
Voice and Speech Review, volume 14, issue 1 (2020) pp. 96–107

Chapter 4
Vocal traditions: Fitzmaurice Voicework
Jeff Morrison, Saul Kotzubei and Tyler Seiple
Voice and Speech Review, volume 11, issue 3 (2017) pp. 339–347

Chapter 5
Vocal traditions: Lessac Kinesensics
Marth Munro, Deborah Kinghorn, Barry Kur, Robin Aronson, Nancy Krebs and Sean Turner
Voice and Speech Review, volume 11, issue 1 (2017) pp. 93–105

Chapter 6
Vocal traditions: Knight-Thompson Speechwork
Philip Thompson, Andrea Caban and Erik Singer
Voice and Speech Review, volume 11, issue 3 (2017) pp. 329–338

Chapter 7
Vocal Traditions: Estill Voice Training®
Kimberly M. Steinhauer and Mary McDonald Klimek
Voice and Speech Review, volume 13, issue 3 (2019) pp. 354–359

Chapter 8
Vocal Traditions: The Roy Hart Tradition
Kevin Crawford and Noah Pikes
Voice and Speech Review, volume 13, issue 2 (2019) pp. 237–248

Chapter 9
Vocal Traditions: The Sharpe/Haydn Method
Edda Sharpe and Jan Haydn Rowles
Voice and Speech Review, volume 14, issue 3 (2020) pp. 342–347

Chapter 10
Vocal Traditions: Miller Voice Method
Scott Miller, John Patrick, Liam Joynt and Kristi Dana
Voice and Speech Review, volume 12, issue 1 (2018) pp. 86–95

Chapter 11
Vocal Traditions: A Voice Pedagogy Based in Middendorf Breathwork
Jeff Crockett
Voice and Speech Review, volume 16, issue 2 (2022) pp. 247–255

Chapter 12
Vocal Traditions: Vocal Combat Technique
D'Arcy Smith and Chaslee Schweitzer
Voice and Speech Review, volume 16, issue 2 (2022) pp. 223–231

Chapter 13
Vocal traditions: Somatic Voicework™ The LoVetri Method
Andrew R. White
Voice and Speech Review, volume 11, issue 2 (2017) pp. 240–248

Chapter 14
Vocal Traditions: Breathwork Africa
Marj Murray and Ela Manga
Voice and Speech Review, volume 16, issue 2 (2022) pp. 232–240

Chapter 15
Vocal Traditions: Steiner Speech
Geoffrey Norris
Voice and Speech Review, volume 16, issue 2 (2022) pp. 241–246

Chapter 16

Vocal Traditions: Seven Pillars Acting Technique
Sonya Cooke, Tiffany Gilly-Forrer, Cynthia Bassham, Victoria Myssik, Adam Thatcher and Thomas Varga
Voice and Speech Review, volume 16, issue 2 (2022) pp. 256–267

Chapter 17

Vocal Traditions: Vibrant Voice Technique
Pamela Prather
Voice and Speech Review, volume 12, issue 1 (2018) pp. 96–104

Chapter 18

Vocal Traditions: Acting and Singing with Archetypes
Bill J. Adams and Christine Morris
Voice and Speech Review, volume 14, issue 3 (2020) pp. 335–341

For any permission-related enquiries please visit:
http://www.tandfonline.com/page/help/permissions

Notes on Contributors

Bill J. Adams, DMA, is an art song specialist, opera and musical theater performer, arts administrator, and associate professor. He has presented Acting and Singing with Archetypes workshops at SETC, the Florida Theatre Conference, and as a guest artist at Belmont University and UNCG, USA. Bill J. is a master teacher of Acting and Singing with Archetypes as well as Estill Voice Training, and he coordinates the performing arts programs in the Department of Performing and Visual Arts at Nova Southeastern University, Fort Lauderdale, USA.

Robin Aronson is a professor of Voice and Acting in the Department of Theatre. As a Lessac-Certified Trainer®, Robin recently served as the vocal coach for *The Tempest Reimagined* project with the Philippine Educational Theatre Association in Manila. Robin has taught International Lessac workshops in Australia, Ireland, England, Croatia, the Philippines, and Austria. Ms. Aronson has also created a Lessac training program to be able to earn Lessac Practitioner Status for graduate students in performance. This past spring, Robin was closely working with the first international intern in the history of Southern Miss from the National Institute of Dramatic Art in Sydney, Australia. Robin is currently serving as the president for the Lessac Training and Research Institute. She has been the voice and dialect coach for the past 13 years for the Southern Miss Theatre main stage productions, has earned four excellence in directing awards from the Region IV Kennedy Center American College Theatre Festival, and is a member of Actor's Equity Association.

Cynthia Bassham has been teaching for over 30 years and has been a professor of Teaching at the University of California, Irvine, USA, since 2005. She has taught and coached at several other institutions including South Coast Repertory, Stanford University, and Oregon Shakespeare Festival. Cynthia received her MFA from the American Conservatory Theater in San Francisco and her BA from the University of Washington, Seattle, USA. She is a lead trainer for the Fitzmaurice Institute and has been the director of Certification since 2015. She is a proud member of AEA, SAG-AFTRA, and VASTA.

Andrea Caban is an assistant professor and the head of Voice and Speech in the Theatre Arts Department at CSU, Long Beach, USA. An award-winning solo artist, she has performed her original works in Colombia, the UK, South Africa, Costa Rica, Spain, and across the US. She is an associate director and master teacher of Knight-Thompson Speechwork, an associate teacher of Fitzmaurice Voicework, and an associate editor for the *Voice and Speech Review*. Her current research interests are as follows: adapting actor voice and accent training for the care of people living with ALS to prolong the ability to speak without the use of assistive devices; arts-based research theatrical performance forms such as auto-ethnography, community-based theater, and investigative theater; and various projects in the medical humanities. She is the dialect expert on HowCast.com demonstrating over 35 accents, a theatrical production coach, and a speaker coach for TED talks. She received her MFA from UC Irvine, USA.

David Carey is currently the Resident Voice and Text director at the Oregon Shakespeare Festival. A voice teacher for over 40 years, David worked as an assistant to Cicely Berry at the Royal Shakespeare Company for four years during the 1980s. David and his wife, Rebecca Clark Carey, have published three books – *Methuen: Vocal Arts Workbook and DVD* (2008); *The Verbal Arts Workbook* (2010, revised 2018 as *The Dramatic Text Workbook and Video*); and *The Shakespeare Workbook and Video* (2015).

Sonya Cooke is an assistant professor of Acting and the head of Undergraduate Performance at Louisiana State University's School of Theatre, Baton Rouge, USA. Founder and author of *Seven Pillars Acting*, Sonya opened and ran two acting studios, namely Seven Pillars Acting Studio: Los Angeles and Actor's Studio of Orange County. Her book, *Seven Pillars Acting*, is the textbook for students of the technique, as well as at a growing number of universities and institutions across the country. A member of SAG-AFTRA, Sonya is a working actor in television, film, theater, commercial, and voice-over mediums.

Kevin Crawford studied under Roy Hart from 1967 until 1975 and is a founding member of the Roy Hart Theatre company. He toured extensively with the company for over 20 years before moving to Ireland, where he was a member of faculty at the School of Drama at Trinity College. In 2001, he was awarded an MA in Voice Studies from the Royal Central School of Speech and Drama. In 2004, he was engaged by the Accademia dell'Arte in Arezzo, Italy, where, until 2018, he directed the MFA in physical theater in partnership with Mississippi University for Women.

Jeff Crockett teaches at USC and Access Acting Academy, a studio for blind and low-vision actors. He was the head of Voice at ACT in San Francisco for 22 years. In Italy, he taught at l'Accademia Nazionale d'Arte Drammatica, Prima del Teatro, and Teatro Due. He has coached at numerous regional theaters and has been a guest teacher at Columbia, DePaul University, University of Maryland, and Stanford University. He trained at the Royal Central School of Speech and Drama, receiving an Advanced Diploma in Voice Studies (distinction), is certified to teach the Alexander Technique, and is a practitioner of Middendorf Breathwork.

Kristi Dana is a visiting assistant professor of Voice and Speech at Penn State University, USA (AY 2017–2018). She served as interim head of MFA Acting, Brooklyn College, CUNY 2016–2017. Vocal coaching includes Liz Lerman's *Healing Wars* and *Marie Antoinette* at Soho Rep. Kristi was mentored by Scott Miller, hosted in part at the Graduate Acting Program at NYU Tisch School of the Arts. She is certified in Knight-Thompson Speechwork and holds a Certificate of Completion from the Michael Chekhov Association. Her degrees include MFA, acting, Brooklyn College, CUNY; MA, theater education, Emerson College; BA, theater arts, Penn State University. She is an associated teacher of MVM.

Tiffany Gilly-Forrer is from Portland, USA, and completed her MFA in acting at Louisiana State University, Baton Rouge, USA, where she earned her certification to teach Seven Pillars Acting. She currently teaches for two studios in North Carolina: Acting Out Studio

NOTES ON CONTRIBUTORS

and In-Studio. Recent work includes a self-produced cabaret at Don't Tell Mama in NYC, dialect coaching for UNCGreensboro, and starring in local commercials. www.tiffany-gillyforrer.com.

Liam Joynt serves on the faculty at the Graduate Acting Program of NYU Tisch School of the Arts where he teaches voice and vocal coaches. He is a certified teacher of Knight-Thompson Speechwork. He has been on faculty at Fairleigh Dickinson University and Maggie Flanigan Studio and taught in the BFA and BA programs at Rutgers University, New Brunswick, USA, where he received his MFA. As an actor he has worked in megabudget and no-budget films, daytime and primetime TV, and Off-Broadway and regional theater. He has produced world premiere productions for playwrights including Lee Blessing, Samuel Brett Williams, and Lia Romeo. He is the co-founder of MVM Studio, co-contributor to Miller Voice Method, and MVM Master Trainer.

Deborah Kinghorn is a Lessac Master Teacher®. She teaches acting, voice, and movement at the University of New Hampshire, USA, where she serves as the director of Acting and where she received the UNH Teaching Excellence Award in 2011. She has been the voice, dialects, and text coach for over 100 shows in many theaters and universities, and she has taught in Croatia, South Africa, Brazil, England, Puerto Rico, and Finland. She is a Fulbright Scholar and the co-author of *Essential Lessac: Honoring the Familiar Body, Spirit, Mind* (2014), which provides simple yet concrete instruction toward well-being. As a long-standing member of the Lessac Training and Research Institute (LTRI), she was honored to receive their Leadership Award in 2009. She continues to act and direct and recently began producing plays with her husband through their company, RMJ Donald Productions.

Saul Kotzubei teaches voice workshops and private clients in Los Angeles and around the world. He is also a lead trainer in the Fitzmaurice Voicework Teacher Certification Program. A performer with a master's degree in Buddhist studies and wide-ranging acting training that includes a year studying clown with Philippe Gaulier, Saul has taught Fitzmaurice Voicework at NYU's BFA program (CAP 21); at the Actors Center in New York; and in workshops throughout North, Central, and South America, as well as Europe. In addition to teaching voice, Saul teaches public speaking and does a wide range of communication-related consulting. He holds an MA from Columbia University, USA, and a BA from Wesleyan University, Middletown, USA.

Nancy Krebs graduated in 1972 with a BA in Theatre from the University of Maryland, Baltimore County, USA, and went on to graduate school at the Dallas Theater Center under the leadership of Paul Baker. She has been a professional actor/singer since 1975 and is a member of AEA, AFTRA, and SAG. She is a Lessac Master Teacher® leading workshops around the US and abroad and has served as the resident voice/ dialect coach for the Annapolis Shakespeare Company for the past 5 years. She is also working in the same capacity for countless professional productions in the Baltimore – Washington region since 1994. She teaches Voice Production in the Theatre Department of the Baltimore School for the Arts and operates her own private studio: The Voiceworks. She is also a singer/songwriter and a recording artist, having released seven albums of critically acclaimed original Christian meditational music, which continue to receive airplay around the world.

Barry Kur is a professor emeritus at Penn State University School of Theatre, Lessac Master Teacher®, and voice/speech specialist for 30 years of Penn State's BA, BFA, and MFA

NOTES ON CONTRIBUTORS

performance programs and served as the school's associate director. For the Lessac Institute, Kur serves as the director of Certification and leads the Teacher Training Workshops and One-Week Introductory Workshops. He has had teaching residencies in South Africa, New Zealand, the UK, and Croatia. He was a founding faculty member of the South Carolina Governor's School for the Arts and Humanities. Kur is the author of the textbook *Stage Dialect Studies—A Continuation of the Lessac Approach to Actor Voice and Speech Training*. He has been the voice, speech, dialect, and text coach for over 100 professional and academic productions. He is the recipient of Penn State's George W. Atherton Award for Teaching Excellence and the Lessac Institute's Leadership Award. Kur is a past-president of the Voice and Speech Trainers Association and the Lessac Training and Research Institute. He currently chairs the VASTA Awards, Scholarships, and Grants Committee.

Amy Leavitt is approaching her seventh year of concentrated study with Patsy, training both in the US and in Europe and has been teaching her work since 2015. She is a member of the first class to be accredited as a Patsy Rodenburg Associate (PRA) and has played an integral part in the development of the Patsy Rodenburg Academy.

Kristin Linklater is the artistic director of the Kristin Linklater Voice Centre in Orkney, Scotland, and professor emerita at Columbia University, USA. Her book *Freeing the Natural Voice* has sold over 150,000 copies and has been translated into six languages. *Freeing Shakespeare's Voice: An Actor's Guide to Talking the Text* was published in 1992. From 1963 to 1996, she taught and coached at New York University; Emerson College; the Stratford Festival in Ontario; the Guthrie Theatre; the Open Theatre; the Negro Ensemble Company; and Shakespeare & Company in Lenox, USA. From 1997 to 2013, she was a professor of Theater at Columbia University, USA. As an actor, she has played most of Shakespeare's women and some of his men, and since 2014, she teaches year-round workshops at her residential center in the Orkney Islands with participants coming from 35 different countries.

Ela Manga is committed to sharing breathwork on the continent and further afield. Her integrated and conscious approach to wellness, alongside her unique focus on breathwork, has been a catalyst for healing and change across many communities and sectors from business to education. Dr. Manga is an integrative medical doctor, specializing in energy management and author of *Breathe: Strategising Energy in the Age of Burnout*.

Mary McDonald Klimek has been a professional musician and singing voice teacher since the early 1970s, an Estill Voice Training® enthusiast since 1990, and a speech-language pathologist since 1995. She currently lives in Maine, but much of her professional life was spent in Boston: teaching in music schools and colleges; performing in recitals, operas, and oratorios; and providing professional voice therapy for injured actors and singers at the Massachusetts Eye and Ear Infirmary. Since that first encounter with Jo Estill, Mary has been committed to promoting the art and science of the human voice. She is an Estill Mentor and Course Instructor, Vice-President of Estill Voice International, and co-author and illustrator of *The Estill Voice Model: Theory &Translation*.

Scott Miller has 40 years in the training universe. Scott's diverse life paths include two sports at the professional level; a law degree from George Washington University; clerking at DC's Public Defender Service; time as a producer, actor, and director; a trainer of lead teachers; training in counseling and holistic practices; and for the last 15 years, a professor at NYU Tisch's Graduate Acting Program. Scott has trained professionals from over 50 countries; these include executives; managers; Oscar, Tony, and Emmy Award winners and nominees; Olympic athletes; news anchors; and the not-so-heralded individuals simply seeking improvement and fulfillment. Scott is the founder of Miller Voice Method.

Christine Morris is an actor, voice coach, teacher, and director based in North Carolina. She is an associate professor at UNCG Greensboro and also resident vocal coach at Triad Stage, an Equity theater in downtown Greensboro. She has been working with Vocal Archetypes since 2011, studying with Janet Rodgers and Frankie Armstrong in three intensives on Cape Cod, and performing in several featured presentations of the work at the VASTA conference in London in 2014. She was certified as a teacher in 2015. She edited the VASTA Newsletter in different capacities during its print incarnation (regional and associate editor; editor) and has served a term on the VASTA Board.

Jeff Morrison teaches voice, speech, and dialects to BFA and BA acting students at Marymount Manhattan College. He has taught at ART/MXAT at Harvard University, the Old Globe School/USD in San Diego, Tufts University, San Diego State University, the University of Northern Iowa, and the Heifetz International Music Institute. He is a certified associate teacher of Fitzmaurice Voicework (2000) and has assisted Catherine Fitzmaurice at workshops and certifications since 2002. He has coached for television and stage in New York, Los Angeles, San Diego, and the Midwest and is the former editor-in-chief of the *Voice and Speech Review*. He holds an MFA. from the University of Wisconsin, Madison, USA, and a BA from the University of Pennsylvania, Philadelphia, USA.

Marth Munro (PhD) specializes in bodymind and voice in behavior and performance. She is a Lessac Master Teacher®. She received the LTRI Leadership Award in 2016. She was one of the editors of the Lessac Festschrift (2009). She was the associate editor of several Voice and Speech Reviews (1999–2006). She has taught in South Africa, the US, Finland, and Croatia. She is a certified Laban/Bartenieff Movement Analyst™, certified NLP Life, Business and Executive, qualified sound therapist, qualified Hatha Yoga teacher, and Bio-, Neurofeedback practitioner. She is a professor extraordinaire at the Drama Department at the University of Pretoria, South Africa, and is rated as a researcher by the National Research Foundation in South Africa. She teaches performance voice, movement, and acting. She facilitates workshops in business communication and emotional competence. She still finds time for various artistic endeavors and practice-based research publications.

Marj Murray is the director at Breathwork Africa and a qualified breathwork practitioner who has a unique gift of working with young people. Her background in communication and coaching, as well as her own life experience, has afforded her deep insight in the human condition. Marj's passion is to equip young people with the ability to experience life fully.

Victoria Myssik is a writer and a professional international actor from Almaty, Kazakhstan, who is currently based in Los Angeles. She earned her MFA in acting at Louisiana State University, Baton Rouge, USA, and was certified as an instructor for Seven Pillars Acting technique. To date, Victoria serves as one of the leading teachers at the Actor's Studio of Orange County. Her research interests include the difference in translation of Chekhov's plays from Russian to English, the evolution of pronouns with gender diversity, and feminist revolution.

NOTES ON CONTRIBUTORS

Geoffrey Norris is an actor, director, storyteller, and teacher of voice, movement, and drama. He trained at the London School of Speech Formation and Dramatic Art, graduating in both English and German Speech, and he is a master teacher of Steiner Speech, Drama, and Movement, with 45 years of experience in the field. He has performed and given courses and workshops worldwide and worked with over 15 languages, applying the universal principles of Steiner Creative Speech. www.speechanddramastudio.com

John Patrick is the head of Voice and Speech for the Professional Actor Training Program at the University of North Carolina at Chapel Hill, USA. JP serves as resident vocal coach for PlayMakers Repertory Company and company vocal coach for Gulfshore Playhouse, Naples, USA. JP has taught for New York University Graduate Acting and NYU Steinhardt School, Rutgers University, Southern Methodist University, The Lyric Theatre and Queen's University in Belfast, Northern Ireland, Theater Academy at the University of the Arts at Helsinki, Finland, and New York Film Academy. He holds an MFA acting, Rutgers University and a BFA acting and musical theater, TCU. He is the Co-founder MVM Studio, co-contributor to Miller Voice Method, and MVM Master Trainer.

Noah Pikes was born in wartime London. He began study with Roy Hart in 1967, performing in inaugural and subsequent Roy Hart Theatre performances. He started teaching in 1973, moving with the group to France in 1975. He studied movement, contemporary dance, clown, and jazz improvisation, and he collaborated in a multi-octave "voice-music" group. In 1990, he moved to Zurich and had informal studies in Jungian and Post-Jungian psychology, developing the "Whole Voice" approach; he authored *Dark Voices: The Genesis of Roy Hart Theatre*. In 2001, with David Carey, he coled the London International Conference on "The Contribution of Alfred Wolfsohn, Roy Hart and Roy Hart Theatre to Vocal Expression."

Pamela Prather is an associate professor of Theater in the Conservatory of Theatre Arts at the State University of New York (SUNY) at Purchase. She has trained actors at the Yale School of Drama, NYU's Playwright's Horizon's BFA program, UCLA, Marymount Manhattan College, AMDA, and The School for Film and Television. Coaching includes Off-Broadway, regional theaters, and over 23 productions at the Tony Award-winning Alley Theatre in Houston. Pamela coaches and leads workshops for actors and professionals nationally and internationally. She holds certifications in Prana Yoga, Laughter Yoga, Fitzmaurice Voicework®, and Vibrant Voice Technique. She created Laughing Voice as a tool for expanding vocal range, resonance, emotional depth, and personal truth. www.pamelaprather.com.

Jan Haydn Rowles was the head of Voice and Dialect at Shakespeare's Globe from 2007 to 2010. She has provided voice and dialect coaching at the Royal Shakespeare Company, the Almeida, the Donmar Warehouse, the Royal Court, the Manchester Royal Exchange, the West Yorkshire Playhouse, Birmingham Rep, and the Salisbury Playhouse. Jan skills have also been employed on American and British films, radio, and TV dramas, such as HBO's *Game of Thrones* and Netflix's *The Alienist: Angel of Darkness*. She has provided accent coaching and teaching for LAMDA, East 15, Rose Bruford College of Speech and Drama, and Central School of Speech and Drama, among others.

Rockford Sansom, PhD, is a voice coach in theater and a voice trainer in business and politics. He is Editor of the *Voice and Speech Review* and has published *The History of Voice Pedagogy: Multidisciplinary Reflections on Training*.

xvi NOTES ON CONTRIBUTORS

Chaslee Schweitzer is an assistant professor of Voice at Oklahoma City University, USA, where she teaches voice, speech, and text in the BFA acting program. She has worked as a voice and/or accent coach for professional theaters and actors. Chaslee holds an MFA in theater voice pedagogy from the University of Alberta, Edmonton, Canada, and a BA in theater performance from Rocky Mountain College, Billings, USA. She is an endorsed instructor of the Emotional Body methodology.

Tyler Seiple is an actor, director, writer, producer, and freelance voice and speech coach in the Los Angeles area. He holds an MFA from the University of California, Irvine, USA, and a BA from the Ohio State University, Columbus, USA. He is an associate teacher of Fitzmaurice Voicework and a certified teacher of Knight-Thompson Speechwork, as well as the founder of his coaching company, *phonetic phreedom*. Tyler coaches productions and private clients throughout the Los Angeles area. He has taught at the University of California, Irvine, USA; California State University, Long Beach, USA; and Chapman University, Orange, USA, and at multiple studios in the Los Angeles area.

Edda Sharpe was the head of Voice and Dialect at The Shaw Festival Theatre in Canada for 20 seasons, where she continues to work as an associate. She has also coached for the Royal Shakespeare Company, numerous productions in the West End, London, UK, and the regions and for film and television. She was the head of Voice at East 15 Acting School and the principal dialect teacher on the MA in Voice Studies course at Central School of Speech and Drama. Edda is an accredited NLP master practitioner, providing high-level voice, personal impact, and communication training to business and public sector clients including Hiscox, Aviva, The Met Police, the Ministry of Defense, Disney, and CNN, among others.

Erik Singer is a freelance dialect coach for film and television. He is a master teacher of Knight-Thompson Speechwork and regularly teaches workshops in voice, speech, accents, phonetics, and text. He taught for a number of years in actor-training conservatory programs, including the MFA program at the Mason Gross School of the Arts at Rutgers University, New Brunswick, USA, and at HB Studio in New York City. His videos for wired discussing accent work in films have been viewed over nine million times and won a Webby award. He has played leading roles at Off-Broadway and at major regional theaters and has voiced numerous television and radio commercials, documentaries, animated shows, and New York Times best-selling audiobooks. Erik was the associate editor for the *Voice and Speech Review*. He is a graduate of the Webber Douglas Academy of Dramatic Art in London and of Yale University, New Haven, USA.

D'Arcy Smith is a professor of Voice, Speech and Dialects at The University of Cincinnati, USA. He brings over 20 years of experience as a professional actor, coach, and teacher of performers, working on well over 100 productions. He has used his vocal combat techniques in numerous professional productions and alongside fight coaches. He has trained extensively in a variety of voice techniques to help serve every level and voice type. He has created and tested Vocal Combat Technique specifically for the video game actor. www.darcysmithvoice.com

Kimberly M. Steinhauer, PhD, is the president and founding partner of Estill Voice International and travels the world teaching and certifying in Estill Voice Training®. She has been on the voice faculty at Point Park University, Pittsburgh, USA, taught in health sciences for Duquesne University, USA, and served as a singing voice specialist for the

NOTES ON CONTRIBUTORS

University of Pittsburgh Voice Center, USA. As a scientist, Dr. Steinhauer was awarded a federal grant to study voice motor learning, published in the *Journal of Voice*, in *Professional Voice: The Science and Art of Clinical Care*, 3rd ed, and has been the editor of The Voice Foundation Newsletter. As a singer, she has performed in a variety of venues and styles thanks to her Estill voice training.

Adam Thatcher is an assistant professor of Voice for the Actor at Ball State University, Muncie, USA. He is a professional actor based in Chicago. Recently, he has been seen at The Goodman Theatre's production of *An Enemy of the People* directed by Robert Falls. Adam earned his certification in The Seven Pillars Acting Program in August 2020.

Philip Thompson is the co-founder of Knight-Thompson Speechwork and a voice, text, and accent coach. He has coached more than 175 professional productions and has coached at five recipients of the Regional Theatre Tony Award: South Coast Repertory (31 productions), La Jolla Playhouse, Denver Center Theatre Company, the Cincinnati Playhouse in the Park (18 productions), and the Utah Shakespeare Festival, where he is the head of Voice and Text and the resident coach since 1999, coaching numerous shows including 28 of Shakespeare's 37 plays. He is a professor of drama, teaching voice, and speech in the MFA acting program at the University of California, Irvine, USA. He was the president of the VASTA as well as a board member and secretary. He also served on the Board of Directors for the University/Regional Theatre Association. He is a master teacher of Fitzmaurice Voicework and frequently teaches in the Fitzmaurice Certification Program.

Sean Turner (PhD) has degrees in Literacy, Special Education, and Theatre Arts. He is a Lessac-Certified Trainer® and has been the managing director of Lessac Training and Research Institute (LTRI) since 2013. He was one of the editors of the *Lessac Festschrift* (2009). He has presented and published nationally and internationally around arts-based research/education. His research interests include interdisciplinary approaches toward Kinesensics, Critical Discourse Analysis, Social Learning, Multimodality, New Literacies, Special Education, and Arts Based Education. Sean currently collaborates with multiple arts-based programs throughout the country and teaches at Hunter College, Mercy College, and Innovation Diploma High School, USA. He is a current member of the LTRI Research Committee and served as the president of LTRI from 2012 to 2013.

Thomas Varga is an actor, writer, and acting teacher based in Los Angeles. His acting credits have included work with the Oregon Shakespeare Festival and New Swan Shakespeare Festival; television airing on Freeform and Lifetime Movie Network; and upcoming appearances on original series for Apple TV+ and Hulu. Thomas also serves as game writer for Ember Lab, an award-winning narrative-focused video game development studio. He earned his MFA in acting from the University of California, Irvine, USA, and has been teaching the Seven Pillars Acting technique as a certified instructor since 2017.

Andrew R. White, BM, MM, AD, DMA, teaches at the University of Nebraska Kearney, USA. Previous faculty positions include Indiana University of Pennsylvania, University of Akron, Hiram College, Lake Erie College, Baldwin Wallace University Conservatory of Music, and Ashland University, USA. He holds certifications in levels I, II, and III of Somatic Voicework™ the LoVetri Method and served as an associate faculty at the Somatic Voicework™ The LoVetri Method Contemporary Commercial Music Vocal Pedagogy Institute in 2015. His article "Belting as an Academic Discipline" was published by *American Music Teacher* in 2011, and his article "Do Men Belt?" appeared in *Classical Singer* in 2016.

INTRODUCTION

Framing the "Vocal Traditions" Series

Rockford Sansom ⓘ

Creating the Series

Ultimately, the "Vocal Traditions" series is a collection of articles in the *Voice and Speech Review* (VSR) from 2017–2022 that focus on varying vocal pedagogies. This project sought to offer voice teachers a deeper knowledge of pedagogical history and a wider understanding of different voice training schools and traditions, which highlighted historically important voice teachers and schools of thought in the world of vocal training, particularly as it relates to voice and speech.

In many ways, I orchestrated the series of articles that I always wanted to read. When I was in an undergraduate actor training program, the voice and speech teacher exclusively taught a singular voice method, but the teacher never told us that. We just had "voice class." And while I grew from the training, I knew even then that the training lacked context to the wider field. The acting teachers acknowledged lineages and variety to acting methods and techniques. "I trained with Uta Hagen," or "We do Meisner in this class." And they also acknowledged that they offered a *perspective* on acting, and the teachers acknowledged that many other perspectives existed. This standpoint was not the case in my voice training classes.

In graduate school, the voice and speech instructor offered training from several different voice pedagogies, which I believe was a great luxury and benefit, but no resource gave a broader context to the field. For a grad school research project (in circa 2003), I wanted to examine different kinds of speech pedagogy. The VSR had just begun publishing at the time, but I neither had access to it nor knew it existed. And even if I had, those early VSR volumes did not include a systematic discussion of varying vocal pedagogies, at least to any significant degree. And even years later when I decided to focus on becoming a voice trainer, I still could not find a text that offered an expansive view of the field. Suffice to say, this gap in the literature has always bothered me, so when I became Editor of the VSR, filling this gap was a top agenda item.

Bartow's (2006) book on American actor training remains a favorite of mine. He edits a volume that looks at the major schools of American acting, as they existed at the turn of the twenty-first century. And without question, his book helped to inspire me to solicit and create this vocal series. I must also credit Saklad (2011) with her book, *Voice and Speech Training in the New Millennium: Conversations with Master Teachers*, since

Series Structure

This six-year endeavor began with an invitation to some of the more objectively well researched vocal pedagogy programs such as Knight-Thompson, Linklater, Lessac, Estill, Fitzmaurice, etc., but as the series evolved, it became an opportunity to include a wider body of vocal traditions. Personally, the more historical pedagogies captivate me like the Central School Tradition, Middendorf Breathwork, and Steiner Speech. My scholarship often centers on historical themes in voice training (Sansom 2016, 2019a, 2019b, 2021), and I delight in learning more about traditions that are almost lost to time. But the Vocal Traditions series makes room for modern training trends as well such as Vocal Combat Technique, Miller Method, and Seven Pillars Acting. And importantly, the series invites perspectives outside of an Anglo-American tradition such as Breathwork Africa and the Roy Hart tradition.[2]

Each article purposely follows the same basic structure. The authors were asked to write an overview, information about the founder(s), key concepts, and exercise examples.[3] If the pedagogy has a certification program, then the authors were invited to write about this element as well. Some authors followed this prompt strictly, while others took more liberties with the proposed outline when it suited their needs. My editing was not overly strict; I wanted the authors to feel they could showcase and represent their pedagogy individually. At the same time, this series unapologetically invites readers to compare vocal teaching theory. Too often vocal training is siloed (Sansom 2016, 2021). This series hopefully sparks curiosity about other pedagogies and pollenates vocal communities. My hope is that voice trainers will read about other kinds of teaching and seek it out, going beyond what they have studied and what they currently teach.

I see this series as an academic exercise; that is true. I wanted to document this moment in vocal training history, and I wanted to capture past and future trends. Simultaneously, I see this series as a gentle way to encourage the voice and speech field to play nicely with each other. The articles are easy-to-read, tangible ways to find new kinds of vocal "toys" and new training paths to explore. I have, of course, written about this series before in various VSR Editor Notes. But it occurred to me that I had never overtly framed the series and discussed it in detail. My six-year journey as Editor closes soon, so I wanted to take this opportunity to elaborate. There have been 13 general issues and 5 special issues during my tenure as Editor; they are all important, and I am proud of them. But this series remains the dearest to my heart because it has been a thread through all the yearly volumes and been with me the entire six years. It is a kind of love letter to the voice field. By learning about the vast span of vocal traditions, I have grown as a trainer, and I hope readers have too.

Notes

1. Certainly, other books and articles have examined different vocal pedagogy programs, but the goal of this series was to be systematic in the approach and broad in historical scope.

2. This article series focuses exclusively on English-speaking vocal training traditions in the performing arts. The discipline of voice pedagogy has roots and branches beyond the English-speaking world and beyond voice training in the performing arts. (See Sansom 2019a for wider resources.) Although pedagogies for many types of voice training certainly exist in a robust fashion beyond the English-speaking world, they are outside the scope of this article series. Moreover, this series is not exhaustive; there are other training programs and traditions. My goal was to capture as many as I could. Over the years, I made several attempts to have articles from various organizations that are not included, but for a variety of reasons, an article never materialized. And I simply may not have known about other programs. My hope is that this series continues beyond my tenure with the VSR to grow the series in perpetuity.
3. The article authors use the terms method, methodology, technique, approach, and tradition in varying ways. Anecdotally, I find that "method" tends to refer to a complete training system, whereas "technique" tends to refer to a body of exercises or a central concept. Nevertheless, I allowed authors the opportunity to define these terms as they see fit.

Disclosure Statement

No potential conflict of interest was reported by the author(s).

ORCID

Rockford Sansom http://orcid.org/0000-0002-9574-1308

References

Bartow, Arthur 2006. *"Training of the American Actor Training of the American Actor."* New York: Communications Group.

Saklad, Nancy. 2011. *Voice and Speech Training in the New Millennium: Conversations with Master Teachers*. Milwaukee, WI: Applause.

Sansom, Rockford. 2016. "The Unspoken Voice and Speech Debate [Or] the Sacred Cow in the Conservatory." *Voice and Speech Review* 10 (3): 157–168. doi:10.1080/23268263.2016.1318814.

Sansom, Rockford. 2019a. "The Emergence of a Profession: The History of Voice Pedagogy." *Voice and Speech Review* 13 (1): 1–4. doi:10.1080/23268263.2019.1573562.

Sansom, Rockford. 2019b. "Answer the Question." *Theatre, Dance and Performance Training* 10 (3): 303–304. doi:10.1080/19443927.2019.1667179.

Sansom, Rockford. 2021. "When Corporate Executives Sing: A Multidisciplinary Invitation." *Journal of Singing* 78 (2): 255–259. muse.jhu.edu/article/819674. doi:10.53830/KJVR1256.

Cicely Berry and the Central School Tradition

David Carey

ABSTRACT

Vocal Traditions is a series in the *Voice and Speech Review* that highlights historically important voice teachers and schools of thought in the world of vocal pedagogy. This article explores the history of the Royal Central School of Speech and Drama and the work of one of its most famous graduates, Cicely Berry. Key features of the pedagogy of the School's founder and early teachers are outlined, and Cicely Berry's unique contributions to voice culture are discussed.

Overview

For much of the twentieth century, the story of British voice teaching was focused on a number of influential institutions, including the Royal Academy of Dramatic Art (RADA), which was founded in 1904 by Beerbohm Tree and provided the first formal conservatory for actor training in the UK. But it is RADA's great rival, the Royal Central School of Speech and Drama, which has been the principal alma mater of voice teachers in the UK. Either directly or indirectly, the vast majority of voice teachers working in Britain in the twentieth century were products of the Central School and its pedagogical ethos.

The Central School of Speech Training and Dramatic Art (as it was then known) was founded in 1906 by Elsie Fogerty, a speech teacher and performer who had trained at the Paris Conservatoire, and Sir Frank Benson, a classical actor and director who managed the Stratford-on-Avon Shakespeare Festival for many years. Initially, the school focused solely on the training of classical actors, but Fogerty appreciated the value of verse-speaking, mime, and movement in the development of both a theatre culture and an educational culture in general. So, by 1908, she had created a three-year teacher-training course to produce speech and drama teachers who would go on to influence generations of children and actors. Among these teachers were such early acolytes as J. Clifford Turner and Gwynneth Thurburn, who both trained at Central shortly after the First World War. Thurburn was to go on to become Principal of Central toward the end of the Second World War, while Turner taught at both Central and RADA. Two other important Central graduates were Rose Bruford and Greta Colson, both of whom went on to be principals of drama schools with a strong focus on voice and speech teaching. My own voice teachers, for example, Jim House and Jacquie Crago, were both products of

Colson's school, the New College of Speech and Drama. More recently, of course, Patsy Rodenburg and Barbara Houseman trained at Central, in the 1970s and 1980s respectively. But the most widely-esteemed graduate from the Central tradition is Cicely Berry who, before her death in 2017, was perhaps the most influential voice teacher of the last 50 years.

Elsie Fogerty and the History of the Central Tradition

Elsie Fogerty was born on December 16 1865 in Sydenham, London. She was the only child of Irish parents. After developing an interest in acting and recitation as a child, she attended the Paris Conservatoire in 1883 where she received training from Louis-Arsène Delaunay, actor and professor of dramatic declamation, and Coquelin *aîné*, one of the leading actors with the Comédie Francaise. Later, in London, she trained with the American actor and teacher Hermann Vezin, who also taught Beerbohm Tree and Sir Frank Benson. Another mentor in London was the Anglican clergyman, Russell Wakefield, later Bishop of Birmingham. Fogerty died on July 4 1945 in Leamington Spa, Warwickshire.

During the 1890s Fogerty taught English and diction at the Crystal Palace School of Art and Literature and also held speech classes on Saturdays at the Royal Albert Hall. When Benson started his London School of Acting in 1901, Fogerty was appointed tutor of diction. These experiences led her to found (with Benson) the Central School in 1906 at the Royal Albert Hall.

Fogerty's approach to speech and diction eschewed the narrow focus of prevailing practice in elocution on the formation of oral postures for speech sounds. Instead, Fogerty developed a more holistic approach that recognized the importance of breathing, physical posture, and movement to voice and speech production as a whole.

Fogerty recognized the essential physiological basis of the voice, and she was therefore keen to root her training in healthy, anatomically correct practice. In 1912 she was introduced to Dr W. A. Aikin, who had recently published a practical book on the voice, which set out the anatomical and phonetic principles of voice and speech production and provided a thorough approach to the vocal development of both speaking and singing. She quickly recruited Aikin to her staff, where he remained for over 20 years. At the same time, Fogerty was deeply concerned with developing the standards and practice of verse speaking in the theatre and in society as a whole. Her mentor, Russell Wakefield, taught her to value the power of speech and the indivisibility of form and meaning in poetry, and to condemn the "false tradition of 'recitation'" which placed personal self-assertion before "all true faculty of poetic interpretation" (Fogerty 1929, x). Thus, Fogerty was establishing a fundamental principle of modern voice teaching: we (as teachers) are developing expressive skill in order to serve the writer's intentions, not the speaker's ego. This requires an imagination that is able to expand to enter the world of the poet and dramatist, not a personality which seeks to reduce the writer's world to one's own boundaries.

Aikin's work also established some fundamental principles which were to become the foundation of a systematic training of the voice and key features of the Central tradition that can be summed up in four words: Breath. Note. Tone. Word. He wrote:

The cultivation of the voice thus resolves itself into a threefold process, to be undertaken in the following order:

(1) The development of the capacity and conscious control of the breath.
(2) The conscious establishment of well-arranged positions and movements of the resonator which are to become half-conscious habits of speech.
(3) The free and unhampered use of the vocal vibrator in its natural relation to mental sound-perception and under the dominion of the breath.

(Aikin 1910, 15–16)

It is interesting to compare Aikin's threefold process with the writings of Fogerty, Thurburn, and Turner. In *Speech Craft* (first published in 1930), Fogerty follows the anatomical order of breath, note, tone, and word (Fogerty 1930). In *Voice and Speech*, Thurburn identifies the same sequence, but she goes on to assert that this is not "the best educational order" (Thurburn 1939, 25). Instead, she states: "The aim in training is to work upon the directly-controlled organs until their action becomes automatic, dealing only in an indirect manner with unconscious movements" (Thurburn 1939, 25). And she presents a pedagogical order of breath, muscularity, tone, and pitch. Turner, who seems to have been one of Aikin's closest disciples, prefers in *Voice and Speech in the Theatre* (first published in 1950) the breath, tone, note, word order implied by Aikin. All the authors also make a distinction between voice and speech, which Turner summarizes by saying, "Voice is instinctive and speech is an acquired habit" (Turner 1950, 1), and elsewhere states that the actor's instrument "is at one and the same time a tone-producing instrument [voice] and a word-producing instrument [speech]" (Turner 1950, 6).

In Aikin's work on breath, note, tone, and word, concepts such as central and rib-reserve breathing, the center note, the open throat and resonator scale, and muscular work on the organs of articulation all came into the voice field and formed central planks of most voice teachers' work in Britain up until at least the 1970s.

Breath

Aikin promoted central or intercostal-diaphragmatic breathing which focused on expansion of the lower ribs surrounding the solar plexus and contraction of the diaphragm, as far as it affected the upper abdominal wall. This was in contrast to other forms of breathing (costal and abdominal), which were seen as unhealthy at the time. He also advocated what came to be known as rib-reserve breathing—the maintenance of an expanded chest (specifically at the level of the sixth and seventh ribs) throughout a speech of some length while breathing diaphragmatically. Rib-reserve breathing was seen as beneficial both for general audibility and maintenance of pitch and tone. Fogerty, Thurburn, and Turner all advise central breathing for effective voice production and the use of rib-reserve for full breath control, although their pedagogical approach is slightly different in each case. Thurburn, for example, is the only writer who makes the point that "All exercises must be done as exercises [...], and never thought about in connection with the speaking of a poem or the reading of a passage" (Thurburn 1939, 58).

Note

The center note (a note toward the middle of one's singing pitch range or "compass") was advocated by Aikin and Turner as the best pitch to use for vocal practice. Subsequently, this has sometimes been modified to refer to the use of a note toward the middle of the speaking range (which is usually lower than the singing range). But in either case, the aim is to develop a speaker's use of a flexible pitch range and not one that is stuck with either too high or too low a center.

Tone

An "open throat"—one which is free from habitual constriction in either a vertical or horizontal dimension—is advocated by all of the voice practitioners discussed. Aikin builds on this open throat concept to develop his idea of the resonator scale, which is founded in the phenomenon produced by whispering through the shapes of the principal pure vowel sounds (monophthongs). Interestingly, Aikin complained that the FACE and GOAT[1] vowels were losing their purity in his day. For him, they were monophthongs, whereas today for most speakers of Received Pronunciation they are diphthongs.[2] Turner, following Aikin very closely, presents the resonator scale as "the means by which tone is developed through the natural working of the resonator" (Turner 1950, 39). Cultivation of the natural working of the resonator involved expansion of the oral and pharyngeal cavities and the acquisition of the ability to pass from one vowel shape to another without affecting the size of the resonator. This often required the use of a bone-prop—referred to by Thurburn as "Aikin's Bone Prop for Vowel Position" available from Bell and Croyden for sixpence in 1939 (Thurburn 1939, 69n). Although use of the bone-prop went out of fashion toward the end of the twentieth century, it has recently made a come-back thanks to British voice teacher and speech therapist, Annie Morrison. Her Morrison Bone Prop is available in eight colors and costs £12.99.

Word

Once freed from habitual tension, the muscles of these speech organs need to develop precision and flexibility of movement for accuracy in word formation. This pedagogical concept is what is often referred to as either articulation or muscularity in voice teaching, and all the Central authors provide very similar exercises for the different articulators and for specific vowel-consonant combinations in conjunction with tongue twisters or appropriate passages of text. In fact, all of the work on breath, note, tone, and word is consistently applied to work on text by each of the Central writers. Much of this text work is devoted to verse-speaking since, as Thurburn puts it, "[p]oetry stimulates the imaginative faculty and gives a heightened sense of perception. It also helps to develop greater appreciation for the happy use of words and choice of phrases" (Thurburn 1939, 84–5).

This is the tradition that Cicely Berry inherited, and it inevitably informed her early work as a voice teacher in the 1940s and 1950s. Before Berry's *Voice and the Actor* was published in 1973, Turner's book was the most widely used text in post-war actor training, and it is still available in a sixth edition edited by Jane Boston, who is currently the principal lecturer in voice studies at Central.

Cicely Berry and the Central Tradition

From her ground-breaking books on voice and text to her radical work with theatre companies, schools, and communities around the world, Cicely Berry's contribution to voice culture has been incalculable.

Born Cicely Frances Berry on May 17 1926 in Berkhamsted, Hertfordshire, she was one of five children. She revealed her independent spirit and passion for poetry at a young age when, as a child of seven, she would lock herself in the bathroom and recite from memory Longfellow's "Hiawatha" or Coleridge's "Rime of the Ancient Mariner" in order to escape her siblings.

She attended Eothen School for Girls in Caterham, Surrey, which she describes in *Text in Action* as "a minor public school [...] where one was not forced to be academic, and where poetry was spoken aloud in class" (Berry 2001, 33). She also recollects taking elocution classes which "awakened my ear to the music of language, to the subtleties of rhythms and cadence, and gave me the chance to practise all this out loud" (Berry 2001, 33).

After leaving school, she attended the Central School of Speech and Drama in London, where she trained as a voice and speech teacher under Gwynneth Thurburn. Thurburn's teaching and socialist philosophy greatly influenced Cicely's later work; and Thurburn must have quickly realized Berry's potential as a teacher of voice and text, for soon after Berry graduated in 1946 she was back at Central teaching voice and diction[3] in the acting program.

In 1951, Cicely married Harry Moore, an American actor who had trained at the "Method School" in New York. It is likely that Berry initially absorbed a Stanislavskian concern for the psychological aspects of an actor's process from her relationship with Moore. During their life together in London, as well as teaching on the acting course at the Central School, she maintained her own studio in Drury Lane, working with actors such as Peter Finch, Sean Connery, and Anne Bancroft. Working with actors in training and professional actors at the same time will have greatly informed her teaching and laid the foundation for her distinctive approach.

She will also have been strongly influenced by the artistic and socio-political changes that affected Britain during the 1950s and 1960s. In theatre training, these changes led to the rejection of established training norms in favor of more psychological, physical, and improvisatory approaches and a more naturalistic style of speaking. While some other Central teachers broke away from the school in 1963 to establish the Drama Centre (a London drama school famed for its Stanislavskian approach to acting), Berry remained loyal to her mentor, Thurburn. Nevertheless, when she wrote in *Voice and the Actor*, "Your voice must be accurate to yourself, so it needs to reflect not only what you think and feel but also your physical presence" (Berry 1973, 16), she was articulating a more nuanced approach to voice training than the older Central tradition; Berry advocated for an approach that spoke very much to young actors of the day.

In 1969, Cicely was hired by Trevor Nunn as voice director for the Royal Shakespeare Company (RSC). The following year she was appointed as Head of Voice, making the RSC the first theatre company to have a permanent full-time voice department. She served the company continuously until 2014, when she became the advisory voice director.

Cicely Berry and the RSC

The transition to the RSC brought Berry into contact with three different directors of classical work: Nunn, John Barton, and Terry Hands. In *Text in Action*, she writes eloquently about the methods she used to help actors develop their vocal potential while working with each director's process:

> I had to get each actor to enter the language on his/her own terms,
> while still being in tune with the overall directive, and so I began
> to find those exercises which would release them [...]. So in a Nunn
> rehearsal I would take individual actors aside and find ways to make
> them discover the extravagance of the language; with Barton I would
> get them to do a task of some sort to take their mind off the pointing
> up of the rhetorical devices; and with Hands I would have to get them
> to speak very slowly and quietly so that they could discover the
> imagery and texture of the language in their own particular way.
>
> (Berry 2001, 37)

This valuable exploration of language in rehearsal was a far cry from her work at Central, but it prepared her to work with Peter Brook on productions such as his famous *A Midsummer's Night's Dream* in 1970. Brook validated her approach and encouraged her to go further in exploring the connections between voice work and the actor's process. As her work developed, she documented its progression through a sequence of highly influential books, beginning in 1973 with *Voice and the Actor*, which was the first British book to provide a modern approach to voice. As Peter Brook observes in his foreword to the book, "Cicely Berry never departs from the fundamental recognition that speaking is part of the whole: an expression of inner life [...] She would never try to separate the sound of words from their living context" (Berry 1973, 3). Her pedagogy at this time, while clearly rooted in the Central tradition of physiological function and imaginative intention, emphasized the expressivity of the voice and muscularity of language in service of both character development and theatrical performance.

Berry recognized that a new generation of actors required a fresh approach to the work —one that eschewed a prescriptive technique for achieving the "right" voice but rather emphasized a method for opening up the potential of an actor's voice, releasing it from the limitations that impede vocal expressivity and transformation. She was particularly concerned with finding "the essential truth of the voice" (Berry 1973, 15), and she specifically felt that rib-reserve breathing produced an unreal voice. While she encouraged strength and muscularity in the intercostal muscles, particularly in association with the lower back ribs, it was the focus on the diaphragm and the abdominal muscles which became more important, and in *The Actor and the Text* (first published in 1987 and revised in 1992) she even notes a development in her own thinking from an upper abdominal focus to a deeper, lower abdominal one that is more in touch with one's feelings.

Her breath-work combined exercises for training the breathing musculature with work on resonance and was designed to help actors find their own vocal energy and quality which could then be connected to the energy of the word for full communication with an audience. For Berry, "the actor has to find the specific measure of the words he is using and relay them with clarity and accuracy [...] so that they can be heard without strain" (Berry 1973, 43). The work on muscularity that this required is rooted firmly in the Central tradition; for example, Berry still refers to the bone prop and uses the same sequences of vowel-consonant combinations as her teachers. With regard to the traditional concept of "note", Berry makes no reference to the idea of a center note, preferring to concentrate on achieving full use of chest resonance. She does, however, encourage the use of singing and intoning of text in order to open out the sound, while she has this to say with respect to an actor's vocal range:

> Inflection and use of range must always come from the specific attitude to your text. However, you can increase the flexibility of range by experimenting with pieces of text that require different pitches, and by consciously making yourself key them at different places in your range.

(Berry 1973, 42)

Beyond the RSC

By the mid-1970s Berry's work for the RSC was expanding beyond its primary focus on the actors into the educational sphere. She worked regularly with secondary school teachers and students, as well as youth theatres in many parts of the UK. And she developed a long-standing commitment to working with high security prisoners at Long Lartin prison in Worcestershire. This work sat comfortably with her political beliefs: a lifelong Marxist (apparently, she declared herself to be a communist while still at primary school), she devoted much of her work outside the RSC to social justice projects. In addition to her work in prisons and with schools, she also worked with the underprivileged across the world, most notably the Nós do Morro youth theatre in the favelas of Rio de Janeiro and the Cardboard Citizens theatre company of homeless people in London.

In parallel with this work, she continued to document her developing approach to text work. While her work on breath, resonance, and muscularity changed little, it was the work recorded in *The Actor and the Text* that broke new ground by providing a method of working on text that replaced a primarily intellectual approach with an emphasis on the physical roots of language and the power of words to effect change in both the speaker and the listener. *Text in Action* followed in 2001, taking as one of its themes a line from Thomas Kyd's *The Spanish Tragedy*: "Where words prevaile not, violence prevails." Subtitled "a definitive guide to exploring text in rehearsal," *Text in Action* provides perhaps the fullest account of Cicely's text work. In it she emphasizes her commitment to the centrality of collective work on text during the rehearsal process because, as she points out, "it not only opens our ears to the possibilities but it allows us to be provoked by the language. It frees the actor from the responsibility of making the sense clear and opens out the humour and the roughness" (Berry 2001, 95). And she argues that this kind of work is just as useful in creating a company as is the now traditional movement work that many directors favor because "it makes us listen in a different way, it makes us bolder in tackling text and gives a spontaneity to the speaking" (Berry 2001, 95).

Exercises in storytelling and passing text around help to develop a sensitivity to language and its physical manifestation in speaking, while engaging actors in listening to each other actively and creatively. Further work involves actors in jostling each other while speaking text or taking time to fulfill the meaning of each word in a speech in order to discover the action and even aggression in dramatic language.

Building on this collective work, Berry goes on to describe her work on subtext, rhetorical structures, and dialogue, using an extensive range of Shakespearean speeches and scenes to exemplify the exercises. In addition, she describes the kind of work one can do with writers such as Tennessee Williams, David Mamet, Edward Bond, Caryl Churchill, and Timberlake Wertenbaker.

Her book *From Word to Play* appeared in 2008, focusing on a detailed set of workshops, strategies, and exercises for directors to use at different stages of the rehearsal process. The stimulus for the book came partly from workshops for directors that Berry had been leading for several years under the aegis of Theatre for a New Audience in New York, but it also brought together much of what she had practiced in her own directing experience. Starting in 1985 with a production of *Hamlet* for the National Theatre education program, Cicely directed a number of Shakespeare's plays, perhaps most notably *King Lear* in 1988, which she liked to describe as Shakespeare's most Marxist play.

Among her many other achievements, Berry was awarded honorary doctorates from Birmingham University (1999)and the Open University (2001). She was honored by the British government in 1985 and in 2009 for her contributions to the arts and society, and she was awarded both the Sam Wanamaker prize for pioneering work in Shakespearean theatre in 2000 and the 2007 Samuel H. Scripps award for her extraordinary commitment to promoting the power of language in contemporary and classical theatre.

Cicely Berry died peacefully in her sleep on October 15 2017 at her Cornish care home.

The Person

A passionate, rigorous, and at times even fierce teacher, Cicely Berry was also warm and generous. Fun and funny, she was a humanist, Marxist, and challenging straight-talker, and she also knew the art of well-placed profanity and the shock of the lewd. But perhaps the most important thing to understand about her is that, for her, being a voice teacher is about the work. She was utterly selfless and tireless in her commitment to passing on her passion for language and for artistic vocal expressivity of the highest order. She sought no accolades and hated to be called a voice guru, for it was always about the work.

Cicely Berry left an immense legacy, both in her written work and in the hearts and minds of all the actors, teachers, children, and directors who came in contact with her. If you were not fortunate enough to know her personally, then you may still catch her spirit and her work through *The Working Shakespeare Library* of DVDs and workbooks that Applause Books published in 2003. This captures a set of workshops that Berry undertook in New York in the late 1990s with a group of British and American actors led by Blythe Danner, Samuel L. Jackson, Emily Watson, and Toby Stephens. In it you may discover the complete woman that is Cicely Berry.

Central Today

Today, The Royal Central School of Speech and Drama is a different institution from the one that Cicely attended, given the passage of time. Among a wide and diverse range of under-graduate and postgraduate courses is the MA/MFA in voice studies under the leadership of

Jane Boston. Boston, who trained at Central on the Advanced Diploma in voice studies (a forerunner of the current degree course), is also a Linklater-designated teacher and an academic with an interest in the history of vocal pedagogy and its documentation. The course, which is designed to serve the needs of graduates who wish to develop a career in voice teaching, takes an eclectic approach to vocal pedagogy while still honoring the Central tradition from which it has grown. Further information can be found by contacting the school:

The Royal Central School of Speech and Drama, Eton Avenue, London, NW3 3HY, UK enquiries@cssd.ac.uk

https://www.cssd.ac.uk/ma-voice-studies

Notes

1. FACE and GOAT are lexical sets (or vowel concepts) from John C. Wells (1982), who defines twenty-four lexical sets as a means to understand and define accents of English.
2. A number of mnemonics exist for the resonator scale; the one I was taught is "Who would know aught of art must learn and then take his ease."
3. At that time, "diction" work centered greatly on the speaking of verse of different styles and periods. Today, the term diction is often used to mean articulation, and in many ways the term diction is now antiquated.

Acknowledgments

Grateful acknowledgment to Gillyanne Kayes of Vocal Process Ltd for permission to adapt my essay "The History of UK Voice Teaching" in preparing this article. And equally grateful acknowledgment to Rockford Sansom for permission to adapt my obituary of Cicely Berry from the *Voice and Speech Review* (Volume 13, 2019) for this wider article on her work.

Disclosure statement

No potential conflict of interest was reported by the author.

References

Aikin, W.A. 1910. *The Voice*. London: Longmans, Green and co.
Berry, Cicely. 1973. *Voice and the Actor*. London: Harrap.
Berry, Cicely. 1999. *The Actor and the Text*. revised ed. Virgin: London.
Berry, Cicely. 2001. *Text in Action*. London: Virgin.
Fogerty, Elsie. 1929. *The Speaking of English Verse*. revised ed. London: J.M. Dent and Sons.
Fogerty, Elsie. 1930. *Speech Craft*. London: J.M. Dent and Sons.
Thurburn, Gwynneth L. 1939. *Voice and Speech*. London: James Nisbet and Co.
Turner, J. Clifford. 1950. *Voice and Speech in the Theatre*. London: Pitman.
Wells, John C. 1982. *Accents of English*. Cambridge: Cambridge University Press.

Linklater Voice Method

Kristin Linklater

ABSTRACT

Vocal Traditions is a series in the *Voice and Speech Review* that highlights historically important voice teachers and schools of thought in the world of vocal pedagogy. In this essay, Linklater Voice Method offers its overview, history, process, exercises, and details on teacher training. Written by the founder of Linklater Voice Method, the article particularly highlights the background of the method and its relationship to artistry and text.

Introduction and History of Linklater Voice Method

I began teaching when I was 21 years old, and the methodology I teach and have trained many others to teach is based in an approach to voice training for actors developed originally by Iris Warren in the 1930s and 1940s in London. Iris was interested in the emotional roots of voice, and she opened up a new world of exploration in a profession that had defined its esthetic parameters and set the boundaries of successful vocal performance. In the early twentieth century, the standards in the English theatre world were clear: sufficient projection to be heard in the back row of the theater, a pleasantly modulated range of vocal dynamics, and crisp articulation. The actor's voice was a musical instrument to be well-managed and expertly played. But Iris was dealing with successful actors on the West End stage in London who were losing their voices through the effort and strain of pushing for those desired effects.

Legend has it that at some time in the 1930s Iris was asked by a Freudian analyst if she could assist a patient of his who was unable to speak about his traumatic experiences. Iris got him to relax, breathe deeply, and feel the sound of his voice in his body. He immediately began crying, and with the flood of tears came a flood of words. That emotion had freed his voice. Iris started adapting her voice exercises to include the sensory impulses of thought and feeling. Time and again, her clients (many of the major West End actors of the day) recovered their voices as their emotional range was released. Her exercises were revolutionized to find their origins deep inside the sensory body rather than be managed by external abdominal and intercostal muscles. The voice was no longer a musical instrument to be beautifully played, but an expressively human instrument.

It took another 20 years or more for English actor training to catch up with Iris. It was not until the 1950s that mainstream English theatre evolved from its somewhat external, boulevard style of performance to an acceptance of the psychological realism of Stanislavski. Since the 1940s, Jacques Copeau's explorations into character work had begun to influence actor training in England, but in my judgment, it was the raw naturalism of American film acting that finally cracked the façade of English acting technique in the 1970s, 1980s, and thereafter.

American acting was steeped in Stanislavsky's methodology and (notoriously) in Lee Strasberg's Actors Studio approach, which dominated American actor training from the 1950s to the 1980s. But training for voice and movement was largely rooted in singing techniques, diction, and dance. These techniques required physical management and manipulation that distanced the performer from emotional and psychological impulse.

Iris died in1963, and that was the year I left London and went to the USA. I had been teaching at LAMDA (London Academy for Music and Dramatic Art) for 6 years and wanted a change. I thought I would visit New York for a year, and I remained in the States for 50 years. Iris's voice work spoke the same psycho-physical language as the Method, and over the next years, I developed her techniques in the fecund climate of psycho-physical exploration that became the human growth movement of the 1960s, 1970s, and 1980s.

The psychological diggings begun by Freud and Jung led to the rich explorations of psycho-physical behavior that branched out from Wilhelm Reich into processes developed by Fritz Perls, Ida Rolf, Stanley Keleman, and many others for releasing trapped emotions and trauma from clenched muscles in the body.

There were several pioneers in practical psycho-physical work. F. Matthias Alexander had great influence on psycho-physical reeducation, which began in the early part of the twentieth century. In the 1920s and 1930s, Mabel Elsworth Todd (*The Thinking Body*) developed somatic exercises to reeducate the body, known as "ideokinesis." And Moshe Feldenkrais brought his ideas to the United States in the 1970s. The work of these body work pioneers has been embraced by actors, dancers, and musicians.

What Alexander, Todd, and Feldenkrais did for the body Iris Warren did for the voice.

The voice work I teach has come to be called "Freeing the Natural Voice" rather than "The Warren Method" because *Freeing the Natural Voice* (1976) is the title of the book I wrote, which was first published in 1976. It has also come to be known as Linklater Voice Method because I am the author of the book. Iris never wrote about her work, saying it would be misunderstood if it were written down. To a certain extent she was right. The work belongs in the live breath of human bodies in a room together. But her underlying ideas were strong enough and true enough to rise above any misunderstanding of the exercises, and the book, revised and expanded by me is now a required text for all serious English-speaking actor training programs (Linklater 2006). It has also been translated into German, Spanish, Italian, Polish, Russian, and Korean with French, Romanian, and Chinese translations pending. The work is voice work, which transcends language difference and thus can travel across national boundaries. After all, voice can communicate without speech, but speech cannot communicate without voice. All human beings are born with breath and emotions and voices. And in that respect voice is universal, while speech is cultural.

This approach to voice and speech is organically linked to the actor training processes that have developed over the past hundred years in the search for performative veracity in the theatre. The Linklater vocabulary of training is umbilically and imaginatively connected to the vocabulary of Stanislavsky, Michael Chekhov, Sanford Meisner, Uta Hagen, and Stephen Wangh, among others.

My own history as part of this history of my voice work includes teaching at the NYU School of the Arts (before it became the Tisch School of the Arts), while also teaching and coaching some Broadway shows (e.g. the first *Hair*), the short-lived Lincoln Center Repertory Company (founded by Kazan and Whitehead), The Negro Ensemble Company, and several of the experimental companies such as The Open Theater and the Manhattan Project. In 1977 I moved to the Berkshires, teaching and acting with Shakespeare & Company for twelve years. From 1990 to 1997, I taught at Emerson College in Boston and began teaching regularly in Germany and Italy. 1997 brought me back to New York as Professor of Theater Arts in Columbia University's School of the Arts, where I was Chair for five years. After seventeen years at Columbia, in 2013 I retired and left the States to return to my native Orkney Islands in Scotland. There, I have built a Voice Centre and teach workshops throughout the year. (See linklatervoice.com for more detail.)

Overview

The Linklater Voice Method goes step-by-step through a practical series of exercises that begin with relaxation, awareness of breathing, and the experience of vibratory sound; then from jaw and tongue relaxation to opening the throat, and then the development of resonance and range. This culminates in an exploration of the articulating activity of lips and tongue. These organic psycho-physical experiences release the voice from inhibitory tension and restore the full gamut of three to four octaves of speaking notes that can reveal the full extent of human emotion and all the nuances of thought.

Dramatic and poetic texts are interwoven with the technical work. First, as the voice becomes free of restriction, we explore the experience of truthful speaking on a personal level. Then with the full range of resonating response available, we explore the versatility of the voice in the service of a wide variety of characters and styles. An organized sequence of text and verse exercises introduces the specific physical, emotional, and imaginative demands that Shakespeare makes of the voice.

Process

A simple picture of how the voice works shows us (1) the impulse to speak, (2) breath entering the body, and simultaneously, (3) vocal folds approximating, (4) vibrations reverberating through resonators, and (5) articulation into speech by the lips and tongue.

An equally simple picture contradicts every step on this easy road. The impulse to speak is halted by an inner voice: "Are you sure you want to say this?" "That's a stupid thing to say!" "Hold on," Wait a minute ..." "Dangerous!" Thus, impulse number two is interrupted, and the free flow of breath to diaphragm halts; the central breathing muscles hold hard, protecting the emotional impulse. If the need to speak is so strong that it overrides the lack of emotional breath response in the diaphragm and demands to be heard, then just enough breath is found under the collarbone to activate the vocal folds, and the muscles of the throat, the tongue, and the jaw provide supportive action substituting muscle for free breath. Occupied with the effort to compensate for breath, they close off access to the resonators, and the natural range and expressivity of the voice narrows.

For the person who wants to be an actor, step one is to free their personal self from the inhibitions of expression that have (almost inevitably) been learned through an upbringing and education that acculturates to societal norms.

Entering a rediscovery of how the voice works, we observe these habitual defensive activities and decide whether they serve our purposes or not. We become conscious of unconscious activity and can make a choice as to whether the observed function is optimal or not, according to the need for vocal communication.

The step-by-step exercises of the method I inherited from my teacher, Iris Warren, provide the means by which one can make that observation.

Key Features

Voice training for actors is paradoxical: one must develop the voice to its utmost potential in order, then, to forget about it, to sacrifice it—to let it be burned through by the heat of thoughts and feelings and moods and emotions. The voice conveys mood, emotion, attitude, opinion, confidence, conviction, restriction, inhibition, and a multitude of subtle shades of meaning that influence the speaker and the listener.

The voice reveals authentic character more than spoken words, because the voice is formed by breath and because breath is intrinsically connected to our senses, our psychology, our behavior, and our emotions; all of which are experienced in the body. Voice training for actors is not a matter of acquiring a skill. Voice is identity. It says, "I am." Voice is made of breath, and breath gives us life; thus, the actor must breathe as the character they are creating and donate their identity to the identity of the character, so that the character lives and is plausible.

Voice work is as necessary for actors who work mainly in television or film as it is for live theatre. The voice is the truth thermometer. Cameras and microphones zero in on the internal truth of a performance, and if a voice is not plugged into the true and transparent inner life of instinct and impulse, then the truth will not be revealed. The truth may be described by a voice that delivers a kind of running commentary on what is happening experientially. (And there are some styles of writing that choose that mode.) But in terms of high-quality acting, description comes a poor second to revelation: Voice is the revelatory channel through which thoughts and feelings are conveyed. Voice is a human instrument with all the complexities that this notion implies.

The intonations and inflections of voice, are collectively gathered in the word prosody.

> In linguistics, prosody is concerned with [...] such linguistic functions as the rhythm, stress, and intonation of speech. Prosody may reflect various features of the speaker or the utterance: the emotional state of the speaker; the form of the utterance (statement, question, or command); the presence of irony or sarcasm; emphasis, contrast, and focus; or other elements of language that may not be encoded by grammar or by choice of vocabulary. (as cited in Wikipedia 2017)

We each have our own personal prosody, and every writer (playwright, poet, prose-writer) also has their own prosody that reflects the backstory of the story, the backstory of the character, and the backstory of the writer. Actors must listen to these prosodic "backstories" while being conscious that their own prosody may distort that of the character. The actor's voice must be alive and elastic and unconfined by the dynamics of personal speaking habits. This demands recognition of habits of thinking as much as consciousness of habits of voice production.

The voice is the musical part of speaking, while speech is the deliverer of organized information. Voice conveys para-verbal and meta-verbal information, and that information comes from many different parts of the brain. The most obviously identifiable structures are the corpus callosum, motor cortex, prefrontal cortex, nucleus accumblens (emotional reactions), amygdala, sensory cortex, auditory cortex, hippocampus, visual cortex, and cerebellum. The nervous system deploys sensory, visceral, respiratory, laryngeal, and pharyngeal musculature to influence the tones, rhythms, and volume that can accurately reveal the inner state of the speaker.

Speech is more "encoded by grammar or by choice of vocabulary." But of course, voice and speech are inter-dependent. Speech involves rhythm, as the interplay of consonants and vowels riff on their intrinsic differences of longer and shorter, sharper or buzzier, murmurous or explosive, higher or lower in musical nature. Speech is governed by two major brain regions: well known as (1) Broca's area activating the lips and the tongue and (2) Wernicke's area that puts words together to make sense. Broca and Wernicke identified these areas in the late nineteenth century. This only matters to a voice practitioner in that it emphasizes the conscious work that must be done to bring speech and voice into a harmonious relationship. Clearly, Broca and Wernicke cannot live without the music of voice, but too often they tend to act as if they are the bosses. These days our voices are mostly imprinted with utilitarian, logical information. We do not speak poetry enough, or sing enough, or sigh out our longings, joys, sorrows, and loves enough to keep an even balance between voice and speech. Training the voice implies demoting Monsieur Broca and Herr Wernicke and promoting the Dionysus within. Or inviting the schoolmasters to join the dance.

From an artistic point of view, this is a fascinating time to be involved in voice and speech training. Neuroscience is shedding light on the brain functions that lead to speaking; the old dualistic view of mind versus body has been roundly challenged by scientists of all persuasions. We know that the body, the senses and the emotions are vital to the intelligence of the whole self.

Nevertheless, we have all grown up in an educational system that has an endemic commitment to dualism. The brain, reason, and rationality are valued over emotion and body. Growing up we do not know how to deal with the turmoil of our emotions; nobody offers us emotional education. Nobody suggests that speaking is a physical act engaging the senses, the emotions, and the breath. The act of speaking words is, thus, conditioned in an environment that exiles emotion. Words go from our rational speech cortex to our mouths, barely disturbing our bodies.

The voice teacher's job is to reunite brain and body experientially.

Voice teachers seek solutions to imperfect vocal communication by spotting the physical manifestations of inhibition, prohibition, and restriction and by reeducating those bodily effects. We teach our students how to relax the throat, the jaw, and the tongue, which have learned too often to clamp down on emotional expression; our students hum and ululate, shout, cry, and sing through a range of many octaves; we restore breathing to the full extent of its involuntary activity from the pelvic floor to the diaphragm and the ribs.

Thinking, feeling, and speaking are thus retrained. We need the word "mind" instead of "brain" when we explore how thinking works its way into speech. For working purposes, "brain" is the thing in the head, and "mind" is the experience of brain in the body. For "mind" to happen, the experience of thinking drops out of the head and into the body. Yes, we need to "get out of the head" (as so many acting teachers remind their students), but this does not mean stop thinking. When you are up in your head, you are thinking "about" something. When you drop your thoughts into your body, you are really thinking because you are feeling what you think.

In the past few decades, we have been led to the knowledge that we have not just one brain but at least (identifiably) three. There is the skull brain, the gut brain (or "enteric brain"), and the heart brain.

Developmentally, words emerged from the body brains into the skull brain, not the other way around.

According to neuro-cardiologists, 60–65% of heart cells are neuron cells, not muscle cells (Chang 2013). Numerically, the skull brain wins the neuron count with 86 billion neurons, versus 100 million neurons in the gut and 40,000 in the heart. (I suspect these numbers may not be set in stone.) However, the heart generates the largest electromagnetic field in the body. As measured by electrocardiogram, the heart's electrical field is about 60 times greater in amplitude than the brain waves recorded by electroencephalogram. The gut and the heart surely constitute the playing field for actors and singers. This information sheds the light of science on the subjective experience of the psycho-physical work of *Freeing the Natural Voice*. In practical terms, rerouting the balance of the activating impulses that govern speaking from skull brain dominance to body-brain dominance is a delicate reeducation of neuro-physiological pathways.

It cannot be repeated often enough that the breathing muscles and vocal muscles are part of the autonomic nervous system. They can be controlled voluntarily, but they function at their best on the involuntary circuits of mind and body. Thus, the first step in voice work needs to be the gradual development of an awareness that can detect counterproductive effort and tension in the conscious musculature and decide to let go of both. Muscular tension is there for a purpose; it is there to protect. It is holding on to energy. When that protection is no longer needed, the muscles can be persuaded to let go, and the energy can be redirected to more enlivening activity, such as breathing freely or letting the throat open up.

Exercises

In order to arrive at this place, first comes physical awareness with particular attention paid to the spine as the two-way message channel between brain and body and the essential support for the three main areas of breathing musculature: diaphragm, diaphragmatic crura, and intercostal muscles. These muscles are part of the involuntary systems of the body. You cannot tell your involuntary muscles what to do, but you can influence them through imagery—anatomical imagery, imaginative images, abstract images, and sensory imagery. In Linklater Voice, we spend a long time observing the anatomy of our natural, everyday breathing rhythm without organizing, interfering, or labeling "right" or "wrong." We banish the active verbs "inhale, exhale" or "breathe in, breathe out." With my hand on each student's abdominal wall, I say

> Relax this. Now relax here. Now here. Picture the center of the diaphragm; it drops as the breath enters, then the breath immediately escapes out. Then, there is a tiny pause, not a holding. Then you feel breath wanting to enter again, and all you can do is *yield* to that need.

I say "You don't have to breathe in. Breath will enter." I say "Let it happen. Let the air breathe you." I say, "Don't lengthen the breath; don't control it." Consciously giving up that unconscious breath control can be a disquieting mind–body moment. This is the first practice of how to prepare the ground for the shock of inspiration. After the outgoing breath, there is a moment where nothing happens; then breath reenters. I am inspired. Then immediately I expire. There is a moment of nothing. I have faith, and lo and behold breath comes in. I live. The organizing, controlling, logical brain goes quiet and merely observes. We observe the action of the diaphragm and know that the solar plexus, the emotional receiving and transmitting nerve center, is connected with it.

Floor work deepens the experience of relaxation and awakens consciousness of the action of the diaphragmatic crura, which run from the diaphragm down the spine and lead into the pelvic floor. In inspiration the crura assist the descent of the diaphragm. Imagery that includes the spaces in the pelvis and hip joints enlivens the connection between these deep breathing muscles and their engagement with the sacral plexus, which houses instinct and intuition.

When sound emerges from clear embodied imagery and is freed from auxiliary effort in the throat, sound finds its natural resonance.

Iris Warren's organically logical progression of exercises, which I embodied and expanded over the years, restores our birthright of a voice that can express the full range of human emotions and all the subtleties and nuances of thought through a three-to-four octave range of voice.

A series of large umbrella headings can map out the route:

(1) Physical Awareness (becoming aware of habitual tensions in order to choose and experience relaxation)
(2) Awareness and Release of Natural Breathing (observing, not controlling)
(3) The Touch of Sound (a visualization and tactile sensation of sound originating in the body)
(4) Freeing the Vibrations (releasing vibration as one relaxes lips, neck, head, and whole body with sound)
(5) Freeing the Channel (releasing inhibitory tensions from jaw, tongue, and soft palate in order to allow the breath to take responsibility for the voice)
(6) The Resonating Ladder: Chest, Mouth, Teeth (exploring the sensation of resonance in the bony cavities of the body that corresponds to different energies and pitches of the voice)
(7) Breathing Capacity (opening the ribs, stimulating the intercostal muscles, and strengthening the organic response between impulse and breathing musculature)
(8) Sinus Resonance (awakening the resonating cavities of the mid-face that strengthen the mid-range of the voice)
(9) Nasal Resonance (awakening the extrovert, carrying power of the bony nasal cavity that strengthens the top part of the speaking voice)
(10) Skull Resonance: Falsetto (releasing into the ecstatic voice)
(11) Range (becoming familiar with every resonating bone from the bottom to the top of one's three-to-four octave speaking range)
(12) Articulation (exercising the lips and tongue that articulate the free voice into words)

This is all sensory work, redirecting goals from any kind of auditory judgment to the visualization and tactile experience of the sounds of the voice in the body, trusting the rightness and pleasure of sensation rather than the judgment of the ear. The work only works as the voice is embodied, as the enteric brain of the senses and emotions overthrows the authority of the skull brain. This is thinking and feeling as one thing, rather than thinking about something. Once the full extent of the vocal potential has been absorbed, the speaker or singer's job is to activate the desire to communicate, think clearly, and commit whole-heartedly to the voyage of the communicative event.

Voice into Language

"Sound & Movement" is the name given to a sequence of improvisational voice and body exercises designed to provide a visceral link between voice, speech, and body. This organic progression of exercises explores the roots of language experientially, which I created to reroute Shakespeare's words from the contemporary head to the Shakespearean body. The work is, however, effective in a wide range of stylistic writing from Shakespeare to the present day. From primal sound to emotion, image and word impulses awaken the appetite energies of vowels and consonants. Group exchanges and partner improvisation open the flow of vibration between bodies. Listening and sounding become whole-body experiences. Neuro-physiological pathways between brain and body are reinvigorated and the actor's agility and sensitivity in responding to imagery is exercised. Vocal impulses galvanize physical movement. Voice and body provide the intellect with information. Meaning and interpretation emerge. The actor experiences "Let the words play you" rather than "Play with the words."

Text work

The transparency of the mid-voice is one of the keys to open communication. We explore devices such as speaking with the tongue outside the mouth, whispering, and speaking text on vowels only to continue the reconditioning of voice and speech from a head/brain-centered experience to an embodied, sensory experience.

Shakespeare is the Olympics of the art of acting. Shakespeare's text is the emotional, intellectual, physical, vocal personal trainer for actors. In *Freeing Shakespeare's Voice: The Actor's Guide to Talking the Text* (1992), I outline a step-by-step approach to the embodiment of Shakespeare's words and imagery, how to deal with the iambic pentameter and unravel the clues of figures of speech, rhetoric, and verse forms within the context of Elizabethan culture. In practice, all this is explored in physical, on-your-feet activity leading to sonnets, speeches, and scenes.

Singing

The anatomy of the voice is the same for speaking and singing. Singing is heightened expression. One can argue that singing happens when emotions can no longer be well expressed in prose or poetry. The demand upon the vocal anatomy is intensified by heightened emotional content. While many singers find freedom in their practice of my work, I am not a singing teacher. For singers I heartily recommend the book *The Naked Voice* (2007) by W. Stephen Smith. He was an early teacher of the great opera singer Joyce DiDonato. He has taught at Juilliard, Northwestern University, the Aspen Music Festival, and the Houston Grand Opera Studio.

Teacher Training

I have been training teachers since 1965 when the Rockefeller Foundation supported a year-long teacher training for 10 applicants. Over the years, the process has evolved. There are now more than 250 Designated Linklater Teachers (DLT) worldwide. Currently, a candidate must have substantial prior personal training in Linklater work before being considered as a trainee. Prerequisites for acceptance into the Teacher Training include: evidence of the seriousness and success of such prior work, assessment by a senior Designated Linklater Teacher, at least 50 hours of private lessons with a DLT, observation of a semester (or equivalent) of a senior DLT teaching, and a competitive audition.

Our English-speaking teacher training takes place every two years at my Voice Centre in Orkney, Scotland. Part One comprises three weeks within which trainees demonstrate their ability to lead a warm-up, and I teach the specifics of the progression of exercises. These sessions are filmed. Trainees practice-teach for a year. Part Two follows a year later and consists a demonstration of ability to teach the detail of exercises with practice students. As Master Teacher, I supervise these sessions with the support of other Senior DLTs.

When there are enough German and/or Italian candidates, teacher-training is organized in those countries.

Contact

- Information on the Orkney Kristin Linklater Voice Centre can be found at www.linklatervoice.com
- In New York, the Linklater Center for Voice is run by Andrea Haring and offers classes and workshops. See www.thelinklatercenter.com
- The European contact is linklater.eu

Disclosure statement

No potential conflict of interest was reported by the author.

References

Chang, Pao. 2013. "Scientific Evidence: The Heart is an Intelligent Electromagnetic Field Generator That Thinks." *Energyfanatics*, July 26. http://energyfanatics.com/2013/07/26/scientific-evidence-heart-intelligent-electromagnetic-field-generator-thinks/.

Linklater, Kristin. 1976. *Freeing the Natural Voice*. New York: Drama Book Publishers.

Linklater, Kristin. 1992. *Freeing Shakespeare's Voice: The Actor's Guide to Talking the Text*. New York: Theatre Communications Group.

Linklater, Kristin. 2006. *Freeing the Natural Voice: Imagery and Art in the Practice of Voice and Language*. New York: Drama Book Publishers.

Smith, W. Stephen, and Michael Chipman. 2007. *The Naked Voice: A Wholistic Approach to Singing*. Oxford: Oxford University Press.

@ OPEN ACCESS

Rodenburg Voice and Speech

Amy Leavitt

ABSTRACT
Vocal Traditions is a series in the *Voice and Speech Review* that highlights historically important voice teachers and schools of thought in the world of vocal pedagogy. This essay introduces the reader to Patsy Rodenburg's teaching processes and artistic philosophy; her innovative marrying of voice, presence, and text work; and her distinctive approach to speaking Shakespeare.

Overview

There is no Rodenburg method as such, but rather a series of discoveries Patsy has made over her forty-five-year career of teaching. These discoveries have resulted in a clear sequence of work that is practical, thorough, and ever-evolving. An ardent educator, a champion of the human voice, and a world-renowned authority on Shakespeare, Patsy has honed a highly nuanced way to work with the voice, teaching people how to use the entirety of their voices with freedom, intimacy, and power in order to convey truthful passion with clarity of thought. Patsy's work has shaped speakers and awakened audiences worldwide.

Background

Patsy Rodenburg was born in 1953. "As a child, I had a considerable fear of speaking. I was sent to a speech specialist but continued to fear communicating. I do believe that we are called to face our fears. I entered voice work to understand my fear" (Women on Writing 2006, 1). In 1973 she began her training in voice studies at London's Central School of Speech and Drama, where she was mentored by Gwynneth Thurburn.

After Central, Patsy apprenticed with Sheila Moriarty for five and a half years, before Cicely Berry and Trevor Nunn brought her to the Royal Shakespeare Company in 1981. She worked alongside Cicely for nine years and recently completed eight years of service as a Governor on their Board. Also in 1981, she was appointed Head of Voice at the Guildhall School of Music and Drama, in which capacity she served for 36 years and where she currently serves as Professor of Text and Poetry.

In 1990, at the request of Richard Eyre, Patsy founded the Voice Department at the Royal National Theatre, serving as its director for 16 years. Patsy has served for over 20 years as the Director of Voice at the Michael Howard Studios in New York City,

---

This is an Open Access article distributed under the terms of the Creative Commons Attribution-NonCommercial-NoDerivatives License (http://creativecommons.org/licenses/by-nc-nd/4.0/), which permits non-commercial re-use, distribution, and reproduction in any medium, provided the original work is properly cited, and is not altered, transformed, or built upon in any way.

currently under the leadership of Gabrielle Berberich. She organized the voice program at the Stratford Festival Theatre in Stratford, Canada, and she served as a Distinguished Visiting Professor in the Theatre Division at the Meadows Schools of the Arts, Southern Methodist University in Dallas, Texas.

"When I was a child," Patsy recalls, "I wanted to be an archaeologist" (Rodenburg 1997, 37). Looking back, Patsy easily connects her childhood dreams with her adult reality. "Like archaeologists, voice teachers are constantly unearthing, cleaning, and then polishing lost voices. The difference is that to find and release a voice is a living and transforming experience" (37).

Internationally, Patsy has taught and presented her voice workshops in North America, Africa, Australia, Japan, India, and throughout Europe, often with high-profile actors, playwrights, and directors. Her students and clients are among the best-known actors and biggest stars of film and television of our generation, including Simon Russell Beale, Cate Blanchett, Orlando Bloom, Glenn Close, Daniel Craig, Daniel Day-Lewis, Dame Judi Dench, Olympia Dukakis, Paapa Essiedu, Joseph Fiennes, Ralph Fiennes, Hugh Jackman, Glenda Jackson, Nicole Kidman, Jude Law, Damien Lewis, Sir Ian McKellen, Helen Mirren, Gary Oldman, Bernadette Peters, Vanessa Redgrave, Alan Rickman, Fiona Shaw, Patrick Stewart, and thousands more.

She has worked with legendary playwrights, including Samuel Beckett, Caryl Churchill, Sarah Kane, Arthur Miller, Harold Pinter, and Tom Stoppard. She has collaborated with renowned directors, including Mike Alfreds, Declan Donnellan, Peter Hall, Martin McDonagh, Sam Mendes, Mike Nichols, Trevor Nunn, Deborah Warner, and Franco Zeffirelli. She has worked with preeminent theatre companies all over the world, including the Almeida Theatre, Cheek-by-Jowl, Comedie-Francaise, Donmar Warehouse, Moscow Art Theatre, National Theatre of Greece, National Theatre School of India, Peking Opera, Royal Court, Royal National Theatre, Royal Shakespeare Company, and Theatre de Complicite. She coached the original London musical productions of *Cabaret, Cats the Musical, Les Misérables*, and *Phantom of the Opera*, among others, as well as countless Shakespeare productions worldwide. She is the first woman to have taught Kabuki performers in Japan.

Some additional highlights of Patsy's career include:

- In 1995 she became an honorary member of the Voice and Speech Teachers Association (VASTA), receiving a Lifetime Distinguished Membership.
- In 1999 she was appointed an Associate at the Royal Court Theatre, London.
- In 2003 she contributed to the original release of BBC's *Walking with Cavemen*, a television documentary series about human evolution.
- In 2005 she was named an Officer of the Order of the British Empire (OBE) in the Queen's Birthday Honours for her significant contribution to drama and the arts.
- In 2006 she directed an acclaimed production of *King Lear* at the Electric Lodge theatre in Los Angeles.
- In 2010 she was listed at number 15 in the "Top 50 Most Influential People in Theatre" by *The Times* newspaper's "The Luvvie Power List."
- In 2011 she was awarded a National Teaching Fellowship for excellence in higher education teaching.

- In 2015 she established the Patsy Rodenburg Center for Voice and Speech at Michael Howard Studios, and launched the Rodenburg Master Teacher Certification program.
- In 2016 she devised and directed *Go, Make You Ready*, a play performed at the Guildhall School that reimagines Shakespeare's last moments, looking back on his life through selected sonnets and scenes.
- In 2019 she received the Freedom of London, a high honor shared with such guiding lights as Florence Nightingale, Nelson Mandela, and Winston Churchill.

Patsy's study has always been a passionate investigation into how people communicate. She has stayed open to learning, and she has gained vast insight into the qualities that are required for success. She thus has been able to transfer her coaching technique seamlessly from the stage into the realm of everyday life. People from all over the world have sought her out, resulting in an eclectic mix of students and collaborations.

Patsy's focus on vocal patterns and presence extends to those professions that require sophisticated and considered use of language, including speechwriting, lectures, and keynote addresses. In the corporate world, she began by working in call centers and with middle management, eventually coaching CEOs and Boards of Directors of top multinational corporations. In the political arena, she works with the most eminent politicians and states people. She teaches barristers and judges on a regular basis through the Gray's Inn in London. She works with Lewis Pugh in his quest to preserve the planet's oceans.

On a broader scale, Patsy works with groups to create ensembles, from Olympic athletes to professional football teams to Formula One race car drivers. She has helped puppeteers bring the voices of their puppets alive and has taught string quartets to perform in unison.

Perhaps most important, Patsy's work breaks down race and class and gender barriers and seeks to give voice to marginalized and disenfranchised cultures that have been silenced. As an advocate for Penal Reform in the UK, she has staged Shakespeare in maximum-security prisons and worked with the criminally insane for over 30 years. Alongside the treating psychiatrists, she has encouraged prisoners to write and to use their voices.

Patsy has taught her voice workshops in Africa, with the San people and the Maasai, and in underprivileged schools in Soweto in post-Apartheid South Africa; in Australia, with Aboriginal communities, where she was honored with a rare Corroboree; in the most poverty-stricken areas of India; in Northern Ireland, where she taught Shakespeare to mixed groups of Protestant and Catholic women; in Amsterdam, where she has conducted workshops with up to three hundred prostitutes at a time. And finally, Patsy works extensively with children, who do not know (or necessarily care) who she is.

Key Features

Formed under the pressure of performance and in concert with her own pragmatic nature, the through-line of Patsy's work is its practicality. Can you play it? Will it "read"? Is it the right tension for the job at hand? She gives a note only when she deems it can change someone at that moment, and she limits herself to three notes as the most an actor can absorb at one time. Patsy's processes are designed to solve problems as they present themselves. The training, always done on the text, is active and exact, never theoretical or academic, and she eschews generalities and abstractions. The transformations she elicits result from imagination and thought as delivered through breath and diction, and it is in this practical context that all of Patsy's work resides. Coupled with the practicality of Patsy's work is its relevance. She often remarks that "we teach in the times we live in." She brings Shakespeare's themes into the present, connecting his writing to our politics and our humanity today, now. As she draws attention to your feet and adjusts your spine, she speaks of what it means to "stand by your words" or to "be spineless."

The Craft of Voice Is a Structured Sequence that Begins with the Body

At the center of Patsy's teaching is the craft of voice, which she defines as the foundational work that results in a flexible, trained instrument capable of meeting the demands of heightened text. Until the body, breath, support, voice, and speech muscles are thoroughly worked and tuned, it is impossible to realize and release the physicality of language. She describes craft as repetition, as a field to be plowed until you come to know it so well you forget it. Much as a musician, an athlete, or a dancer needs to be trained to a level of fitness, the craft work Patsy teaches underpins an actor's artistic performance.

The overall structure of this craft work is an organized series of technical exercises that begin with the body. How do you walk on stage with the focused energy required to tell an important piece of a story? Your own physical manifestations of fear—shoulders up, breath high and shallow, voice held, text rushed or falsely manufactured—are lodged in the body. Patsy homes in on the whole body, from the meeting of the feet with the floor to the tilt of the head, releasing excess tension to bring into being a naturally placed and centered body. The body is where, she says, "all our emotional, intellectual, and spiritual secrets eventually embed themselves" (Rodenburg 1997, 37). The voice is housed in the body; speaking is a full-body activity.

After the body, Patsy turns to the breath—the core of voice work—to create a system both flexible and powerful. She opens the channel, allowing time for the full breath to drop in deeply, and uses a series of exercises to connect breath to support, ensuring that each word has breath beneath it. She extends breath capacity and quickens breath recovery to meet the arduous demands of speaking classical text. She works on matching the breath to the space and connecting it organically to the thought and the emotion.

The next link in the chain is voice. Patsy stretches and strengthens it to cope with a variety of venues and vigorous texts. Only by discovering your own free and flexible voice can you serve the text. She warms the voice with humming and properly "places" the voice with intoning—shaping and releasing from the front of the mouth the resulting vibrations, not only to travel across distance but also to strike, to penetrate an audience like an arrow. She teaches how to sustain the open, placed, and supported voice, and the use of complete resonance and range. Thus, the voice is freed so that it can readily express emotional and intellectual passion, filling the space with the appropriate energy of the text, and revealing the inner life of a character.

The final step in the craft sequence is speech. Here, Patsy stretches the speech muscles and isolates the articulators, unclenching the jaw, stretching the tongue, and trilling the lips to prepare for muscular articulation. She requires clarity for every sound and every syllable, not half there or forgotten, while emphasizing that English is largely onomatopoeic, with sound and sense intrinsically connected. Vowels bring emotion and consonants reason. As rhythm is syllabic, you must speak each syllable distinctly in order to speak an iamb or anapest effectively.

This sequence, practiced diligently, results in an actor being fit enough to speak the most demanding roles without losing breath or diction, and being flexible enough to respond to impulses and transform into character. Ideally, an actor should have this craft already within her before entering a rehearsal space and facing a director. It is the thoroughness of this voice craft, and how she links it organically to presence and to text, that distinguishes Patsy's work.

By Releasing Habits, You Restore Your Natural Way of Being

A cornerstone of Patsy's process is to troubleshoot for habits, those accumulations of tension and distortion, disempowerment and isolation, that life itself has sculpted into us. Uninterested in the superficial or the cosmetic, she plumbs deeply, seeking the roots of habits (versus their manifestations) and inferring which subtle adjustments will be most effective to release them. Often, with simply a light touch, she shows you how to negotiate from the habit to the natural, from constriction to freedom. She has you vocalize from both those places to hear and feel the difference. And she teaches you how to find that place of freedom for yourself.

Hers is a practical process of self-discovery, working from the outside in, exploring who you are and what you can do without a habit—which may have been originally acquired as a matter of survival, but which may not serve you well now. She likens the process to taking a firehose and spraying all of the coating off you, that you might work from a place of clarity. The goal is not to replace your habits but to allow openness for creative impulses to move through you, to create character from this undefended place, to reveal the truth of the text, not simply your interpretation of it. Your ability to respond to the exactness of the language, letting it change you and the audience, is what is at stake. Patsy asks that you not reduce great text to your habits, that you not merely perform, but that you transform. "What I am offering," says Patsy, "is a choice. The right to speak in your own personal voice, uncolored and unflavored by anything artificial. [...] Affectations always get in the way of honesty and clarity" (Rodenburg [1992] 2015, 34–35).

Second Circle ™ Is the Place of Your Connection and Power

Another original contribution Patsy has made to the discipline of voice and speech is helping people redefine their presence. Refusing to accept the inequality of human charisma, Patsy has discovered that everyone has presence—power—although it often needs to be reclaimed. Presence has to do with your physical alignment and how you conduct your energy. She recognized that there are three ways your energy connects to the world and where it is focused, which she refers to as the Three Circles of Energy.

When you are in the First Circle, you are imploded and focused on yourself. This focus can be seen and heard in a collapsed body, an averted gaze, and a voice that drops back into the speaker. At the opposite pole is the Third Circle. When you are in the Third Circle, you are braced, and your energy is pushed out and generalized. People in the Third Circle look past you, take up disproportionate physical space, and often speak too loudly.

It is when you are in the Second Circle that you are fully present in the world. The Second Circle is the natural human state, the physical manifestation of power, the place of survival, and when you are in it, you are alert and available to others. Your energy is aligned with a specific point outside of yourself, allowing the reciprocity and flow of give and take, with connected speaking and active, accurate listening.

All of Patsy's work in the Second Circle is grounded in specific physicality. Her Second Circle exercises investigate presence, witnessing and meeting another's humanity, exchanging real eye contact and unconditional love, honing the ability to be and to stay present through greater self-awareness of the body's alignments and breath rhythms, and thereby dissolving barriers between yourself and others. Patsy's presence exercises provide this crucial piece of the puzzle, linking speaker, text, ensemble, and audience. There is neither intimacy nor community without an equal exchange in the Second Circle. Patsy says:

> Words are magical, and when they are spoken in Second Circle, they make the world concrete and somehow bearable [...] Inspiration is the intake of Second Circle breath. The parts of your life that matter to you will be lived in Second Circle. (Women on Writing 2006, 1)

Patsy favors ensemble to solo, celebrity status, understanding that while the individual is important, the group is even more important. She uses her presence work to bring out our sameness, our common humanity, instead of our difference. She brings forth what is within each individual and connects this vital energy to something specific outside of the self—a scene partner, a text, an audience. The energy of the ensemble becomes as one, whether in movement, in choral speaking, or simply in being on stage and breathing together.

It is only when we are physically aligned and centered, with habitual tensions released and energy forward and connected, that we achieve the state of readiness that Patsy at times refers to as "ears up—with an internal tail wag!" Hamlet's question "To be or not to be" opens a debate on presence. He gives us a clue to the answer in his advice to the players, "Go, make you ready" and he reveals his answer just before he dies, "The readiness is all." As life's heightened circumstances batter us, Patsy offers us a means to steady our courage: Stay in Second Circle. Breathe low. Be present.

Deliver the Text before You Interpret It

Patsy's text work exists on a continuum. The culmination of voice and presence work is also the beginning of text work—you must deliver the text. She sets this as the bar to cross before you proceed to the next phase of interpreting text and creating character. First, Patsy argues, play what's there, not what you may think might be there. You must be able to play every note of Bach exactly as the score is written before you can begin to interpret the music.

By delivering the text, Patsy means bringing into play all of the preceding craft and presence work: honoring the playwright and the text with every word fully spoken in Second Circle, being both heard (audible) and understood (clear)—no vocal pushing, no emoting, no generalizing tone, no skimming over words, no dropping ends of words, no putting on a Shakespeare voice, no playing the poetry at the expense of the purpose, neither rushing nor lingering. Once an actor can land the text with this honest clarity, attention shifts from the actor to the story being told, and rehearsal can begin.

Complete an Exercise, Take a New Breath, and Immediately Speak the Text: Exercises for Working with Text

Another of Patsy's important innovations is always to put an actor immediately back on the text after a technical exercise. Before there is time to think or consider what the exercise may or may not have revealed, the actor lets a new breath drop in and starts speaking the text. This rhythm of repeatedly pivoting from doing an exercise to delivering the text effectively transfers technique to performance. The very act of shifting language by orally deconstructing and reconstructing a text embeds words ever deeper into the actor's being. Patsy's artistry lies in knowing which exercise to deploy to release the next layer of freedom. Out of a repertoire of nearly one hundred exercises, here is but a sample:

- Build a line with breath under each word
- Intone the text
- Mouth the text without voicing it
- Speak only vowels, or only consonants
- Hum the text
- Explore range
- Examine the length of thoughts
- Walk the journey of a speech
- Own words through the exactness of your unique imagination.

It Is Not a Speech: It Is a Series of Discoveries

Patsy understands that thought, emotion, and imagination in acting all ignite through language. A monologue is not a prepared speech, but a series of discoveries made in the moment as words are minted under the pressure of heightened circumstances. This is the DNA of classical text, that we are compelled to speak, our thoughts taking us forward, each thought leading us to the next, building toward a resolution, with suspension but never a stop until the last syllable is spoken.

All of this work is put to use in performance. When you think, feel, imagine, and speak simultaneously, there is no need to act before the word—else you would not need the word. Apply your unique and detailed imagination to the text, and let it marry with the imaginations of both the character and the playwright through the exactness of the language. And it will, if you get out of the way and let the text play *you*. Let the text speak through you. You are but the vessel.

Character is achieved through the language, with choices supported by the evidence of the text. Patsy wants the joints of a speech, the twists and turns of thought, the structures of rhetoric that Shakespeare wrote, to be audible, to aid you in finding the nimbleness you need in your delivery today. You are not the same person at the end of a speech as you were at the beginning. As Patsy sums it up, "A great actor walks into a speech of Shakespeare and allows the speech to change him (or her)" (personal communication, July 2014). The principles of Patsy's approach include:

- Invent in the moment.
- Discover the *thought* in the moment, rather than the *intention*.

- Let the text change you, rather than leading with emotion.
- Let the text breathe you, rather than you decide where to breathe it.
- Weave the inner life of character intrinsically into the freedom of the voice.
- No character pre-judgments, nothing unsupported by the "evidence of the text."

In the transformation that this approach creates, the actor goes through something very exacting, so the audience can experience in concentrated form the "magic" of performance, which grows in great part out of hard work and mastery of technique. This technical mastery includes the ability to inhabit different characters through the medium of voice. Patsy discovered that allowing the physicality of your finely tuned instrument—rather than your preconceptions—to govern your performance will inspire new possibilities.

Shakespeare Requires the Full Engagement of Your Mind, Body, Heart, and Spirit

Patsy says:

> Do you think you have to add something to the text? Shakespeare is only boring when the actor tries to make it interesting. It is interesting! Reveal and discover and trust and honor the text. Every word, every end of words, every syllable matters. Release the energy of the text. (personal communication, July 2014)

Patsy ranks with the greatest champions of Shakespeare of all time. She has an encyclopedic, profound understanding of Shakespeare's texts, not only noticing every sound and syllable but also having a thorough grasp of the context and structure of each play, speech, and sonnet. She examines his language with a forensic eye. Patsy's classes on Shakespeare are a particularly enlightening display of the principles she embraces as all of her work comes together in speaking Shakespeare. A leading luminary in the theatre has asked Patsy, "What is it you do? How is it that the actors you train connect with and speak Shakespeare verse so well?" (personal communication, April 2019).

Patsy avers that Shakespeare is the only playwright she has experienced who requires our full bodies, minds, hearts, and spirits, and that speaking his words requires that we rise up to him, not bring him down to us, to meet his humanity and enlarge our own. She challenges her students to serve the play and to be precise—there are no "sort ofs" in great acting—to be genuine rather than falsifying or pushing emotions, and to engage fully *through the language* in the heightened emotional situations in which Shakespeare's characters find themselves.

As Patsy puts it, "Shakespeare is life with all the boring bits cut out" (Rodenburg [1993] 2018, 25). He probes the eternal themes that resonate across the planet: the use and misuse of power, the test of conditional or unconditional love, the difference between man-made and divine justice, the conjoining of the epic with the domestic, complicity, unrequited love, forgiveness, and redemption. He believes in us and teaches us the miracle of being alive.

Teaching Style

Patsy says, "I feel useful when I teach and therefore, I teach" (Women on Writing 2006, 1). From the moment Patsy enters the room, she establishes both her quiet authority and the safety of the space, where risk-taking and creativity can flourish. All she asks of a student is a willingness to try to do the work. She teaches with optimism and has a minimalist teaching style. She guides you to where you need to work, but she leaves you alone to do the work yourself.

Patsy's teaching style is organic but not random. Refreshingly, she adapts her work to the student, not the student to her work. She is keenly responsive to the people in the room and how they proclaim themselves from moment to moment and is constantly changing her teaching while keeping the form. Just as no two live performances are ever identical, no two of her classes or workshops are ever the same.

Patsy's classrooms are inspiring and creative spaces, experimental laboratories where complex artistic experiments are being conducted and where revelation after revelation is being made. After an exercise she asks, "What did you discover? How does that change your connection to the ground ... the text ... the audience? What happens if you do this?"

Patsy's teaches with both exquisite courtesy and a completely unpretentious formality. She has the courage to be moral but without moralizing. She has strongly considered opinions but is not an ideologue. She asks guiding questions, allowing students to process information without judgment or analysis, and offers both feedback and modeling, sparingly. She is exacting but not fussy; pragmatic, not dogmatic; curious, not intrusive; intimate, not confessional. She does not privilege herself to know students' secrets. She asks permission to touch.

At the same time, Patsy is vigilant at not allowing a student to tear down another's work. Similarly, she dislikes actors criticizing other actors and voice teachers denigrating other voice teachers. She believes that any teacher who can heal your voice is worthwhile. "Whoever can release your voice, use that technique" (personal communication, November 2016). Unassuming and shunning the limelight, preferring to concentrate on the work at hand, Patsy claims not to have invented anything but to have inherited a lot. Her presence is warm, alert, intelligent, generous. She has a trove of delightful stories, anecdotes, even parables, expertly told, which illuminate her pedagogy through this informal yet binding medium. Her students have called her brilliant, sensitive, compassionate, and the most present person they have ever met. Her classes are a paradox: the freedom of play joined with the seriousness of everything being at stake—an inviting blend of joy and gravitas.

Evolving Focus of Work

Patsy says:

> In all truth at this moment of time I am excited and optimistic about a powerful renaissance of language and storytelling. We have extraordinary evidence from neurology, anthropology, and education research that embodied speaking, dialogue, and full presence, as we communicate, is not only part of our humanity but contributes to our well-being. It is not a quaint or eccentric need but a vital one. (Rodenburg [1993] 2018, 2)

Patsy continues to clarify her work, fine-tuning her ideas and methods in dynamic environments worldwide. She maintains a large private practice and takes on a wide and varied range of new pupils to keep in touch with the reality of the beginner's situation.

In 2015, Patsy launched the Patsy Rodenburg Master Teacher Certification Program at the Patsy Rodenburg Center for Voice and Speech in New York. To date she has certified 30 Registered Rodenburg Teachers, with another 18 on pace to earn their designations in 2020.

Passionate about the need for knowledge to be spoken, Patsy is spearheading initiatives to bring oral learning back into schools. She has recently built a spoken learning and rhetoric curriculum for schools through The Laurus Trust in Manchester, UK, and is expanding this work into primary and secondary schools throughout Wales and in the City of London. The curriculum is designed to teach the skills developed in creative arts, such as the art of debate, speaking extemporaneously, stage presence, and rhetoric, and, crucially, to harness them in real-world settings. Her initiative has already shown results, as a growing number of students from schools that have embraced this work have gained admission to universities such as Oxford and Cambridge for the first time.

Patsy helps world leaders to create presence and speak eloquently, to craft and communicate their stories with maximum impact and engagement, offering them the skills and confidence to share their stories and inspire audiences around the world. Using Shakespeare and other classical texts, Patsy opens conversations on the ethics of leadership and brings the power of unconditional love into the boardroom, provoking meaningful debate on the good use of power and inspiring reflection upon how these principles should be applied today. Her methods change the culture in organizations, and most recently those methods have been helping women in various fields negotiate top-tier leadership positions.

Patsy's new book with a working title of *Women's Lost Power: Stories of Binding and Unbinding the Voice* is forthcoming in 2020. A second edition of *The Actor Speaks* was recently published, to be followed by a revised edition of *Speaking Shakespeare.*

Teacher Certification

Patsy has established The Patsy Rodenburg Master Teacher Certification Program to train the next generation of voice teachers in her pedagogy. The program offers rigorous, personalized training in Patsy's teaching methods, principles of vocal production, the connection of voice to text, and the technical demands of all theatrical forms, leading to certification as a Registered Rodenburg Teacher (RRT).

The program revolves around practical hands-on work and discussions with Patsy. Training is done personally by her and with a small, hand-picked cadre of other top innovative teachers of the performing arts. As with all of Patsy's teaching, specific curricula are organic to the needs of each class and reflects her evolving work. Training takes place in two phases spanning a thirteen-month period, at the Patsy Rodenburg Center for Voice and Speech, housed at the Michael Howard Studios in New York.[1]

Connecting with the Organization

How to Get Involved

There are many ways to get involved with the organization:

- Take part in one of Patsy's workshops in Portugal or New York.

32 VOCAL TRADITIONS

- Apply to become a Registered Rodenburg Teacher. Attend an open house information session with Patsy at Michael Howard Studios in New York.
- Patsy offers voice and speech consultations and seminars. Contact her to speak to your organization, deliver a keynote address, give a master class, or to work with her on ethical leadership, speechwriting, and presentation skills.
- Contact Patsy for privately arranged professional coaching.

Contact Information

Patsyrodenburg.eu (Europe) and patsyrodenburg.com or michaelhowardstudios.com (United States) are the best places to keep current on Patsy's upcoming workshops.

You may also e-mail her administrative assistant at info@patsyrodenburg.eu or prodenburgassoc@aol.com.

Resources

Patsy has written six books articulating her voice training methodology:

- *The Need for Words: Voice and Text* (Rodenburg [1993] 2018)
- *The Right to Speak: Working with the Voice* (Rodenburg [1992] 2015)
- *Power Presentation: Formal Speech in an Informal World* (Rodenburg 2009)
- *Presence: The Three Circles of Energy*, also titled *The Second Circle* in the US (Rodenburg 2007)
- *Speaking Shakespeare: Speaking Shakespeare's Words* (Rodenburg 2004)
- *The Actor Speaks: Voice and the Performer* Rodenburg ([1997] 2020)

Patsy has released an eight-disc DVD series that chronicles the first 30 years of her work, titled *Shakespeare In the Present* (Rodenburg et al. 2011).[2] Her other media includes the following:

- You may watch Patsy's TED Talk: *Why I Do Theatre*[3]
- And her YouTube clip on *Second Circle*[4]

Notes

1. Throughout the article, the author has often chosen to use Patsy's own words in describing her work. The author has made every attempt to fully credit all of her sources and asks that readers contact her should they notice any unintended omission.
2. See http://shakespeareinthepresent.com./.
3. See https://www.ted.com/talks/patsy_rodenburg_why_i_do_theatre?.
4. See https://youtu.be/Ub27yeXKUTY.

Acknowledgments

I offer much gratitude to David Landon, PhD, RRT, for your open hand and your expertise, particularly with respect to Shakespeare's rhetoric and Patsy's text work. This essay would have been much poorer without your considerable contribution. Thank you to Lawrence Kessenich and Donald Stewart for your editing excellence.

Disclosure statement

No potential conflict of interest was reported by the author.

References

Rodenburg, Patsy. 1997. "Re-Discovering Lost Voices." In *The Vocal Vision: Views on Voice*, edited by Barbara Acker and M. M. Hampton (pp.37-42) . Milwaukee WI: Applause.

Rodenburg, Patsy. 2004. *Speaking Shakespeare*. London: Palgrave Macmillan.

Rodenburg, Patsy. 2007. *The Second Circle*. New York: Norton & Company.

Rodenburg, Patsy. 2009. *Power Presentation: Formal Speech in an Informal World Presence*. London: Penguin-Michael Joseph.

Rodenburg, Patsy. [1992] 2015. *The Right to Speak:*. Working with the Voice Abingdon-on-Thames: Routledge.

Rodenburg, Patsy. [1993] 2018. *The Need for Words: Voice and Text*. Abingdon-on-Thames: Routledge.

Rodenburg, Patsy. [1997] 2020. *The Actor Speaks: Voice and the Performer*. London: Macmillan-St. Martin's Griffin.

Rodenburg, Patsy, Gabrielle Berberich, Dave Hall, and Joseph Fiennes. 2011. *Shakespeare in the Present. DVD*. New York: Michael Howard Studios.

Women on Writing. 2006. "20 Questions Answered by Patsy Rodenburg." *Women on Writing*, January 8. https://wow-womenonwriting.com/17-20Q-PatsyRodenburg.html

Fitzmaurice Voicework

Jeff Morrison, Saul Kotzubei and Tyler Seiple

ABSTRACT

Vocal Traditions is a series in the *Voice and Speech Review* that highlights historically important voice teachers and schools of thought in the world of vocal pedagogy. In this essay, Fitzmaurice Voicework offers its overview, history, principles, and certification process. The key features of Fitzmaurice Voicework are explored including: Destructuring, Restructuring, Presence Work, Applications, and Play. The essay discusses connections between Fitzmaurice Voicework and *bel canto* singing technique, the importance of an anatomically accurate understanding of the voice, and the significance of experience-oriented (as opposed to goal-oriented) teaching and learning.

Overview

Fitzmaurice Voicework explores the dynamic interactions of body, breath, imagination, language, and voice. This holistic approach to the voice supports the development of vibrant voices that communicate intention and feeling with an economy of effort. The work is a synthesis of Catherine Fitzmaurice's classical technical voice training, her adaptations of other modalities, and her own experiential insights. It also includes significant contributions from voice teachers she has trained.

Students of Fitzmaurice Voicework usually begin with a focus on breathing by learning *Destructuring* and *Restructuring*. These two parts of the work guide students to experience the distinction between the autonomic (involuntary and reflexive) nervous system and the central (voluntary) nervous system. Harmonizing these two aspects of the nervous system helps students embody and communicate their full humanity while also developing relevant skills with greater ease, specificity, and adaptability.

To help students integrate and use the work of Destructuring and Restructuring, students also learn Fitzmaurice *Presence Work*. In Presence Work, students gradually cultivate their ability to be seen, heard, and felt by others. A key part of this work involves expanding the capacity to be present by developing a fluid awareness of internal and external experience and honing the ability to focus on and react to what matters in the moment.

History

Students then explore *Applications* of Fitzmaurice Voicework in various contexts of performance that involve the voice. As students explore these Applications, they engage their sense of creative *Play* to experiment and innovate with the work, incorporating it into their own individualized practice as performers and communicators of all kinds.

History

The work began in the explorations and teaching of Catherine Fitzmaurice. From age ten to seventeen, she studied voice, speech, verse speaking, and acting with Royal Central School of Speech and Drama alumna Barbara Bunch, who was also one of Cicely Berry's childhood teachers. Catherine then attended the Central School (which was founded in 1906 by Elsie Fogerty to teach her adaptations for stage actors of the classical Italian *bel canto* voice training method).

Catherine was a scholarship holder for three years at the Central School. Her teachers there included Cicely Berry, Gwyneth Thurburn, and J. Clifford Turner. While at Central, Catherine won multiple prizes including a national competition: the prestigious English Festival of Spoken Poetry, sponsored by Edith Sitwell and T. S. Eliot.

In 1965, Catherine began teaching voice, verse speaking, and prose reading at the Central School. When teaching the acting students there, she found that some of them seemed incapable of being fully vocally expressive. She saw the primary problem as inhibition caused by tension, particularly around breathing. As she explored ways to reduce these habituated limitations, David Kozubei introduced her to the work of Wilhelm Reich and his therapeutic use of reflexive tremors. After further study with Alexander Lowen and others, she began to adapt some of Reich's work for voice training and incorporated it into her classes, where she immediately recognized its effectiveness. These discoveries initiated a process in which she began to build upon and differentiate from her Central School training.

Since then, Catherine has continued to study somatic, mindfulness, and energy-oriented disciplines (including yoga, shiatsu, meditation, and healing techniques such as Brennan Healing Science and Reiki). Through these and other explorations, Fitzmaurice Voicework has evolved into a vocal pedagogy with a unique approach to voice and with a cultural inheritance and perspective that span centuries and continents.

Since leaving London, Catherine has taught voice and text at the Yale School of Drama, Harvard/American Repertory Theatre/MXAT, the Juilliard School's Drama Division, New York University's Tisch School of the Arts Graduate Acting program, and many other actor training programs, as well as in numerous workshops and seminars around the world.

Beyond the classroom, Catherine has lectured and conducted workshops for theatre, academic, and medical colleagues at international theatres, actor training establishments, universities, and conferences on five continents. She has worked as voice, speech, text, and dialect coach and consultant for award-winning directors JoAnne Akalaitis, Robert Wilson, Molly Smith, and many others, at such venues as the Guthrie Theatre, Stratford/Canada, Arena Stage, and Lincoln Center. Her roles as a performer include Goneril in Robert Wilson's Lear in Los Angeles and Prospero in Molly Smith's The Tempest at Perseverance Theatre, and she was a member of the company at the American Conservatory Theatre for three years.

Key features of Fitzmaurice Voicework

Throughout her teaching, Catherine has championed a basic reality: breathing in-the-moment that is responsive to inner and outer circumstances is the foundation for vibrant and expressive voices. This focus on breath (as opposed to vocal "quality") as the key to expressive potential helps students of Fitzmaurice Voicework engage in a deep and wide-ranging exploration of the underpinnings of the human voice and communication.

In Catherine's terms, "survival breathing" refers to the autonomic or reflexive breathing that responds dynamically to the body's need for oxygen, and "intentional breathing" refers to the voluntary use of breath to power vocal communication. Rooted in a keen awareness of anatomy, neurology, and physiology, Fitzmaurice Voicework incorporates the latest scientific insights to assist students in communicating with depth and clarity by harmonizing the involuntary with the voluntary, rather than allowing these forces to remain isolated or in conflict with each other.

Destructuring and *Restructuring* are the two primary practices associated with this exploration. Fitzmaurice Voicework further utilizes *Presence Work,* various *Applications,* and *Play* to support communication and performance in all of its dynamic variability.

Destructuring

Destructuring helps students open to their involuntary impulses, release excess tension, and increase a felt sense of flow. It "prepares students to allow autonomic, uncontrolled physiological shiver-like oscillations to pass like a wave through their entire bodies," during which "chronic tension blocks are made very apparent" (Fitzmaurice 2015, 3). These "shiver-like oscillations," or "tremors," are "induced initially through hyper-extension of the body's extremities only, thus leaving the torso muscles free to respond with a heightened breathing pattern" (1997, 249).

By triggering reflexive responses in the autonomic nervous system, Destructuring opens students' awareness to changes in their survival breathing and other involuntary impulses. Tremors can be explored, either through self-guided practice or with instruction, following a "Sequence" of exercises that have been developed over time, but "there is no exact, prescribed regimen or set of exercises to be followed in this work" (2015, 5). Instead, students' individual experiences are paramount. Ultimately, the practice of Destructuring is "self-regulatory," in that the students determine "how much, and when, and where" they experience release in their own body and breath (3).

Catherine refers to some of her exercises as "dynamic efforts," rather than "positions" (as in yoga), in order to emphasize that each individual will engage with them differently rather than aiming for an idealized external physical image, and that the transitions between each are as important as the efforts themselves. Teachers of Destructuring are encouraged to develop sensitivity to individual student growth and experience, in the moment and over time, rather than adhering to a fixed set of repeated exercises. Students of Destructuring are encouraged to develop "autonomy, authenticity, and authority" while exploring this work (1997, 249). This mindset extends well beyond the classroom.

As summarized in Catherine's writings, most notably "Breathing Matters," the benefits of Destructuring include:

- releasing muscle tension (and reducing stress and limitations on movement, circulation, breath, and vocal expressivity);
- sensitizing the body to vibration (and ultimately to resonance);
- stimulating autonomic (survival) breathing (and cellular oxygenation) without causing hyperventilation;
- creating a simultaneously relaxed and receptive state of awareness by encouraging the brain to slow into alpha and theta wave frequencies; and
- inducing the pleasurable feeling of energy flowing through the entire body (2015, 4).

Destructuring also introduces "fluffy sound" through the minimal effort of semi-approximated vocal folds. This encourages the "engagement of the vocal folds to coordinate with the exhalation, developing a kinesthetic rather than auditory relationship with the participant's voice" (4).

A subjective exploration of sound accompanied by the release of habitual tensions also enables (but does not aim for) the release of repressed emotion. Any such emotion generally is channeled into play with text.

During Destructuring, the interplay of the deliberate with the involuntary can extend to articulator activation, impromptu speaking, and fully embodied explorations of text, creating opportunities for spontaneous, personal responses to inner and outer circumstances.

Restructuring

Restructuring develops further awareness of breathing, and it can be used after, alongside, or even before Destructuring. Destructuring serves as a helpful foundation for Restructuring. But even alone, Restructuring is useful in developing an embodied knowledge of rib and abdominal anatomy, function, and flow as they apply to communication.

During Restructuring, students activate the central nervous system, and therefore an intentional breath pattern, to communicate. Rather than suppressing the breathing or other impulses accessed by Destructuring, Restructuring harmonizes the expression of thought and other facets of communication with "the individual's physical and/or emotional needs for oxygen moment to moment" (1997, 250).

The specific flow of muscular use and release in Restructuring is an evolution of Elsie Fogerty's *bel canto* method (which she called "rib reserve") and seeks to preserve the best of her work while also incorporating nuances found in organically open and expressive bodies.

Restructured breathing begins with "the use of the external intercostals and release of the abdomen for a fast inhalation responsive to a desire to express a thought—an *inspiration*" (2015, 7). The expansion of the lower third of the ribcage, where the bones and costal cartilages are most free to move and the lungs are largest, allows students to draw in "as much air as needed phrase by phrase without undue effort in the upper chest but also without inhibiting any movement that may occur there as a result of physical need or emotional involvement" (1997, 250). The coordinated movement of rib muscle engagement and abdominal muscle release during inhalation enables efficient movement of the diaphragm, as it moves down and out in all three dimensions and increases lung volume.

The Restructured exhalation (with sound) begins with a contraction of the deepest, most internal abdominal muscle, the *transversus abdominis*. This muscle compresses the abdominal organs back into the abdominal cavity and upwards, into the underside of the diaphragm, rather than compressing the ribcage to force air out. This specific use of the *transversus abdominis*, without overuse of the oblique or *rectus* abdominal muscles, provides sustained support in the Restructured exhale. The result is a versatile flow of breath and voice that can respond to autonomic needs and communication goals, without introducing unnecessary—or potentially harmful—tension in the ribcage, abdomen, shoulders, or neck. Or anywhere else in the body!

Restructuring is a distillation of an organic process that follows from and fulfills the need to communicate. Students often find that Restructuring emerges spontaneously from the process of Destructuring—an "order out of chaos" that parallels similar emergence patterns in the biological and physical sciences.

Unlike "rib reserve" and *bel canto* singing techniques, during Restructuring the ribs are not held open, and the *transversus abdominis* is engaged as a response to imagination, emotion, text, spatial context, and other realities affecting communication. Restructuring supports the needs of the performer, rather than tying students to a "correct" or "proper" way to use their breath to create "good" sound production. While there is a clearly discernible pattern in the sequence of muscular actions of Restructuring, the manner in which these movements unfold is infinitely variable. Timing, duration, and sense of effort and release in Restructuring are intuitive and improvisatory, responding to the in-the-moment needs of performance.

Restructuring also involves the use of the "Focus Line," an awareness of connection to the listener and audience that "involves receiving as much as sending" (251).

Presence

The foundation of *Presence Work* is the gradual invitation to students to be present with others, themselves, and the space they are in. Through this exploration, a natural vibrancy or presence emerges—perceivable by audiences—as students learn to reveal their expressivity with more ease. An appreciation and care for the strength and tenderness of students' humanity supports them in recognizing their own willingness to be heard, seen, and felt by others. The process is unforced, respecting the individual rhythms and impulses of students. As students explore opening themselves to others, they also clarify their own boundaries and their right to have boundaries.

Part of the Presence Work is focused on learning to be with nerves and stress in useful and healthy ways. As a natural by-product of this work, performing can become easier and more pleasurable.

Applications

The *Applications* of Fitzmaurice Voicework have been taught and explored in myriad ways in theatrical, cinematic, professional, and scientific fields. Some of the applications taught during Fitzmaurice Voicework Teacher Certifications include: vocal range (pitch, rate, volume, and resonance); heightened emotion (laughing, crying, wailing, shouting, screaming, and more); character voice (including voiceover); voice with movement (including stage combat); singing (all styles); speech (based in physical exploration, limberness, and specificity, rather than "correctness"); text, stylized text (including Shakespeare), and acting; diversity training; and teaching practice.

Fitzmaurice Voicework has also supported the creation of many new performance pieces through the interplay of Presence Work, Destructuring, Restructuring, and Play.

Bringing it all together …

When combined, Presence Work, Destructuring, and Restructuring—followed by explorations with various Applications—encourage students to "invite a combination of freedom and choice," a powerful blend of flexibility, adaptability, possibility, and specificity (2015, 7).

The integration of the intentional with the involuntary does more than add up to a unique skillset. Fitzmaurice Voicework helps students "access the almost infinite number of options available to them," creating the opportunity to "tap into expressing the whole range of their humanity as needed" (7).

… to Play!

Students and certified teachers of Fitzmaurice Voicework bring their individual life experiences and curiosity to the work and are encouraged to improvise and innovate with the principles and exercises of Presence Work, Destructuring, and Restructuring. The Applications of these practices are therefore as varied and adaptable as the people who use them.

This embrace of diversity and continual evolution gives rise to the last major aspect of Fitzmaurice Voicework: *Play*. Students and certified teachers are encouraged to "regain both freedom and focus," to trust themselves "to make healthy, appropriate, fearless, brilliant, and very personal choices," and "to truly listen" as they apply this work to performance and communication of all kinds (8).

Discussion of teaching style

Certified teachers of Fitzmaurice Voicework move away from the classical authoritarian model of information delivery towards a mutual sharing of experience between teacher and student. Teachers learn to recognize that the nervous system responds differently to commands, even internalized commands, than it does to exploration motivated by one's own curiosity and passion. Instead of focusing on control, competition, and "getting it right," teachers, during and after their training, seek to develop a greater acceptance of what is—with a focus on deepening awareness and perception—and then a curiosity about what could be.

The certification process in Fitzmaurice Voicework helps teachers develop their capacity to teach "what's in front of them," embracing their own humanity and in so doing serving as a model for their students. As certified teachers develop an understanding and experience of Presence Work, Destructuring, Restructuring, Applications, and Play, they are encouraged to develop innovative curricula that respond to their own passions, interests, and needs. They are also encouraged to study widely with teachers of other voice training methods and in related fields.

This focus on teacher and student autonomy extends to a sensitive, personal, and political awareness of diversity, inclusion, and cultural difference. Teaching voice is an opportunity not only to recognize but also to embrace diversity and inclusion. Naturally, no single Fitzmaurice Voicework classroom is ever the same.

Goals of the organization

The Fitzmaurice Institute is responsible for preserving the legacy of Catherine's work and guiding its continued evolution. Broadly speaking, the goals of the Fitzmaurice Institute and teachers trained in Fitzmaurice Voicework are:

- to foster healthy, clear, adaptable, and passionate voices;
- to develop students' unique voices without narrowing towards a default, standardized "good" voice;
- to foster diversity and inclusion of difference;
- to offer practical means for students and teachers to be embodied and present;
- to encourage students' self-regulation and self-trust based on self-perceived cues from within and outside the body;
- to engender curiosity and patterns of learning and practice that lead to deep and sustainable growth;
- to maintain and further develop the body of experiential and practical knowledge called Fitzmaurice Voicework that without care could be lost in our often fast-paced, stressed-out, technologically-oriented world; and
- to create community through clear, direct, and open-hearted communication and collaboration.

Certification process

Teacher certification in Fitzmaurice Voicework began in 1998. Applicants to the Teacher Certification Program must have previous experience with Fitzmaurice Voicework. This experience can include one or more years of study in an academic or conservatory environment, or multiple group workshops taught by Master Teachers. Exceptions have been made for those who show extraordinary promise with the work or who have extensive experience teaching voice in other traditions.

The Certification Program takes place over two years, with a total of ten weeks of group instruction plus regular individual mentorship in the intervening year. Weekly curricula are coordinated and led by Master and Associate Teachers providing instruction in their areas of expertise. Instruction during certification supports the curiosity, perceptiveness, specificity, and adaptability that teachers need to embody in order to encourage the same in their students. To help participants internalize the work and develop practical skills, there are also ample opportunities for teaching practice.

Master and Associate Teachers individually mentor those participating in the certification process. Mentorship creates an opportunity for dialogue about the unique challenges and opportunities each participant encounters as they incorporate Fitzmaurice Voicework into their lives and careers. Participants are expected to teach aspects of the work between the two years of the program, using their practical experience to test knowledge and unearth questions for the second year. Written work, including introspection and candid feedback, is also an essential part of the certification process.

Teacher certifications in Fitzmaurice Voicework have been conducted in the United States and Europe and will soon also be coming to South America, Australia, and Asia.

In addition to taking advanced coursework that is offered post-Certification, certified teachers can participate in the Fitzmaurice Voicework Teachers' Symposium (offered bi-annually). They are also invited to teach and perform in the public Freedom & Focus Conference, also offered bi-annually, in which certified teachers teach and learn with the public in various international venues.

Contact information, resources, and how to get involved

Visit our website at: www.fitzmauricevoice.com

Representatives of the Fitzmaurice Institute are happy to share information about our international community, resources, ongoing classes, workshops, conferences, teacher certification, private study, and performances spanning six continents.

Our website is regularly updated with public workshops and opportunities for private instruction with certified teachers—including voice, speech, singing, acting, public speaking, Balinese mask, and others.

Hundreds of university training programs that offer Fitzmaurice Voicework (including NYU, Yale, Harvard, and UC Irvine) are listed on the website, as are publications that reference or explore the work and its applications. You can also find information on the evolution of the work through the writings and public offerings of Catherine's past students, including Dudley Knight, Joan Melton, Saul Kotzubei, Phil Thompson, Micha Espinosa, Michael Morgan, Heather Lyle, and Christopher DuVal.

Reach out to the Fitzmaurice Institute or individual teachers through the website, or write to info@fitzmauricevoice.com. We hope you will visit us soon to learn more about our work.

Disclosure statement

No potential conflict of interest was reported by the authors.

References

Fitzmaurice, Catherine. 1997. "Breathing is Meaning." In *The Vocal Vision*, edited by Marian Hampton, 247–252. New York: Applause Books.

Fitzmaurice, Catherine. 2015. "Breathing Matters." *Voice and Speech Review* 9 (1): 61–70. doi:10.10 80/23268263.2015.1014191.

Lessac Kinesensics

Marth Munro, Deborah Kinghorn, Barry Kur, Robin Aronson, Nancy Krebs and Sean Turner

Overview

Lessac Kinesensics (LK) is a well-established and holistically developed approach that is ever emergent (and continuously evolving) as a bodymind approach toward optimal and an effective body and voice usage in behavior, communication, performance, and well-being. It is rooted within inherent elements present in human development. Lessac Kinesensic training acknowledges the object/subject intersect (i.e. the anatomy and physiology of all humans, and the social yet unique identity present in all humans)[1] and therefore follows an embodied pedagogy.

Lessac Kinesensics, as we prefer to refer to this approach, denotes, acknowledges, and honors the founder of this approach, Arthur Lessac. Kinesensics, a neologism created by Lessac himself, represents the multimodal concepts embedded in the work, namely:

- a continuous process of becoming, of movement, in and of the human bodymind (*kine*),
- the organic and undisputable process of being as a bodyminded gestalt (*esens*),
- the continuous sensing of organic processes within the bodymind, as well as the shifts in these processes, due to fluid and continuous interaction between the self and the environment (*sens*),
- while honoring the original, organic, and authentic self in behavior, communication, performance, and well-being (*sic*).[2]

Given the concepts and tasks embedded in the name Lessac Kinesensics, it is appropriate to trace (succinctly) the development of the approach as well as the formalization of the Lessac Training and Research Institute (LTRI).

Arthur Lessac, founder of Lessac Kinesensics

Arthur Lessac was born in Palestine in 1909. He immigrated with his parents to the United States of America around the age of two. His parents divorced soon after arrival in the States, and Arthur was left to the haphazard care of extended family and friends, resulting in frequent changes of abode. According to Arthur, there was no consistent or fulltime parental care and he lived an orphaned life. It was this loveless childhood that triggered in the young Arthur a need and desire to self-soothe, to calm and fill the inner as he weathered the storms from the outer. He organically discovered that actions innate to all humans like rocking, humming, moving, dancing, and singing filled that void, counteracted the constant sense of rejection, and made him feel safe. These innate actions became familiar events that he could access at any moment and in any situation. These familiar events became his passion, and marked the beginnings of his bodyminded way of life. Throughout his lifetime, Arthur never stopped searching, seeking, questioning ... indeed he explored "beyond wilderness" (Lessac 1990, 19), beyond the mediocre and habitual, until he passed away in 2011. It was this continuous research on himself and through his teaching that led to what is now known as Lessac Kinesensic Voice and Body Training (also referred to as Lessac training, the Lessac work, Kinesensics or simply Lessac).

Arthur Lessac began formally defining and shaping his work with a voice scholarship to Eastman School of Music and went on to earn a BS and an MA in Voice–Speech Clinical Therapy from New York University, as well as a clinical certificate from ASHA. From the 1930s to the 1950s, he made his living as a singer, actor, director, and voice teacher, achieving recognition for his unique training approach through his work on Broadway musicals such as "Pins and Needles" and "From Vienna," working with patients at Bellevue hospital, and teaching at the Stella Adler studio and Jewish theological seminary in New York. Perhaps his first worldwide recognition was his training of the original Lincoln Center Theater company, along with Robert Lewis and Anna Sokolow in 1962–63. In 1970, he accepted a full-time university position at SUNY Binghamton, from where he retired as Professor Emeritus in 1981. From 1967 to 2000, he conducted more than 65 intensive annual workshops and training programs throughout the United States, Puerto Rico, Germany, Yugoslavia, and Mexico. During this time, he trained various scholars, artists, and practitioners, some who started to teach his work alongside him, some who researched the application of the work in various fields, some who contributed to the evolution of Lessac Kinesensics. It was indeed this group of committed role-players who impressed on Lessac the need to formalize his work, this "team," and the training in a structured manner.

Arthur Lessac received great recognition for his seminal texts *The Use and Training of the Human Voice, A Bio-Dynamic Approach to Vocal Life* (1997)[3] and *Body Wisdom, The Use and Training of the Human Body* (1990),[4] in which he notates his research in the areas of body and vocal energy, movement, and health. *Essential Lessac: Honoring the Familiar in Body, Mind and Spirit* an introductory booklet about Lessac Kinesensics, which he co-authored with Deborah Kinghorn, was published in 2014.

The Lessac Training and Research Institute

Adhering to the above-mentioned call of his supporters, in the summer of 1998 Arthur Lessac invited a group of Lessac-Certified Trainers and other practitioners of the work, to meet to discuss the future of the work. As a result of this meeting, a new certification program began in 2000 and, along with it, a mentoring program for new teachers of the work. This certification program has continued to adapt and grow. In 2004, another meeting launched the basis for the current Lessac Training and Research Institute (LTRI), establishing a Board of Directors elected by the group. The group in attendance charged the Board with establishing a viable working Institute which could realize the hopes of all those represented at the meeting. In 2006, the Institute presented the Inaugural Lessac Conference, co-sponsored with the University of Denver at Colorado. The Lessac Conference now occurs annually and is a place to share critical and practical insights into the Lessac work. Topics have included theatre performance and production, theatre pedagogy, community building, English as a second language, clinical speech therapy, vocal coaching, communication, somatic studies, and neuroscience.

The mission statement of the Institute is as follows.

The Lessac Training and Research Institute® is a worldwide organization devoted to the pursuit, growth, and evolution of Arthur Lessac's Kinesensic Voice and Body Training. By providing workshops, training, and certification in Kinesensics, we promote, strengthen, and disseminate our work to a diversified global landscape.[5]

As its name implies, the Institute has two overarching goals, namely training and research. Most people interested in, and investigating and committing to, Kinesensic training are seeking a holistically integrated and comprehensive training pedagogy that addresses body, voice, mind, and spirit, whether in life or in performance. From a training perspective the Institute's goal is to train excellent practitioners and trainers for this purpose, and provides multiple avenues for those who wish to gain access to the training. With regards to such training, The Lessac Training and Research Institute® has continued to develop its teacher certification process, and recently added expanding training opportunities. Future goals in this regard include training and certifying more Lessac trainers, and expanding teaching opportunities for trainers by creating a wider variety of short, intermediate, and intensive opportunities to learn the Lessac Kinesensics.

In order to maintain the highest standards of training, the institute is deeply invested in research. The LTRI has actively documented the Lessac philosophy and the development of and research on the work. In 2009, the Lessac Research and Training Institute® released a collection of published works by Lessac practitioners, certified trainers, and scholars entitled *Collective Writings on the Lessac Voice and Body Work: A Festschrift*, edited by Marth Munro, Sean Turner, Allan Munro, and Kathleen Campbell. The members of the LTRI are committed to maintain and develop the work, aligning its evolution with the basic principles outlined by Lessac in the seminal sources, workshops, writings, musings, and discussions. We are also committed to assessing the efficacy of the work on an ongoing basis, continuously aligning the pedagogy with the ontological principles encapsulated in the work itself. Evidence of this commitment is the forthcoming 2017 publication by the LTRI entitled *Play with Purpose: Lessac Kinesensics in Action*. This publication reports on new research demonstrating the efficacy of Lessac Kinesensics in the performing arts domain and in contributing to well-being.

The institute is of the opinion that its dedication to research provides the means whereby the training can continue to evolve and grow. Lessac-Certified Trainers are encouraged to remain open and curious about the many ways in which Kinesensics can be applied, in which it intersects with, or relates to, vocology, somatics, neuroscience, and psychology, and with various populations, such as special needs groups, early language learners, and trauma survivors to name a few. Critically, Lessac Kinesensics is an approach that is applicable to all languages and therefore to all human behavior, because it draws on all developmental aspects, processes, and patterns clustered around action/interaction and communication.

LK has realized the importance of imbedding itself within different first language communities and as such is developing workbooks for those multiple languages. Opportunities to present their findings are provided by the institute through several avenues: short articles in the quarterly newsletter, presentations, workshops, and panels at the annual LTRI conference, and articles in other field-specific journals and presentations at other conferences. The Research Committee and Master Teacher Council are available, at no cost to members, for consultation, advice, and editing assistance.

It is through these continuous and growing critical interactions with the work that we confidently claim a situating of Lessac Kinesensics as an embodied pedagogy.

Lessac Kinesensics (LK) as an embodied pedagogy

As a pedagogical approach that specifically aligns with embodied learning principles, Lessac Kinesensics mindfully and deliberately acknowledges and engages with kinesthetic, collaborative, and multimodal learning strategies, honoring human congruencies while celebrating the personally unique. At its core is the premise that we, as bodyminded beings, possess a naturally superb ability to engage ourselves physically and vocally because we are created/designed for optimal functioning and have an ingrained desire to do so. Patterning and conditioning from the external world (within LK this is referred to as the Outer Environment) potentially blocks or limits us from realizing our full potential and creates tension, stress, and fatigue, which over time erode the body's natural and organic responses and usage, until we become mired in habits that are neither effectively functional nor clearly expressive.

In order to retrieve the unique function and expression[6] we are born with (or, as Lessac referred to it, our "original voice"),[7] LK trainers guide clients through a series of evolutionary processes to re-discover the way the body (and therefore, the voice, as it is part of the body, from here on referred to as body-voice) is meant to perform when free of adverse conditioning. These processes are underpinned by the following principles:

(1) The body and mind are not separate but a bodymind functioning holistically and organically in fluid and continuous relation to the Outer Environment.

(2) The Inner Environment (the aforementioned bodymind) contains innate wisdom which we can access to teach ourselves better functioning in action.

(3) All learning begins with information from the senses which, when received and interpreted by an inner sensing modality called Inner Harmonic Sensing, creates new awareness and perceptions, resulting in altered behavior and communication.

(4) Each instruction begins with a Familiar Event, which is a healthful use of the body when performing an action, and therefore pleasurable, graceful, and efficient.

(5) Each Familiar Event provides an opportunity for Organic Instruction, also called self-teaching or the Teacher Within. This provides the chance to use that pleasurable, graceful, and efficient action to dispel restrictive habits which impede vocal and physical expression and performance of self by choice.

(6) All teaching and learning is pursued in a spirit of productive play (playing with purpose). Invitations, requests, or instructions, such as "explore" or "experiment," are used to encourage a lively sense of discovery, openness, and child-like curiosity, releasing self-judgment or pursuit of perfection.

(7) In honoring each client as a unique bodyminded being, respecting their lived experiences and various contexts, the client's "choice" in all training moments and application is recognized.

Embodied training begins with experiencing the basic pain relievers innate to the body and mindfully observing how they relieve tension and bring ease. This understanding is expanded to an appreciation of those actions of the body which provide both relaxation and energy, thus forming a natural balance between action and rest, referred to, in Lessac Kinesensics, as Relaxer-energizers. Once these sensations are felt and registered in the bodymind, they are the Familiar Events from which Organic Instruction, as the mindful facilitation of the Familiar Events, can be obtained. From these experiments, we derive three foundational kinesthetic strategies for exploring movement: sensing weightlessness in motion, or floating, called Buoyancy, sensing rapidly changing motion like vibration, or shaking, called Radiancy, and sensing muscular extension and release, like yawning, called Potency. These are denoted as "energies" or "NRGs," an abbreviation representing Energies but simultaneously referring, due to the presence of brain and body plasticity, to neurological regenerative growth (Lessac 1997, 276), thus a body-voice continuously becoming/emerging. Mindful engagement with the energies/NRGs releases physical blocks and diffuses habitual holding patterns, resulting in improved functioning and behavioral change.[8]

Vocal training occurs simultaneously with body training, as body-voice is perceived as a monist manifestation or expression of self. Vocal training recognizes the elements inherently present in human development of voice, speech, and language. Instead of primarily listening to their own voices or trying to imitate the teacher, thus aligning themselves with the Outer Environment, clients are encouraged to become aware first of the sensing of the changes in the Inner Environment during vocalization. Clients are guided to revel in the feeling of vibration primarily in the alveolar ridge, hard palate, teeth, cheek bones, nose bone, and forehead, thus experiencing the bone conduction present in all voice. These sensations, and the facilitation thereof, become seminal in developing good tone, and are called Tonal NRG. Speech is developed through attention to the vibration of humming in sustained voiced consonants and the delicate, rhythmic tapping present in plosive consonants, here called Percussives. This is referred to as Consonant NRG. Consonant NRG explorations experiment with the various places and types of constrictions within the oral cavity to create all possible hums and taps. Classical musical instruments are assigned as metaphors to various consonants to facilitate the awareness of the presence of musicality and rhythm in speech. Finally, Structural NRG gives priority to the muscular sensations that accompany the formation of vowels, although structure is also present in the other NRGs. The focus is thus initially on the mindful facilitation of the inherent elements of voice and speech, in and through the inner environment. Because the voice is felt, sensed, and shaped within the body through these NRG states, voicing, speaking, and singing become pleasurable experiences, which inspires confidence and higher self-esteem. Both body and vocal NRGs, when engaged with mindfully, contribute to well-being and healthy functioning in behavior, communication, and performance.

Teaching style

Lessac Kinesensics respects the bodymind as holistic and continuously becoming. Because the pedagogy recognizes behavior and communication as a/the performance of self-identity, LK acknowledges body and voice as *subjectively* shaped and performed. The approach acknowledges the relative stability of the anatomy and physiology of body and voice, and as such engages with body-voice as object, respecting and upholding effective functioning of the body-voice as instrument. It is the balanced navigation between body-voice as object *and* subject that forms the crux of each teaching moment.

During a session a safe space is created and various aspects of body and vocal NRG's are mindfully explored with an orientation of child-like curiosity. Although the LK trainer is always listening, observing, and analyzing in the moment, the LK trainer invites the client to sense, feel, and enjoy the organic actions in the Inner Environment. Such Familiar Events, generated in that moment, once rekindled and recognized as familiar, form the baseline for organic instructions, which the Teacher Within can then mindfully facilitate toward the most effective actions, honoring the body-voice as simultaneously object and subject, facilitating the performance of self within context. From this perspective there is certainly a best practice when dealing with the body-voice as instrument but, due to the body-voice as subject, the "lived experience" inscribed on the bodymind is honored and embraced in teaching. This object/subject interface leads to each session with each client being shaped according to the needs and desires of the client. Due to this client-centered approach, the trainer can start with explorations situated anywhere in the work since Lessac Kinesensics forms a holistic gestalt. Explorations are done in a playful, yet purposeful, manner. Clients are guided to sense and perceive the smallest possible shifts in the Inner Environment, to have a heightened awareness of, and to respond to these shifts as chosen within context. From the LK perspective, the smaller the shifts perceived and steered, and the stronger the sensing of these shifts, the more effective the inner facilitation of body-voice actions and, as a result, the greater, more effective, and holistic the output. Such output not only leads to optimal behavior, communication, and performance but may also contribute to healing and well-being.

Examples of process

It is important to begin this section with the acknowledgment that the bodymind is a gestalt. Though we address each of the areas below separately, we recognize that they all function simultaneously, in synchronicity with one another, and that each area is at all times affected and supported by the others. A certain amount of repetition is present in the descriptions provided below. This is due to the nonlinear profile of LK.

Breath

To develop and deepen the awareness of the effects of breath in the body, we begin with an experiment which asks the clients, drawing from their lived experience, to choose a scent which is pleasurable to them (e.g. flowers, coffee, oranges, freshly baked bread are all choices that come up frequently). The focus is simply to smell the fragrance and enjoy the sensations which arise from that experience. By doing this, we establish breath as a Familiar Event. As clients immerse themselves in these sensations, they are guided to awareness of fundamental aspects of breathing which informs all movement and vocal production, including experiencing the expansion of the rib cage, the movement of the pelvic floor, and the elongation of the spine. This awareness of the sensation of breath in the body then transforms to an Organic Instruction, allowing the client's Teacher Within to use the breath sensation to release holding patterns or to improve functioning as required. Further exploration over a course of time will introduce the clients to their breath response in various behavioral and emotional states (called E-motivated breathing) and ensure that unwanted tension does not restrict the body (and therefore, the breath). Awareness of breath as Familiar Event will carry through and be deepened in all subsequent explorations during body-voice training. Below we provide a trajectory of a few exploratory processes present in body-voice training.

The Body NRG's

The Body NRG's derive from the acknowledgment that the bodymind has intrinsic means by which it deals with pain and stress, and that those means can inform behavior and movement. These are the pain relievers referred to above. Three of these pain relievers are stretching, shaking, and sighing. Each one promotes a release of tension while also enlivening the body with energy; thus, they are known as Relaxer-energizers. One example of an experiment to feel these sensations is to imagine getting out of a car after driving for a long time. Clients find themselves organically stretching, shaking, and sighing to relieve weary muscles and improve circulation and respiration. Acknowledging these sensations as the feeling of energy moving in and through the body, acknowledging that energy is present at all times, and acknowledging that all energy is in motion, each of these Relaxer-energizers is explored to further uncover their unique characteristics, including how they arise from, stimulate or change movement, breath, and emotion. These Relaxer-energizers become the Familiar Events as pre-cursors of the Body Energies, which are then used as Organic Instructions to the bodymind to dispel tension and create new awareness and expression of behavior in action. The names of the NRGs—Potency, Radiancy, and Buoyancy—reflect the many qualities of emotion and embodied behavior that emanate from mindful use of these NRGs in communication, performance, and eventually well-being.

Concurrent with explorations of the Body NRGs is the recognition of and experimentation within the spheres around the body, including the personal sphere, the public sphere, and the spheres in which the various body part functions. For example, following the natural development of humans, LK trainers begin by having the client explore the Small Ball—a curled, fetus-like position which can roll and rock and access the smallest possible sphere. In this small sphere, the client discovers that due to the design of the body movement is inevitably winding or curved, thus curvo-linear. Further exploration reveals that all joints in the body feel loose and free when we honor the curvo-linear design of the human body. From the Small Ball, LK trainers invite clients to explore the body moving in and through the Expanded Sphere while mindfully engaging with its curvo-linear design. Such engagement with the expanded sphere occurs in hundreds of movements in everyday life, from squatting to reaching to bending to sitting. These explorations gradually develop into the full upright alignment of the body, referred to as an Upright Parenthesis, a phrase which honors the curvo-linear extension of the head and tail in opposite vertical directions, providing ease of movability in the joints. In combination with the Body NRGs, sphere work incorporates all possible movements of the body and can be used to discover hidden tensions, habitual usage and breath blockages, as well as ways in which these detriments can be mindfully dissolved or released. Sphere work also incorporates the exploration of balance and rhythm, two experiences which unite seemingly unrelated separate movements into a dynamic expression of the whole self.

The Vocal NRGs

As both an intimate and public manifestation of the bodymind, voice has the unique ability to reveal our inner selves to the outer world. This expression of identity (voice as subject) must be honored even as we strive to improve our understanding and use of the voice (as object). Respect for individual uniqueness, and the celebration of each client's identity are the reasons why LK trainers guide clients to refrain from imitation, mimicry or copying others, or even from listening to their own voice, thus challenging clients not to rely primarily on an "outer perception." These outer influences can be misleading when it comes to understanding and connecting with the inner sensation that is the voice in action. Lessac Kinesensics bridges the potential divide between subject and object by, as mentioned above, approaching training through the awareness of inner sensations (inner energetic motion of the body), during voicing, primarily in the oral cavity, facial and head bones, pharynx, and larynx. The separation of these various body areas is artificial and solely for discussion or for study purposes and does not negate the understanding that the voice is the bodymind expression and performance of self. Indeed, all training of the bodymind influences voice.

The acknowledged human vocal development process begins with the babbling of a baby, with her experimentation with sounds of all kinds, and in particular, with tone. Lessac Kinesensics returns to this developmental process via explorations and experiments first with humming, which is identified as a Relaxer-energizer, in order to establish the sensory experience of the vibration (in this case, on the lips). Further exploration will deepen the client's awareness of vibration in other hard surfaces of the oral cavity, such as the teeth, the hard palate, the nasal bone, the cheekbones, and the forehead. While other vibrations (in the throat and chest, for example) also occur, the client is guided to focus on the face and head vibration as the Familiar Event which will guide her to healthy vocal production, in this case known as Tonal NRG. Moving from closed mouth to open mouth without losing the sensation of vibration is facilitated by humming on the consonant y (/j/), which reveals its vowel-like nature by producing a combination of the consonant y and the vowel "ee" (/i/). Continued playful exploration allows the client to focus the vibrational energy mentioned above, creating a good tone with minimal breathiness. This initial experiment will eventually result in the well-known Y-buzz, and indeed this tone forms the Organic Instruction for experiencing all other tonal development. The client will over time recognize and sense vibration in the hard palate, the nose bone, and the forehead, and these sensations as kinesthetic markers will replace the ear as primary auditory marker for determining pitch and quality of tone. The feeling of the vibrations moving upward in the face aids in preventing huskiness and throatiness and stimulates a healthy use of the voice, as it results in effective functioning of the voice as object through shaping of the air resonator and healthy vocal fold activity.[9]

As clients become more experienced in being guided by and guiding the vibrational sensation, rather than relying primarily on their ears, a new energy, the aforementioned Structural NRG, is introduced. This energy adds the sensation of the movement of the muscles of the face as a means to shape the oral cavity and thus the shape of the tone, whether it is into a specific vowel, or into a held musical note. Returning to the Relaxer-energizer of yawning, participants explore the initial feelings of the yawn, experiencing the subtle but forward movement of the cheek muscles (zygomatic and levator), and the resulting release of the jaw and lift of the soft palate. These muscular movements create the structure in which tone can freely re-sound. These different shapes and sizes of the lip openings and oral cavity will then create specific vowels, leading the client gently into elements of articulation and the preparation toward clear and intelligible speech.

Tonal and Structural NRGs are then joined by Consonant NRG, in which the client physically explores and experiences the obstructions, frictions, and impedances that result in consonant formation. Returning again to the Relaxer-energizer of humming, voiced sustained consonants are hummed and explored to sense the unique quality of each consonant, again drawing on the developmental phases of voice, speech, and language. To facilitate identifying the different qualities, the participant is introduced to the musical metaphor, mentioned above—that of the classical orchestra, in which every consonant is matched with an instrument that possesses similar qualities. For example, plosive consonants are matched with percussive instruments (such as the /t/ with the snare drum, or the /d/ with the tympani drum) and are executed with the artistry that a drummer has when playing the drums: the drumstick springs away from the drumhead, resulting in a light tap and a clean sound. In this metaphor, the tongue functions as the drumstick, the teeth or the alveolar ridge as the drum, and the client, via focus on this physical sensation, playfully produces clear, clean plosive consonants. It is the interactive use of Tonal, Structural, and Consonant NRG that ensures clear and intelligible speech, irrespective of the linguistic paradigm.

Concurrent with these explorations is a continual application to text. Sequencing may vary, but in general, one explores the sound element for its unique qualities, then moves to words, phrases, sentences, and poetry that contain the sound being explored, and then all is combined in many different applications to poetic and prose texts. This trajectory is apt irrespective of the language which is used. All explorations are supported and enhanced by simultaneous experimentation with Body NRGs. Throughout the entire training process, clients switch between two communicating modes: self-to-self, building personal awareness of the intersectionality of all the NRGs with the physical, vocal, emotional, and cognitive experiencing systems; and self-to-other, building the connection of the inner with the outer and finding the balance between uninhibited speaking and active listening as needed within the context of communication or performance.

The LK trainers are all skilled to engage respectfully with each client. They are trained to listen, observe, and analyze the client's usage of body-voice in action and to facilitate the client's journey toward optimal use of body-voice, adhering to best practice within the object/subject intersect. The purpose always is to guide the clients to perform themselves optimally in context—whether in behavior, for communication, in performance or toward well-being.

Lessac Training and Research Institute® training designations

The Lessac Training and Research Institute® offers the opportunity for individuals to be designated as *Practitioners, Certified Trainers,* and *Master Teachers* of Lessac Kinesenics. All of the procedures for these accomplishments were developed by the Master Teacher Council. All master teachers are members of this wing of the institute which oversees pedagogical procedures and development.

These designations indicate levels of competency; the levels begin with self-awareness, practice, and effective application of Lessac Kinesensics and develop into teaching the work to others and finally obtaining a level of mastery to be able to train teachers and contribute to the ongoing evolution of Lessac Kinesensics, its pedagogy, and its application.

Lessac Practitioner

Lessac Practitioners[10] have successfully completed assessment procedures demonstrating comprehensive, self-reliant awareness, and application of the Lessac Voice and Body Work. Practitioners usually have completed full-time study in two Lessac-Intensive Workshops and successfully completed a practical examination, administered by at least one Lessac Master Teacher. Individuals participate in the Practitioner assessment procedures only by invitation or after consultation with a master teacher. While the institute acknowledges that there are specific benchmarks for obtaining practitioner status, there is no set timeline for this, respecting and celebrating each candidate's unique profile. The aim is to obtain self-efficacy in practice and not to complete a course for qualification purposes.

Lessac-Certified Trainer

Lessac-Certified Trainers are Lessac Practitioners who have successfully completed assessment procedures demonstrating the ability to train others in the comprehensive Lessac Voice and Body Work. Only Lessac Practitioners may apply for Certification Candidacy. Upon acceptance as a Candidate for Certification, the candidate is assigned a mentor. The mentor is a master teacher appointed by the Master Teacher Council. During the mentoring period, the candidate communicates the development of his/her teaching skills and periodically provides recorded or on-site observations of teaching the voice and/or body work. During this period of time, the candidate will also participate in a Teacher Training Workshop and must successfully complete a comprehensive written exam of Lessac Kinesensic concepts and tono-sensory "phonetics." When the candidate and mentor mutually agree, again based on the unique profile of the candidate, recorded teaching experiences are shared with the Master Teacher Council for final assessment. There is no set timeline for the mentoring procedures.

Lessac Master Teacher

After at least 15 years as a practicing Lessac-Certified Trainer, demonstrating commitment and excellence, the Master Teacher Council may invite a certified trainer to become a candidate for master teacher. Candidacy is usually a two-year period of time in which the candidate co-teaches with Master Teachers at Intensive Workshops and private studies with master teachers. This individual is chosen because he or she models the practice of the work with exceptional consistency, has contributed to the extension of the work in demonstrated practical creative activity or research, and can eventually fulfill the responsibilities of mentoring others and leadership workshops.

Contact information, resources, and how to get involved

The Lessac Training and Research Institute is eager to interact, share, facilitate, teach, and learn from all people who are committed to improve their own behavior, communication, performance, and well-being. The approach upholds and respects the intersectionality of human congruencies and the personal and unique performances of selves. As such, Lessac Kinesensics is non-language-specific and embraces people from all cultural paradigms. We view humans as bodyminded beings continuously being and becoming. We simultaneously train the body-voice object/subject interface. Indeed, we honor the emerging gestalt of self in action. If the above is of interest to you, we invite you to engage with us in one way or another:

- Through our website (www.lessacinstitute.org). There, you can find general information about the Lessac Kinesensic training, our upcoming workshops and summer intensives, resources, the Lessac Institute organizational makeup, information on the annual conference, how to become a member, the list of board members, and more.
- Alternatively, those interested can contact one of our practitioners, certified trainers, or master teachers (e-mail addresses of all our members are available on our website). Indeed, our members would love to talk to you one-on-one either on e-mail, phone, SKYPE, FaceTime, or any other form of communication of your choice.
- And finally, feel free to follow the Lessac Institute Facebook page, which includes information on upcoming workshops, performances, annual conferences, and updates from members around the globe. Once you are a member, you are welcome to have your updates on the page.

At the LTRI, we celebrate each other's unique strengths as we engage in practice-based, creative, and scholarly research; teaching and sharing of Lessac Kinesensics. We invite you to explore Lessac Kinesensics.

Notes

1. As an example, and focusing on the vocal, Steyn and Munro (2015, 106) note: "Voice culminates from the holistic interrelationship of two substrata: (1) voice as physiological construct which is primarily responsible for the functional properties of the voice; and (2) the social-cultural voice which reflects and expresses the identity of the self. This interrelationship simultaneously presents voice as object and subject …"
2. See Lessac (1997, 4) for his description of this neologism.
3. First version of this book appeared in 1960. It was reworked and revised in 1967 and again in 1997.
4. First version of this book appeared in 1978 and again in 1980. The second edition appeared in 1990.
5. The Lessac Training and Research Institute. 2017. Mission Statement of the Lessac Training and Research Institute. Accessed July 15, 2017. http://lessacinstitute.org/about-us/mission-statement/.
6. We acknowledge that we borrow this term from Hackney (2002).
7. See Arthur Lessac's VASTA 2009 keynote address.
8. See Lessac and Kinghorn (2014, 1–6) as well as Lessac (1990, 56, 57).
9. An in-depth discussion of the validity of the use of Lessac Kinesensics toward vocal health and improved acoustic output falls outside the scope of this article. See Munro et al. (2009) for a collection of articles reporting on the efficacy of Lessac Kinesensics in these fields.
10. The Lessac Master Teachers may grant exceptions to the candidacy procedures for individuals who may have acquired equivalent training opportunities with Lessac Master Teachers or -Certified Trainers.

Disclosure statement

No potential conflict of interest was reported by the authors.

References

Hackney, Peggy. 2002. *Making Connections: Total Body Connectivity through Bartenieff Fundamentals.* New York: Routledge.

Lessac, Arthur. 1990. *Body Wisdom: The Use and Training of the Human Body.* San Bernadino, CA: L.I.P.CO.

Lessac, Arthur. 1997. *The Use and Training of the Human Voice: A Biodynamic Approach to Vocal Life.* 3rd ed. Mountain View, CA: Mayfield.

Lessac, Arthur. 2009. "VASTA Keynote Address." Presented at the VASTA Conference, New York, August 3.

Lessac, Arthur, and Deborah Kinghorn. 2014. *Essential Lessac: Honoring the Familiar in Body, Mind and Spirit.* Barrington, IL: RMJ Donald.

Munro, Marth, Sean Turner, Allan Munro, and Kathleen Campbell, eds. 2009. *Collective Writings on the Lessac Voice and Body Work: A Festschrift.* Coral Springs, FL: Llumina Press.

Steyn, Morné, and Marth Munro. 2015. "Locating the 'Voice-as-object' and 'Voice-as-subject' for the Entry-level Theatre Voice Teacher." *South African Theatre Journal* 28 (2): 105–116. doi:10.10 80/10137548.2015.1033377.

The Lessac Training and Research Institute. 2017. Mission Statement of the Lessac Training and Research Institute. Accessed July 15, 2017. http://lessacinstitute.org/about-us/mission-statement/

Knight-Thompson Speechwork

Philip Thompson, Andrea Caban and Erik Singer

ABSTRACT
Vocal Traditions is a series in the *Voice and Speech Review* that highlights historically important voice teachers and schools of thought in the world of vocal pedagogy. In this essay, Knight-Thompson Speechwork offers its overview, history, principles, and certification process.

Overview

Knight-Thompson Speechwork (KTS) is a skills-based approach to speech and accent training for actors that places emphasis on developing the speaker's detailed awareness of—and deep engagement with—the precise physical actions which make up speech. By combining a rigorous investigation of those actions with playful, experiential exercises, this work moves efficiently past the usual interference that can make speech training difficult for many students (Thompson 2007).

History

Dudley Knight moved at the age of six from New Orleans, Louisiana, to Middletown, Connecticut, and this might be considered the inciting incident of his lifelong fascination with speech and accents, and in particular, his awareness of the stigma attached to non-standard forms of speech. He trained as an actor at Yale Drama in the early 1960s, and during that training, he encountered very little organized instruction in speech designed for actors. It was only later, when he began teaching speech himself, that he became familiar with the prevailing approaches used in American acting schools. In the 1980s and 1990s, while teaching speech and voice at the University of California, Irvine (UCI), Dudley began to ask some fundamental questions about the dominant system of speech pedagogy. Where had it come from in the first place? Why was it such an entrenched, universal feature of American actor-training programs? What did its claims to clarity, correctness, superiority, and euphony rest on? And perhaps most importantly, was it effective?

In answering this last question, Dudley found it necessary to make some assertions about what the goals of speech training for actors *should* be. He was certainly well-prepared to investigate the question. He had been acting for decades in every medium—on stage, on television, in films, and on the radio. He had also been a dialect coach for many years—for longer than he had been teaching speech in an institution. Through these experiences, he was well aware of the many different demands placed on an actor's speech and embodiment of language. It was clear that some of these demands arose from the work itself, and others were imposed from outside. The principles he saw as essential to an actor's speech training could be grouped into three categories: utility, flexibility, and intelligibility. The speech skills taught to actors should have a *utility* for their artistic work. They should integrate with the rest of the actor's skills, and they should be taught in such a way as to maximize the actor's growth rather than the teacher's convenience. Actors must adapt the way they speak to the circumstances of the character, the language, and the world of the production. They must work under a wide range of acoustic conditions, and because language itself is in a constant state of flux, there is no constant form of speech that will always meet these needs. This means that training for *flexibility* in adopting appropriate physical skills and responsiveness to the needs of the moment is of far greater value than training for conformity to a fixed standard. Finally, the only goal that actors can rely on as a constant throughout their work is *intelligibility*. Whatever each role or each moment might demand, it can be taken as a given that an actor's speech must be understood by an audience.

Dudley recognized that the pursuit of intelligibility in speech training has often been invoked along with a call for correctness or beauty, so he sought to isolate intelligibility and those skills that promote it as a goal independent of other concerns. In fact, he felt if speech trainers pursued ideals of beauty and correctness as though they were the same as intelligibility, then they could seriously interfere with the utility and flexibility of actors' speech skills.

Dudley's practical experience as a teacher and a coach led him to feel that drilling a specific, rigidly prescribed speech pattern was not the way to build a useful speech pedagogy. As he experimented in his classroom with other approaches to developing the skills he saw as necessary for actors, he also read more deeply into the field of linguistics, and he found in the growing literature on phonetics, speech perception, second-language acquisition, and sociolinguistics, abundant support for his approach.

Another powerful influence on Dudley's redefinition of speech training was the work of Catherine Fitzmaurice[1]. They two worked closely together in the early stages of Fitzmaurice's development of her work, and Dudley continued as a teacher of Fitzmaurice Voicework throughout his career. In particular, the key Fitzmaurice concepts of destructuring and restructuring fit well with the approach that he was finding most rewarding in speech.

In the late 1980s, Philip Thompson came to UCI as an MFA acting student and entered into the study of speech in the midst of Dudley's experimentations. When he returned to UCI as a professor of voice and speech in 2001, he found that Dudley had made tremendous progress in defining this new approach. They two began working together on further developments, and starting in 2002, they began presenting workshops to introduce the approach to other speech teachers.

In 2012, they held the first KTS Teacher Certification course. In addition to offering more advanced training to teachers who wanted to make KTS the center of their approach to speech training, Knight and Thompson had a secondary goal to train teachers who could join them in the teaching of KTS workshops, thereby expanding the organization's reach.

Out of that first class, they selected two outstanding teachers, Andrea Caban and Erik Singer, planning to bring them on as assistant teachers in upcoming workshops.

With the untimely death of Dudley Knight in the summer of 2013, Caban and Singer were suddenly charged with a much more central role in the teaching, organization, and planning of KTS, and they continue as master teachers and key figures in the work.

What is Knight-Thompson Speechwork (KTS)?

KTS is Curious

The primary guiding principle is curious, attentive interrogation—interrogation of what speakers are doing physically when they speak; interrogation of what physical habits we may bring to the act of speaking that inhibit free and flexible expression; interrogation of what it is that makes speech intelligible or unintelligible; thoughtful investigation of what any text, moment, character, or medium might require from the actor in terms of skilled speech; interrogation of what, precisely, makes up what we call an "accent"; interrogation of what allows actors to most efficiently, skillfully, and accurately adopt accents, or otherwise make adjustments to their speech.

This inherent questioning aspect of the work demands of its practitioners a certain tolerance of ambiguity and a willingness to remain in a state of unknowing. We build in to our practice a consciously adopted ignorance as starting point for our investigations. This might be compared to the Zen Buddhist concept of Shoshin (初心) or "beginner's mind." At each step, exploration precedes explanation. Description precedes prescription.

KTS is Developmental

The process through which each one of us came to be skillful users of our first language was not a didactic one. For the vast majority of people, language is spoken long before it is written, and it is felt and embodied as a skill long before it is explained through grammar. When we return as adults to explore and expand this skill, it is useful to approach it in a similar way.

A Knight-Thompson Speechwork workshop or class usually begins with a study of anatomy. Through active play and close attention to specific physicality, the course of study then proceeds to delve into *descriptive* (as opposed to *prescriptive*) phonetics. Students learn all of the International Phonetic Alphabet as defined by the International Phonetic Association—all of the speech actions, all of the descriptive terminology, and finally, all of the symbols and diacritics[2]. Students experience and learn the specific physicality of all possible speech actions before they learn the symbols; this pedagogical strategy aids in the learning of the symbols and reinforces kinesthetic awareness of speech actions. As students gain mastery of phonetics, they proceed to use the IPA to carry out narrow phonetic transcription of speech. Throughout, the rigor of our work is infused with playful and exploratory exercises to encourage students to own and integrate their new skills, as well as to continue cultivating their curiosity about their own and others' speech.

KTS is Playful

A playful approach is certainly more appealing to students, but there is more to this aspect of the teaching than simple relief from the monotony of hard work. The unstructured and unpredictable process of engaging in play yields tremendous dividends in the speed and efficiency of learning new skills and awareness. Play is in fact the primary mode of learning and skill building for children (Ormrod 2011), and when we return to play as adults, we are able to access again that mode of learning that served us so well when we first discovered language. One key exercise in this work involves speaking a fictitious improvised language called Omnish. Students take their newly gained knowledge and skills in the broad range of physical speech actions and combine them in a fluent and fantastical exploration. Students are tasked not only with the execution of all possible actions of human speech, but also using this "language" to express their own complex and immediate thoughts. This work strengthens actors' skills of articulation and awareness of the physical gestures of speech while simultaneously connecting this activity with their human, communicative needs. Actors are, of course, players as well, and by studying speech in an environment of fluent experimentation and play, KTS reinforces and integrates this work within the larger context of an actor's skill.

KTS is Rigorous

The notion of learning all human speech sounds may seem daunting, even unrealistic, particularly if our view of speech training is limited to actors working in a single language or in a narrow range of possible accents. KTS sees such limitations as unhelpfully constraining to an actor, both because it leaves many possibilities of artistic speech unconsidered and because a fuller awareness of what speech can do necessarily enriches our experience and skill, even if we then choose to remain within the constraints of what we usually do.

The scope of this project then necessitates a rigorous and systematic understanding of human speech. Fortunately, our colleagues in the field of linguistics continue to work to refine our understanding of speech and the International Phonetic Alphabet as a way of communicating very precisely about the details of pronunciation. KTS embraces the rigor of that system and brings this rigor to actors in the full confidence that a rational system of thinking is not always made easier to understand through simplification. Some simplification is necessary, of course, but our goal is to find a useful balance between explanatory simplicity and a respect for complexity. This is a difficult task, but it is essential if we hope to bring our students to a richer and more skillful experience of how they speak.

KTS is Sociolinguistically Aware

Variations in language are a part of a social landscape. Our particular set of speech behaviors communicates something about our identity, history, and cultural context. This information is judged by those around us as carrying positive or negative value (Hudson 1996). The pressure of those judgements—together with our sense that our speech is representative of our identity—makes work on speech uniquely challenging. KTS acknowledges this landscape of social pressure and seeks to equip actors with tools for awareness and skills for making strong, personal, and meaningful artistic choices relating to speech and accents.

Traditional methods of speech training[3] have focused on teaching actors some variety of "standard" speech.[4] This goal has often (though not always) come together with a claim that this variety of speech is superior to—and more "correct" than—other "nonstandard" ways of speaking. Though there may be admirable rigor in the classroom practice of teachers of this work, KTS sees this traditional approach as fundamentally limiting to actors, as well as being linguistically and pedagogically unsound. By leading with prescription, the teacher will inevitably add to the perceptual confusion about speech that all students bring to the table. If, on the other hand, actors are first asked to experience their own vocal tracts in a thoughtful way and taught to be able to both feel and understand exactly what is happening in the vocal tract in order to produce the full range of speech sounds that exist in human languages, then they are vastly better equipped to do everything an actor needs to do, from connecting viscerally to language to acquiring and truthfully embodying other accents.

KTS is Skillful

An acknowledgment of the pervasiveness of bias in our judgements about speech does not prevent us from setting some positive goals and values. For us, the first goal or "standard" for an actor's speech is intelligibility. This is not a fixed property of some idealized and prescribed accent model, but a constantly negotiated process between speaker and listener, within conditions set by the acoustics of the space and the familiarity of the audience with the language style. Students explore this negotiation without set targets of pronunciation, and from this exploration, they draw conclusions about the most effective features for increasing and decreasing intelligibility.

People make these adjustments intuitively by attending to the opposing values of fluency and detail. If actors wish to be more intelligible, our chief strategy is to increase linguistic detail, often at a cost to fluency. These are largely unconscious adjustments, but after initial exploration into making the adjustments, we can begin to focus on the specific strategies or skills we employ. These strategies can then be enumerated and studied as separable skills with a range of possible executions. With increased physical awareness and flexibility and with a solid foundation in descriptive phonetics, students are well-equipped to make subtle adjustments in their speech in accordance with the needs of the play, character, medium, and moment.

Crucially, in addition to building skills in perceiving, describing, and embodying the sounds of speech with precision, KTS work also explores the actor's skill in balancing and transforming the complex stream of speech as a fluent totality. Students learn to make finely tuned adjustments both up and down the scale of linguistic detail, providing more or less energy in their speech actions. It is essential that actors develop a sensitivity and skill in increasing or decreasing the activity, energy, and range of motion of their speech without locking in to one particular accent or style of speech. No one speech register will suit all occasions, just as no one accent will serve all characters an actor might play.

KTS is Accents

Contained within the set of possible patterns of speech activity are the varieties of speech that we would call "accent" or "dialect." This is, of course, an enormous part of what actors are interested in when they seek training in speech. For KTS, work on accents flows naturally from the preceding work on awareness, articulatory skill, and confidence in fine-tuning the flow of speech. In particular, working through awareness of the physical actions of articulation and encountering all the sounds of human speech equips students to quickly perceive and reproduce the details of an unfamiliar accent.

Acting in accent is a complex task and requires a great deal of analytical and descriptive understanding, but it is also a performance task that must be embodied and integrated with the totality of an actor's performance skills and sensitivities. KTS is concerned with developing an actor's ability to perceive and analyze the component parts of an accent, while strengthening the skills that lead to fluent and authentic performance.

KTS addresses accents under four headings: *People*, *Posture*, *Prosody*, and *Pronunciation*.

People, also called cultural context, refers to an investigation of the world in which an accent is spoken, the societal, historical, and geographical context of the accent. Exploration of the cultural context provides actors with imaginative links to the character and assists actors in identifying personally with the character's circumstances and behavior. A connection with the people also prepares the actor to approach their performance with a fitting respect for the culture and humanity of the people whose identities they are representing.

Posture refers simply to the configuration of the vocal tract during speech (Knight 2012). Through the preceding work, actors develop awareness and the ability to exercise fine motor control over the speech mechanism. This is essential for an understanding of the way speech features flow from the arrangement and state of engagement of the parts of the vocal tract. Making adjustments to this configuration provides a powerful means of effecting changes in accent. This is also the aspect of accent performance that allows actors to manage and remain connected to the other skills of accent in performance. Having invested in the other features, posture is often the handle or interface with the felt experience which guides the rest.

Prosody refers to the rhythmic and melodic aspects of accent. This has long been recognized as a central identifying feature for the perception of accent, but language for the objective analysis of prosodic features remains elusive. In the KTS approach, actors build up an inventory of melodic and rhythmic behaviors for an accent and practice deploying them in the improvisational stream of free speech.

Pronunciation is the aspect of accent analysis most commonly addressed in other approaches to accent. Under this heading, it is important to distinguish clearly between the characteristic sounds of an accent (phonetics) and their distribution (phonology). Actors need to develop a physical and perceptual sense of precisely how a speech sound is rendered in an accent, but it is equally important to know under which conditions that sound is deployed.

By addressing characteristic sounds with reference to the speaker's system of sound categories, the inherent variability in the realization of these sounds, and the relation of these sounds to the speaker's vocal tract posture, actors can more confidently achieve an accent performance that authentically represents the speech of the character.

Certification Process

Dudley Knight and Philip Thompson offered their first workshop in 2002 to introduce their work to speech teachers. Over the years, the workshops—and the work itself—grew, as did the audience it was reaching. The workshops drew the interest of actors, speech language pathologists, linguists, and dialect coaches as well as theatre voice and speech teachers. Each workshop inspired new ideas and deepened the body of work that eventually came to be called *Knight-Thompson Speechwork*. A second workshop, *Experiencing Accents*, was added in 2010. In 2012, the first Teacher Certification program took place, and KTS has gone on to expand our offerings to include a shorter, intensive workshop in phonetics and numerous workshops focused on training in specific accents.

In the summer of 2017, we completed our 4th Teacher Certification program, and we currently have 25 certified teachers. Many more have been introduced to KTS through our workshops and integrated various parts of the work into their teaching, coaching, or acting practice.

We continue to make refinements in our workshops and have plans for new workshops to add to our list of offerings, but we are guided by the desire to balance the interests of participants with a judgement on our part as to the most effective way to move through the material. Everyone interested in attending a Knight-Thompson workshop will have their own specific interests and goals, and some workshops may be more appealing than others for those reasons. Nevertheless, in order to be sure that each workshop can build on a foundation of shared ideas and skills, some workshops are prerequisites to others. The following is an overview of the regularly offered, foundational workshops.

Experiencing Speech

(No prerequisites)

Experiencing Speech is the introductory Knight-Thompson workshop and is designed for actors, voice/speech teachers, clinicians, and coaches. A six-day intensive, Experiencing Speech delves deeply into the work laid out in Dudley Knight's (2012) seminal text *Speaking with Skill*. The workshop is structured in two parts. The first three days focus on the physical actions that produce all the sounds of the world's languages. This first section contains no phonetic transcription, but prepares the participant through a series of *experiential* exercises for the introduction of phonetic symbols. The second three days continue the exploration into even greater specificity through the use of narrow phonetic transcription. Participants then use these skills to explore formal and informal speech actions while building skills of intelligibility. This workshop is the prerequisite for *Experiencing Accents* and the *Phonetics Intensive*. Not infrequently, we are asked if potential participants may skip *Experiencing Speech* as a requirement and go directly to other workshops. We are frustratingly firm in our reply. The essential first step of this work is experiencing. No matter what the participant's expertise or past work, we need to bring the exploration of this work back to a starting condition of self-imposed ignorance and experiential investigation.

Phonetics Intensive

(Prerequisite: *Experiencing Speech*)

This intensive three-day workshop offers focused instruction on narrow phonetic transcription, consistent with the approach laid out in the *Experiencing Speech* workshop. This intensive includes detailed instruction and practice with IPA diacritics, including those found on the "Extended" IPA chart.

Because the Knight-Thompson approach is not centered on any mission of regularizing the pronunciation of English, the work in phonetics uses the entirety of the International Phonetic Alphabet to describe a range of pronunciation possibilities, in English as well as other languages.

We continue to place a special emphasis on the physical actions that produce speech sounds, and this intensive is designed to develop participants' skills in hearing, modeling, and transcribing these sounds. This workshop is also an opportunity to resolve questions about details of phonetic transcription that participants may have from their previous phonetic training.

We strongly recommend taking a *Phonetics Intensive* before taking *Experiencing Accents*; however, this is not an absolute requirement.

All three workshops—*Experiencing Speech, Experiencing Accents,* and the *Phonetics Intensive*—are prerequisites for *the Teacher Certification Program.* (Prospective applicants to the *Teacher Certification Program* who feel that their skills in phonetic transcription are strong may opt to "test out" of the *Phonetics Intensive* requirement.)

Experiencing Accents

(Prerequisite: *Experiencing Speech. Phonetics Intensive* recommended.)

This intensive six-day workshop carries the techniques of the previous workshops into the acquisition of accents. This marks a conceptual shift of sorts, from approaching the process of increasing awareness from a *descriptive* standpoint, to looking at a specified set of accent features as a *prescriptive* target. What keeps this shift to the prescriptive from becoming limiting is our focus on skill building. Our grounding in physical experience and rigorous description of speech actions prepares us to feel, hear, analyze, and execute the features of an accent. The use of improvisation and playful exploration throughout the workshops keeps us connected to the fluent, performative skills of the actor.

Accents Intensive

(No prerequisites)

While it certainly helps to have taken the *Experiencing Speech, Phonetics Intensive,* and *Experiencing Accents* workshops, our goal in these short workshops is to connect with participants in the same way we would with a coaching client or a student. The information is focused and delivered for maximum impact on skill building. For someone following a path toward certification, we may advise taking one or more of these workshops if we feel that accent performance skills need improvement prior to certification.

Certification Program

(Prerequisites: *Experiencing Speech, Experiencing Accents,* and *Phonetics Intensive*)

While we are committed to making the path toward certification achievable, these three workshops are the absolute minimum requirements. We realize that applicants' schedules may not intersect perfectly with the KTS schedule of workshops, so the certification prerequisites may take some time in order to complete them in the required sequence.

Nevertheless, if your long-term goal is certification in Knight-Thompson Speechwork, the slow approach is the most beneficial. The workshops are dense and information-packed. It is best to take each workshop in turn, with time in between to assimilate new knowledge and skills and to practice implementing new techniques in the classroom, studio, or production.

The three-week certification course is at least, in part, a review of the extensive material covered in the prerequisite workshops, but more significantly, the course addresses the skills of teaching the material to others. Participants teach short demonstration lessons throughout the course and receive detailed feedback from the course leaders. Teaching anything as complex and sensitive as speechwork requires a dual investment in expertise and in presence. This requires mastery of the material, but it is also a very personal investment in developing one's teaching style. Our approach in the certification course is to address both essential and ongoing teaching needs.

Contact Information, Resources, and How to get Involved

Our organizational email is knightthompsonspeechwork@gmail.com. The Web site http://ktspeechwork.com holds extensive information about the work, including contact information and a calendar of upcoming workshops. There is also a Readings & Resources section with articles by Knight and Thompson and a growing list of interesting and informative links. The most important text for KTS is Dudley Knights' (2012) *Speaking with Skill*. In this book, Dudley takes the reader step by step through a practical and physical introduction to the work. The KTS Blog is another excellent resource for more in-depth discussions of aspects of the work. Go there to read posts and comment from members of the KTS community on topics related to the work. Another location for discussion and connection between members of the KTS community is our KT Speechwork Facebook Group.

Finally, KTS is currently offering webinars on various topics of interest to KTS teachers and students and to the KTS-curious. These are always announced on the Facebook page and through our mailing list. You can register for them on the ktspeechwork.com Web site for a small fee. This fee in 2018 is $10.

Notes

1. For an overview of Fitzmaurice Voicework, see Watson and Nayak (2014).
2. Some systems of speech training employ a simplified form of the IPA, intended to convey only the level of detail necessary for teaching a target pronunciation. While the IPA can be effectively used in this way, it has the capacity to describe speech in a much richer way, and KTS makes use of that full range of detailed description.
3. Dudley Knight (2000a) describes in great detail the traditions that led to the dominance of one particular approach to speech training at the end of the twentieth century in his "Standard Speech: The Ongoing Debate."
4. Knight (2000b) addresses the tradition and theory behind establishing standards for English speech.

Disclosure Statement

No potential conflict of interest was reported by the authors.

References

Hudson, R. A. 1996. *Sociolinguistics*. 2nd ed. Cambridge: Cambridge University Press.

Knight, Dudley. 2000a. "Reprint Standard Speech: The Ongoing Debate." *Voice and Speech Review* 1 (1): 31–54.

Knight, Dudley. 2000b. "Peer-reviewed Article Standards." *Voice and Speech Review* 1 (1): 61–78.

Knight, Dudley. 2012. *Speaking with Skill: An Introduction to Knight-Thompson Speechwork*. New York: Bloomsbury Methuen Drama.

Ormrod, Jeanne Ellis. 2011. *Human Learning*. 6th ed. Upper Saddle River, NJ: Pearson.

Thompson, Philip. 2007. "Peer Reviewed Article Phonetics and Perception: The Deep Case for Phonetics Training." *Voice and Speech Review* 5 (1): 349–358.

Watson, Lynn, and Sadhana Nayak. 2014. "Fitzmaurice Voicework: Theory, Practice, and Related Research." *Voice and Speech Review* 8 (2): 149–156.

Estill Voice Training®

Kimberly M. Steinhauer and Mary McDonald Klimek

ABSTRACT

Vocal Traditions is a series in the *Voice and Speech Review* that highlights historically important voice teachers and schools of thought in the world of vocal pedagogy. In this essay, Estill Voice training offers its overview, history, key features, goals, and details on teacher training.

Overview

Jo Estill, creator of Estill Voice Training® (EVT), believed that everyone has a beautiful voice. She also believed that this beauty is revealed by understanding the moving parts of the voice and how to control them. In Estill Voice Training there are 13 moving parts with options that contribute to voice quality (timbre). Training progresses from Craft to Artistry to Performance Magic.

In Craft, students begin with simple exercises to build mind-body connections and muscle memory. Craft is for all speakers and singers in studios, in classrooms, on stages, in call centers, or in clinics. The following common vocal questions are often addressed in Craft. Under which circumstance is my voice loud, soft, clear, breathy, high, low? What are the moving parts that make my voice loud, soft, clear, breathy, high, low? How can I structure my practice to enhance my ability to make my voice loud, soft, clear, breathy, high, low? Once the basic skills and understanding are available, Artistry becomes possible.

Artistry is applying Craft to make communication more effective. Do I want my voice to comfort or disturb? What must I do with my voice to persuade my customer to purchase; convince the director that I am perfect for this role; trick the listener into believing that I was born with this regional accent? How can I remove distracting parts of "me" so that my audience surrenders to my character, the power of my poetry, the message of my song?

Performance Magic takes Artistry to a metaphysical level. The performer gets into "the zone" where the ego fades, time slows, the player is one with the game, the performer one with the audience. This Magic is more likely to happen when the speaker or singer has mastered Craft and Artistry. Teachers and clinicians also find Performance Magic as they collaborate with their students and patients.

In athletics, dance, instrumental music, and even woodworking, there is respect for training basic skills before attempting complex projects or activities. These principles of motor learning and systematic practice apply to the voice as well, even though the moving parts are inside the body. The human body is complex and wondrous. The human voice, across cultures, produces an astonishing range of pitches and voice qualities. Estill Voice Training reveals the beauty in every voice by asking speakers and singers to honor the physiology of their breathing, their phonation, and the variables in vocal tract shaping. Students must understand how to work the body in order to find a new way to use the voice.

The innovative core of Estill Voice Training is found in the curriculum of two standardized courses. In EVT Level One: Figures for Voice, the Craft of speaking and singing is taught. During this 3-day course, students explore the 13 vocal structures that influence voice quality. Each structure produces a range of different vocal sound effects. The Figures for Voice are exercises used to develop control of each structure's options. Participants practice their new Figure skills in small group sessions. In open coaching, students work on their personal speech or song and apply Figure solutions to any artistic or technical challenge. The skills developed in Level One expand vocal strength, clarity, and stamina.

Level Two: Figure Combinations for Six Voice Qualities builds on the knowledge and skills from Level One. Students learn to combine different Figure options to mix "recipes" for six basic voice qualities. Speech, Falsetto, Sob, Twang, Opera, and Belt are the qualities researched by Jo Estill and provide the foundation for the Estill Voice Model. This 2-day course highlights limitless possibilities of the human voice, along with how to keep it vibrant and healthy.

History

The Estill Voice Model was developed by Josephine Antoinette Vadala Estill (1921–2010) over a lifetime of singing, teaching, and researching. The Model grew out of the simplest of questions: "How am I doing this?" The answers were informed by a lifetime of experience.

As she searched for answers, Jo Estill collaborated with elite researchers in medicine, voice, and speech science, and she became a member of a distinguished group of creative thinkers. She was fascinated by the extraordinary variations in voice quality heard throughout cultures from around the globe, not just Western European concert stages. She felt, saw, and heard things differently. She never lost her sense of wonder and enthusiasm for new insights. When Jo Estill asked her simple question ("How am I doing this?"), she was willing to consider any answer she found. She narrowed her answers down through the scientific process: observation, hypothesis, research. In her effort to de-mystify the complex human activity called "singing," she developed a wide range of principles and exercises, called Figures, that apply equally to everyday speaking, elite performance, and the treatment of injured voices.

Jo Estill experienced some degree of frustration with the gap between voice science and voice teaching. She devoted decades of her life to bridging that gap. The core training principles and exercises of Estill Voice Training were developed between 1965 and 1991. Jo Estill's vision was that vocal knowledge is vocal power. She wanted to share *her* vocal knowledge with everyone—every child, speaker, teacher, prisoner, auctioneer, crooner, operatic diva, and pop belter. Jo Estill's mission was to "teach the world to sing." She believed that all voices are beautiful and recognized that vocal "beauty" resided in the "ear" of the beholder. Both "soft and loud," "bright and dark," "strident and soothing" could be heard as beautiful. Her plan was to teach the world to sing through simple exercises built on physiology, acoustics, and perception.

The more she learned about the voice, the more excited she became. With further study also came an appreciation for the complexity of voice production. "Teaching the world to sing" was an easy concept for her to say, but it is challenging to do. Jo said:

> During those years when I was a singing student, I remember I could feel that there were a number of ways I could make a tone, but only one way was "right"—only one voice quality was reinforced. Why were these other ways bad? I was one of those "natural" singers. When I would do something particularly "right," the teacher would become excited and say, "That's it! Do you understand?" and I would nod my head up and down and say, "Yes." And I didn't have a clue. Neither of what I had done nor how I had done it, whatever "it" was. I never knew what I was doing to sing so beautifully.

I began teaching voice for the same reasons most voice teachers begin—I needed the money. And like many beginning voice teachers I knew nothing about teaching voice, so I collected many books and thought I would learn. All I learned was (a) I didn't understand the books any more than I had my voice teachers, (b) there was little agreement among them, either in their language or in their concepts, and (c) that was I was reading was not what I thought I was doing when I sang so beautifully. I decided to ignore the books, to analyze what I was doing, and if I could make my students sing as well as I, then I would be a good teacher. (Steinhauer, McDonald Klimek, and Estill 2017, 2)

As Estill Voice Training spread throughout the world, the company Estill Voice International, LLC, was formed to continue and protect the research, education, and certification processes that were developed by Jo Estill. The Estill Voice Model is continually evolving and updated by integrating new principles founded in current voice research.

Key Features

Estill Voice Training is universal, efficient, and liberating.

Universal

Estill Voice Training approaches speaking and singing like athletic endeavors. Speaking and singing have physiological parallels in walking, jogging, running a sprint, running a marathon, tumbling, dancing, and walking on a high wire. Simple exercises that attend to body mechanics and movement patterns are used for basic training in Craft. The genesis for EVT's Figures for Voice Control are the Compulsory Figures once part of Olympic ice skating competitions. Each Figure for Voice is named for a structure that makes a significant contribution to voice quality as observed in the research of Jo Estill and other prominent voice scientists. Each structure can move in different ways, producing an array of sound effects. In other words, the Figure Structures are named for anatomy, and the Figure Options for movement arise from physiology. In the Figure for Larynx (anatomy) control, the options are High, Mid, and Low (physiology). Larynx movements change the length of the vocal tract and apply treble-bass effects on tone.

In Level One, students learn the Figures for Voice Control to train complex muscular coordination of respiration (Power), phonation (Source), and resonance (Filter). In Level Two, students learn to recognize and control the options for each structure that contribute to Six Voice Qualities. Jo Estill chose the following qualities for Level Two to represent a distinctive range of human expression in speech and song: Speech, Falsetto, Sob, Twang, Opera, and Belt.

Efficient

The focus on Craft supports another principle of Estill Voice Training, group learning. When freed from aesthetic standards or restrictions, individuals with a wide range of interests and experience can explore the inner workings of their voice and compare them with others in the group. Three questions are asked constantly throughout the training of each Figure and Quality: What do you feel? What do you hear? What do you see? Kinesthetic learners are encouraged to feel for muscle activity and movement of sound. Emotional learners connect a specific feeling with a corresponding sound quality. Auditory processers focus on identifying and re-producing the complexities of each voice quality. Visual learners re-map their internal models of how the voice works using feedback that includes the mirror, video-endoscopies of each Figure and Voice Quality. Both visual and auditory learning are enhanced via Estill Voiceprint Plus©, an acoustic feedback program with analysis and replay features. Student of EVT record their practice and compare their productions with the male and female models of Estill Figure and Voice Qualities provided in the program. As they train, all learners begin to replace the question "Am I making the 'right' tone?" with "Am I making the tone I intended?" Furthermore, Open Coaching Sessions in all courses offer students an opportunity to present personal vocal challenges as the instructor, collaborating with the group, explores a variety of solutions available in the EVT Figures.

Liberating

Estill Voice Training is student-centered and free of aesthetic bias. Any non-abusive voice quality is accepted and nurtured. Students are encouraged to explore cultural and musical diversity and learn where the risks lie and how to avoid them. EVT teaches all to sustain vocal health by attending to the simple principle of "most comfortable vocal effort."

Goals of the Organization

The mission of Estill Voice International, LLC, is to shift the paradigm of vocal training and rehabilitation by providing simple tools that enable speakers and singers to achieve their personal vocal goals. Estill Voice International provides unparalleled educational opportunities through its world-renowned courses and certification in Estill Voice Training (also known as Estill Voice Craft in some regions). Central to its mission is the balance of vocal health and aesthetic freedom. Estill Voice International accomplishes its goals by merging science and art through progressive research, accessible technology, and innovative teaching techniques. Whether training or rehabilitating performers, everyday speakers, avocational choir singers, or corporate speakers in board rooms or call-centers, Estill Voice International offers unsurpassed products and training for unlocking the vocal potential in everyone.

Certification Process

Estill Voice International, LLC, was founded to promote the principles and spirit of the Estill Voice Model. EVI maintains a rigorous Certification Program with the support of its international Certification Advisory Board to assure that teachers of Estill Voice Training® are qualified and committed to developing and applying their understanding of the voice through research, remediation, pedagogy, and performance. The value of certification through EVI is enhanced by its high standards. Certification assures consistent quality and expertise in the delivery of Estill Voice Training concepts and exercises throughout the world, thus protecting the integrity of this unique system.

EVI offers three sequential levels of certification: in demonstration, training, and mentoring. The Estill Figure Proficiency (EFP) certificate is earned by individuals who can perform the basic options for voice control and voice qualities taught in Estill Voice Training Level One and Level Two courses. Estill Master Trainer (EMT) status is earned by individuals who develop a command of EVT theory and practice and demonstrate an ability to teach Estill Voice Training effectively in the private studio or classroom setting. An Estill Mentor and Course Instructor (EMCI) demonstrates advanced understanding of the Estill Voice Model and its applications to performance, training, and/or therapy, together with a commitment to "teaching the teachers." EMCIs present EVT in courses open to the public and attended by participants with wide-ranging interests and challenging questions. The EMCI must be able to discuss the anatomy, physiology, acoustics, research, and performance applications that are the foundation of the Estill Voice Model. They also play a vital role in the certification process as coaches, examiners, and mentors.

Estill Voice International (EVI) is proud to make effective voice training accessible to everyone by supporting the members of its Estill Voice Training Community. We are empowered by our knowledge of Estill Voice Training to become agents of change in our students' lives and agents of a paradigm shift in vocal pedagogy. Holding any level of certification in Estill Voice Training is both an achievement and a privilege.

Contact Information, Resources, and How to Get Involved

The Estill Voice Training Community welcomes everyone to share in our journey to vocal empowerment. Enroll in a course, find an Estill Voice Trainer, or look for Estill Voice Training in a university program. Our website, www.estillvoice.com, is a good place to start.

Disclosure statement

No potential conflict of interest was reported by the authors.

Reference

Steinhauer, Kimberly, Mary McDonald Klimek, and Jo Estill. 2017. *The Estill Voice Model: Theory and Translation*. Pittsburgh, PA: Estill Voice International.

The Roy Hart Tradition

Kevin Crawford and Noah Pikes

ABSTRACT
Vocal Traditions is a series in the *Voice and Speech Review* that highlights historically important voice teachers and schools of thought in the world of vocal pedagogy. This article explores the history of Roy Hart, the creators, and the training lineage. Key features and a discussion of teaching style are also included.

Overview

The Roy Hart tradition traces its origins back over a 100 years to Alfred Wolfsohn—singer, musician, writer, philosopher, and Roy Hart's teacher. In his autobiographical book, *Orpheus, or the Way to a Mask*, Alfred Wolfsohn vividly describes his World War I experiences and how they spurred him on to conceive a revolutionary approach to the human voice. His closest student, Roy Hart, carried forward his work, and 50 years ago he directed the newly founded Roy Hart Speakers/Singers at the World Theatre Festival of Nancy, France. Since then Roy Hart Theatre teachers and subsequent generations of teachers have continued to consolidate and apply Wolfsohn and Hart's discoveries in a host of contexts.

Wolfsohn brought his unconventional approach to the voice to London as World War II accelerated to a close. From a hermetic and intensely close-knit group of students dedicated to Wolfsohn's re-visioning of how we conceive the voice in relation to both psychic and artistic phenomena, the work further matured under Hart's direction, attracting an ever-increasing number of students. Over these post-war years, important breakthroughs occurred: a woman could sing very low guttural notes, a man could sound high fluttering tones, both men and women could howl like beasts or cry out with broken sounds, and a single singer could scale all the voices of Mozart's *Magic Flute* from the depths of Sarastro to the heights of the Queen of the Night. Vocal specialists documented their work and published their findings. The theatre company founded by Roy Hart amplified and orchestrated his work after his death in 1975, by finding a myriad of connections with contemporary advances in somatic study and dance, in personal development, and in the fertile soil of myth and cultural studies.

Currently, the work is recognized as being of great value in diverse fields, from its application in performance and training to its profound role in personal development.

History and Founders

Alfred Wolfsohn

Alfred Wolfsohn was born into a Russian Jewish family in Berlin in 1886. As a child he loved music, learned piano and violin from the age of six, and later sang in a choir. In 1914, at the beginning of World War I, Wolfsohn was conscripted into the German army, and in 1917 he was injured and seriously traumatized by the high-pitched screams of a dying comrade. That event became the starting point for his life-long questioning of the ideas and conventions greatly limiting the adult human vocal range, incidentally illuminating why he had not developed as a singer although he had a promising voice.

After several years of rehabilitation, Wolfsohn took singing lessons. His teacher sometimes accepted his need to shout out his agony, and Wolfsohn realized that a new approach to singing was needed. The experience of the war, his subsequent illness, and eventual recovery through his particular way of using the voice evolved into a lifetime's quest and astonishing discoveries.

From the early 1930s, Wolfsohn rejected the classical categories of being a tenor, soprano, bass, or contralto. He followed his guiding idea: the voice is an expression of both a person's body and soul and has the potential for both male and female registers. He called this the "unified voice," and over several years he gave innovative singing lessons where he explored vocal range extension. It is important to note that Wolfsohn's approach was not an early version of Janov's (1970) *Primal Scream* popularized in the late 1960s; rather, Wolfsohn's approach was a return to soul. Wolfsohn (2012) affirms, "I found that the sound of the human voice gained its fullest expression exactly at the point where the singer--having found the right balance of concentration and tension--could express it bodily" (45). He reiterates, "I see the voice as a direct form of the manifestation of soul" (59).

Close to the start of WWII, Wolfsohn escaped to England and served in the Pioneer Corps, before being discharged due to ill health. From 1943 onwards, thanks to the support of friends, Wolfsohn began teaching in London, where a group of students formed and committed themselves to regular lessons and meetings. Pupils at this time included Peter Zadek, who went on to become one of Germany's most renowned post-war theatre directors. Zadek (1998) wrote in his autobiography *My Way*, "He is training not only my voice, but my whole body, my whole self. His method is remarkable, quite beyond description" (133).[1] In 1956 Professor Luchsinger of the Zurich Otolaryngological Clinic examined Jenny Johnson, one of Wolfsohn's students, and Luchsinger confirmed that her voice could reach a range of five octaves and six notes with no abnormalities in the anatomical structure or physiological functioning of her larynx.[2]

In the same year, Folkways Records released the influential *Vox Humana: Alfred Wolfsohn's Experiments in Extension of Human Vocal Range* (Wolfsohn 1956). From this point, Wolfsohn's work becomes a focus of interest for both vocal science and media coverage. Radio and television as well as lead articles in magazines introduce his ideas and the exploits of his students to an ever greater public. Referring to Jenny Johnson, an article from *Der Spiegel* on January 1 1958 affirmed, "The most surprising thing in this is not so much the height but the sheer peerless entire range of the voice which exceeds all normal limits also in terms of depth."

Unfortunately, by this time Wolfsohn was already suffering from complications from tuberculosis. He died February 5 1962, leaving behind a legacy of unpublished writings in German that eloquently expressed his life's work and its multifaceted philosophy. His was a vision that drew its inspiration from Jungian psychology, but it also brought together an intense observation of himself and others, combined with a wide knowledge of painting, music, and cinema.

Roy Hart

Roy Hart (originally named Reuben Hartstein) was born in South Africa and arrived in London in 1945 at the age of 19, having studied the history of music, philosophy, and psychology at the University of Johannesburg. He had a beautiful voice, an innate talent for theatre, and major roles in theatrical productions on his resume. However, Hart had difficulty making friends, and he felt in conflict about being on stage. In a 1971 interview for the magazine *Primo Acto*, Hart spoke with Jose Monleon, the foremost theatre critic in Spain. Hart stated, "I knew there was something seriously wrong inside me [...] because I appeared to be completely and perfectly sane, not neurotic. There was a conflict between my innate desire to go on stage and my family."

His religious sense and his desire to succeed in theatre seemed contradictory to him, but meeting Wolfsohn showed him a way. In the same interview, Hart elaborated:

> When I arrived in London, I was awarded a scholarship from the Royal Academy of Dramatic Arts. My first meeting with Alfred Wolfsohn was surprising, because I suddenly realized that for the first time, I was dealing with someone who could be called a human being.

From here on, Wolfsohn became his most influential mentor, shaping the course of his development in a most profound manner. Hart continued in the interview, "I thought I had to forget everything I had learned up until that moment; it appeared to me that I must abandon the Word, for what could be called the Sound."

In 1948 Hart made a fundamental break with professional theatre, and from 1952 he began teaching under Wolfsohn, leading a weekly evening group, combining movement with music and exploring dramatic texts from Shakespeare.

After a six month pause following Wolfsohn's death in 1962, Hart accepted requests to lead the small circle of students who wished to pursue the work they had initiated with Wolfsohn. While maintaining a busy schedule of private lessons, Hart further developed his small group sessions and devoted time to discussions and meetings with students, raising their personal and social awareness of how this work was affecting their lives. In 1964, Hart directed a 30-minute documentary film of the group called *Theatre of Being*.[3] In this film Hart explained:

> We know that everyone has a voice, not simply a speaking voice but a voice which is pure energy and comes from the whole body. In all other expressive fields, what the individual is doing is external to himself, but in this type of voice production, he is going inward. Because of this, it is an intensely personal experience.

He sometimes referred to his training as "a biological re-education of the personality through the voice" (Pikes 2019, 104).

In 1968 The Abraxas Club opened in Hampstead, North London. It included squash courts, movement and gym rooms, a restaurant, and a dedicated space for Roy Hart and (as it was called at that time) "the group." From this point on, the rigorous and often daily training of members of this group included movement, ballet, and contemporary dance classes. Innovations were regular cabaret-style performances called *"Cathédrales"* and a regular workshop that was open to the public. Several of the students subsequently became members.

For 20 years, Hart had concentrated on his own vocal and personal development, which had led him in turn to be the undisputed director of a diverse and international group of 30 individuals; some were from performing arts backgrounds while others had little or no experience in this realm. However, from 1967 Hart executed a gradual return to his first passion: theatre. He began work with his group on the *The Bacchae*, by Euripedes. In April 1969, it performed under the name *Roy Hart Speakers/Singers* in Nancy, France. *l'Est Republicain* wrote in April 25 1969 that it was "A magical and fascinating spectacle! [...] The event of the festival"! One reviewer for le *Monde* in April 1969 found it "An astonishing mixture of gesture and sound." By December it had transmuted into *The Bacchae as The Frontae* (subtitled *Language is Dead, Long Live the Voice*) under the group's new name of Roy Hart Theatre. During this time, Hart, who was no longer giving individual lessons, asked senior members to teach the younger generation. This practice developed substantially over the years and became an essential part of Roy Hart Theatre's survival after his death.

While Hart opened up the company to a wide international audience, he began exploiting his astonishing talents as a soloist in three different works written explicitly for him. *Versuch Uber Schweine* by Hans Werner Henze premiered in The Queen Elizabeth Hall in February 1969. *The Sunday Times* on April 22 1969 wrote, "It was an uninhibited, confident, astonishing performance." *Eight Songs for a Mad King* by Peter Maxwell Davies, now recognized as a seminal work of music theatre, also premiered with Hart in The Queen Elizabeth Hall. Hart also performed in *Spirale, Aus den Sieben Tagen* and *Abwärts* by and with Karlheinz Stockhausen, which was performed at St. Paul de Vence. Nevertheless, Hart's solo career was marred by eventual discord with these composers, and he subsequently focused on projects with his company.

Between 1969 and 1975, Roy Hart Theatre created 10 different performances in English, French, and German, which toured the United Kingdom, Spain, Switzerland, Tunisia, and France. During the Festival *Music and Vocal Art of our Time* one reviewer for *Regional Newspaper, Angers* in 1971 wrote:

> The Roy Hart Theatre blew into the theatre with such a presence, such a protesting violence, in the cries and songs, the gestures, the attitudes, the movements, that their performance could only be described as total art, never seen or heard before.

Hart and his closest collaborators realized that their work was better received in a European rather than a British context, and a concerted search was made to find a suitable property. Finally, they stumbled on an abandoned hamlet called Malérargues

74 VOCAL TRADITIONS

tucked away in the green hills of the Cévennes, and in July 1974 the company began to install itself there, while continuing to work intensively on what was to be Hart's final performance project, "L'Economiste." This piece went on an extended tour to Austria, but it was cut short by the tragic death of Roy Hart, his wife Dorothy, and Vivienne Young in May 1975.

Roy Hart Theatre

Roy Hart's untimely death left a company of almost 50 persons from 15 different countries precariously housed in a complex of rural buildings that required substantial renovation. Many members did not speak French fluently, and the company found itself confronted with enormous challenges: how to survive in a new culture and above all how to re-articulate its artistic heritage and the future of the community. Initially, a collective leadership composed of nine of the more experienced members oversaw an astonishing galvanization of creative energies, allowing the company to sustain a period of great artistic creativity and producing over 20 original performances in the next 15 years. This creative upsurge was made possible by a rigorous training ethic inherited from the years with Roy Hart, coupled with collaborations and periods of study with artists from a variety of fields. The performances during this period reflected this cross-fertilization as the company members absorbed new skills, created smaller groups, and produced works that highlighted the potential of the vocal work, while refining its theatrical and musical expression. It was in those years that the company began to receive official funding for the first time from French national and regional sources. This support included grants for investment, daily operations of a professional theatre company, and funds to tours abroad.

In the summer of 1977, the Roy Hart Theatre offered its first open workshop at Malérargues. Hart and a few select members had already taught internationally in previous years, but this workshop and others that began to take place in France marked an important step forward into the future for the company. Teaching commitments began to play a role in the lives of its members, who were increasingly able to both gain economic independence and (importantly) find their particular pathway to applying the skills garnered through their years with Hart and with the Roy Hart Theatre. Teaching and performing took the company to the Americas, Europe, Israel, north Africa, and east Asia. Students from diverse fields came to study with the company in ever greater numbers, not only in Malérargues but also in a host of other locations. They included performers and individuals curious to discover their own vocal potential or pursue their personal development. Gradually, members of the company asserted their own distinct artistic and teaching identity, and by the middle of 1980s a number of independent groups appeared, ushering in a new era. In 1991, the Roy Hart International Artistic Centre (CAIRH)[4] was created in order to sustain the legacy of Hart and the Roy Hart Theatre in Malérargues. Some members had previously created small centers for the Roy Hart tradition in cities in France, but this center now accelerated growth. A number of the foundering members of Roy Hart Theatre were also now based elsewhere in Europe or in North America. They found fertile ground and often institutional recognition to teach their synthesis of the work and apply it in a host of artistic frameworks, as well as pursuing their own performing and directing careers.

During the years of Roy Hart Theatre at Malérargues, a small number of participants in workshops were drawn to continue their studies with the company, in many cases moving to the region. These individuals constituted a third generation of teachers and contribute to the dissemination of the work today.

Key Features

The pioneering work of Alfred Wolfsohn, Roy Hart, and Roy Hart Theatre has achieved considerable recognition in many fields, particularly for its profound work on the voice. The transmission of this legacy is a fundamental objective of this body of practitioners. This transmission unfolds in two main forms. The first is the Roy Hart International Artistic Centre (CAIRH) in Malérargues, France. It is a permanent residence that enables teachers and practitioners to develop a comprehensive program of workshops, festivals, and performance creations. The second form is an immaterial one; this is the knowledge, experience, and skill of a body of teachers who now disseminate teaching and theatre practices throughout the Americas, Europe, Middle East, Africa, and Asia. These two lines of transmission (one rooted in the stones of a Cévennes hamlet and the other a vascular network of practitioners across the world) offer a wealth of opportunities for meeting the Roy Hart tradition.

The Roy Hart tradition is relatively rare in the sense that it does not refer to a specific opus or manual that lays down a series of exercises or strategies based on practice and theory that serve as a roadmap for its practitioners. Rather, the main pathway of transmission in the Roy Hart tradition has been through personal direct experience in the form of apprenticeship. Roy Hart received his training from Alfred Wolfsohn. While Wolfsohn's writings discussed an original and revolutionary approach to the voice, he did not go into great pedagogical detail.

Hart, in turn, offered a comprehensive teaching that focused on the voice as the essential medium for expression of the protean range of the human spirit, but Hart was also drawn toward personal and societal development. He extended the training his students received by inviting dancers from the company (and other guest artists) to give regular movement and dance classes, and he embarked on collective training sessions that emphasized intense physical and vocal plasticity—a literal unchaining of the performer's potential. But he did not undertake a formal teacher training program for his students.

Therefore, it can be confusing for someone who does not have first-hand experience of this work to understand the particular nature of the Roy Hart tradition and how it fits within other approaches to the voice that have been developed in the twentieth century. Nevertheless, despite the obvious differences in teaching style and focus of a varied body of teachers, many students iterate that there is often a common root between these teachers and their diverse approaches or strategies.

Discussion of Teaching Style

As teachers we believe that some of these common roots are as follows:

- We believe in a fundamental engagement with listening to the student; absorbing a host of information that the voice, body, gestures, and facial expressions give and through these observations, intuiting how best to answer the demands of the student. The teaching strategy or didactic is primarily experiential, guiding students to awareness through sensorial, proprioceptive, and emotional experience.

- We use a non-prescriptive approach: using a variety of strategies to discover and develop their voices. It is an approach to the phenomenon of the voice as being one of sound, distinct from the more specific and culturally defined uses that humans make of voice in speech and song.
- We support an eschewal of a conventional approach to what is beautiful or what is ugly in vocal expression, by approaching it simply as sound. This allows the student to open up raw and, in some cases, very surprising vocal areas. Students are encouraged to delve deep into their own sound matter and to put aside easy definitions of what a male or female voice should be. This approach to the voice therefore tends to break up traditional compartmentalization of vocal types.
- Students are offered the possibility of testing their vocal extremes, not only in terms of pitch, but also of volume, intensity, and timbre. Students access vocal areas that require an intense concentration of energies: the scream, lamentation, and chorded or double-stopping sounds, and the students explore a spectrum of sound that stretches from the darkest growl to bird-like "flutey" pitches, well below and above "normal" ranges. Roy Hart referred to this as "The 8 Octave Voice."
- The Roy Hart tradition favors physical engagement. The full mobilization of the body brings a vital energy to the voice and releases the student's imagination. Subtle somatic awareness, balancing forces of relaxation and tension, enables the student to gauge and refine their vocal experience.
- Overall, teachers in the Roy Hart tradition have a fundamental commitment to a humanistic and holistic view of the voice. Vocal expression takes place in a multidimensional context where balance is sought between a person's life journey and their artistic fulfillment.
- Teachers often use the piano as an objective reference for their work and, depending on their musical skills, this can include basic work on pitch, range, and timbre, but also may serve as an accompaniment and stimulus for improvisation with vocal sound or song interpretation.

Over the years, the founder members of Roy Hart Theatre who worked directly with Hart (including Kaya Anderson, their "doyenne," who also studied under Wolfsohn) have each in their own way furthered and re-invented the work, not only through their own research, but also through symbiosis with other strands and traditions: be they *bel canto*, polyphonic song from many traditions," new music," jazz and improvised music, exposure to approaches to text, somatic studies, or the clarifications of vocal science and anatomy. Many other cultural and artistic currents, such as the field of personal development, the study of myth, Jungian, and archetypal psychology, have all made significant contributions to the evolution of the Roy Hart tradition. Some Roy Hart teachers have had direct contact with leading exponents of other voice-training approaches, in particular Cicely Berry and Kristin Linklater. These experiences and similar exchanges with other practitioners working in this field have broadened their expertise and given them new perspectives on the work. Specific groups, born out of the original Roy Hart Theatre company, have created their own structures in order to further their own research and development.

Broadly speaking the Roy Hart tradition gravitates around two epicenters: (1) one-on-one work (which can take place either within a group setting, or as a private session "À *deux*") and (2) ensemble classes. In the individual work, the student receives a lesson, most often with the teacher at the piano in an in-depth exploration of their vocal potential, which at a later stage can include the full reach of interpretation in both singing, text work, and other forms of performance. This "primary" exploration, which probably favors the sound over any literal semantic meaning in a word or text, is also a precursor for a return to the value of the word. As Hart explained in a letter to a television producer on August 31 1973, "It is therefore necessary that your program should take into full account the way in which RHT [Roy Hart Theatre], as related to the late Alfred Wolfsohn, has come out of the *cry* to reinstate the *word*."[5]

Concomitantly with the one-on-one lesson, Hart created with Roy Hart Theatre an approach to ensemble work that eventually formed the foundation for performances created both in his lifetime and after his death. This approach was partly in response to the growth in group membership, which made it impossible for him to teach each person individually, but also in order to foster the creation of a company that was tuned and sensitive to each member. Hart and his company absorbed a wide field of influences in this ensemble work: from several forms of dance to musical improvisation, from subtle corporeal movement to avant-garde textual expression. Hart's insistence on empathetic awareness and synchronicity, as well as a spirit of research and self-interrogation in ensemble work, has left a deep imprint on the Roy Hart tradition today.

Ensemble work emerged in different forms by both the generation of teachers who worked with Hart and also by subsequent generations of teachers, who bring their own experience and knowledge. The group work prepares body and voice for the demands of a workshop and may turn to a musical or textual resource as material for interpretation or improvisation in an atelier style setting.

As the Roy Hart tradition has moved into the twenty-first century so has the work expanded amid an on-going spirit of renewal, that encourages both senior teachers and younger exponents to continually review and refresh their teaching and artistic practice. The Wolfsohn/Hart philosophy of what constitutes a holistic approach to the voice, their intuition about its importance both artistically and on a human level, continues to find new avenues of application and relevance.

Goals of the Organization

The Roy Hart International Artistic Centre (CAIRH) has an important role in the dissemination and transmission of the Roy Hart tradition, but it is complimented by teachers, whose center of interest is no longer in France, but are based elsewhere in Europe and the Americas, promoting their work independently. The CAIRH has the status of an association (similar to a non-profit status in the United States). Teachers and students at the center alike pay a yearly membership fee. This gives them the right to attend the association's statutory meetings during which, among other business, the

President and the Administrative Council are elected. The President and the Council, in consultation with the members of the association, put into practice policies that further both long- and short-term aims of the association.

The statutes of the association clarify its aims:

- Develop artistic and pedagogic activities of the CAIRH,
- Promote, protect, manage, and transmit the artistic and intellectual heritage of Alfred Wolfsohn, Roy Hart, and Roy Hart Theatre,
- Lead, encourage, and transmit artistic research particularly in the domain of the human voice,
- Create and receive theatre and musical performances, organize workshops and cultural events.

Based on these four primary goals the CAIRH organizes, with the assistance of its members, programs of workshops, classes, and seminars that address the demands, both of those individuals and groups wishing to acquaint themselves with the work, as well as persons who wish to make an in-depth study with a view in some cases to teaching this work. Aside from this, the individual members, depending on their own status (some work independently; others work for diverse associations and institutions) organize and deliver their own workshops and classes, in many cases collaborating with other artists or creating their own performances. The CAIRH has a part to play in producing works of its members: it makes available (when it is able) studio space for rehearsal and offers a polyvalent performance space to receive and promote performances particularly during the summer months. Small subventions are sometimes available to creators through local government grants.

The Centre is active for most of the year with a concentration of workshops and events in the summer months. It plays host to the *Myth and Theatre Festival* directed by Pantheatre, with conferences, performances, and master workshops. Annual meetings of teachers take place in the spring for one week, providing a forum and opportunity for CAIRH teachers of diverse generations to meet, discuss, and exchange practice. A similar event takes place bi-annually in the USA.

Certification Process

Deepening Studies

The CAIRH offers possibilities for deepening the practice and philosophy of vocal expression inherited from Alfred Wolfsohn and Roy Hart. There is no single, prescribed curriculum, and each teacher offers a view of the work built through their own experience. The primary source and common heritage come from decades of experiential research into the human voice and its connection to the individual.

There are multiple avenues for those who have already had significant experience with the voice work and who seek to go further. Access to in-depth training groups is made by selection and each one offers an attestation of completion of their particular training. An annex document with specific details is available on demand from the CAIRH.

VOCAL TRADITIONS

Apprenticeship Toward Teaching

After extensive work in one or more of these training groups, or through a program of individual study, a person may request to be nominated by a senior teacher of the CAIRH to embark on an apprenticeship process leading toward becoming a teacher of the work that is recognized officially by the CAIRH. Agreement to begin the apprenticeship must be supported by at least two more recognized CAIRH teachers and must include the nomination of at least one senior CAIRH teacher as a mentor. The length and content of the apprenticeship is defined by the mentor's evaluation of the needs of the student and may include further avenues of study and collaboration or supervision. A mentorship fee is established by the CAIRH.

The student may begin to teach in the name of the CAIRH upon recommendation by the mentor, with the endorsement of at least four more recognized CAIRH teachers. An annex document with specific details is available on demand from the CAIRH.

Contact Information, Resources, and How to Get Involved

The following are resources for the organization:

- CAIRH: Full information on workshops in Malerargues, performance events, deepening studies, and administrative details are to be found at http://roy-hart-theatre.com. The CAIRH website includes substantial information on the teachers at the Centre, as well as photographic and historical resources and a selection of articles written by members. Some of the workshops outside the CAIRH are also presented.

For general information please contact:
CAIRH/Roy Hart International Arts Center
Chateau de Malérargues
F-30140 Thoiras, France
Telephone:(33) 466854598
e-mail: cairh_office@orange.fr

- Pantheatre (Paris): The website has extensive information on their activities including archival material, reflections on pedagogy, and policy for mentoring potential teachers recognized by the CAIRH. See http://pantheatre.com.
- Paul Silber and Clara Harris have created a website dedicated to Alfred Wolfsohn, Roy Hart, and Roy Hart Theatre containing valuable archives. The site offers digital recordings that illustrate the work of Roy Hart and Roy Hart Theatre, some of which can be downloaded through iTunes. See http://www.roy-hart.com/.
- There is a photographic archive tracing the entire history of the Roy Hart Tradition from Alfred Wolfsohn to the present day. It includes a Roy Hart Theatre photo and ebook that is downloadable from iTunes. It also offers facilities to donate toward the editing and publishing of a full-length photo book. *Orpheus or The Way to a Mask* by Alfred Wolfsohn is available as a download from this site. It is curated by Ivan Midderigh. See https://www.royharttheatrephotographi carchives.com/

- YouTube has many resources and examples of Roy Hart, Roy Hart Theatre, and workshop extracts. For an example, see https://www.youtube.com/results?search_query=roy+hart+theatre+arno+peck.

There are additional books and articles as well:

- *Dark Voices: The Genesis of Roy Hart Theatre* by Noah Pikes. The third edition of this seminal work traces the history of the Roy Hart tradition from its inception with Wolfsohn through to its embodiment in Roy Hart and his group of students, subsequently developing into Roy Hart Theatre. It is written from several different viewpoints, including the autobiographical one, beginning with Pikes's struggles as he began to study with Hart (Pikes 2019). For more information, see wholevoicepublishing@gmail.com.
- *Roy Hart Theatre at Malerargues* by Ian Magilton. This book is a colorful and personal recounting of the Roy Hart Theatre story from its early days in London to its establishment in Malerargues, France and the various phases of its evolution as a cultural, artistic, and residential center. It is available in both English and French (Magilton 2018). For more information, see magian@me.com.
- *The Mystery Behind the Voice: A Biography of Alfred Wolfsohn* by Sheila Braggins. This is a valuable contribution to our knowledge of Wolfsohn, the man and the visionary (Braggins 2012).
- *Singing with Your Own Voice* by Orlanda Cook. This is a practical guide to awakening and developing the hidden qualities in your own singing voice (Cook 2004).
- *Roy Hart by* Kevin Crawford and Bernadette Sweeney. This biography of Hart includes a detailed examination of key theatrical works produced during his lifetime and a selection of exercises proposed by leading teachers in the Roy Hart tradition (Crawford and Sweeney forthcoming).
- "The Roy Hart Theatre: Teaching the Totality of Self" by Laura Kalo, George Whiteside, and David Midderigh. This chapter from *The Vocal Vision* examines the history of the Roy Hart Theatre (Kalo, Whiteside, and Midderigh 1997).

Notes

1. The quotation is translated by Susie Croner.
2. See Luchsinger and Dublois (1956) for more details.
3. The film was directed by Roy Hart with camera by Denis Miller and sound by Leslie Shepard.
4. The French name is the *Centre Artistique International Roy Hart.*
5. The italics are from the author. See http://www.roy-hart.com/pauls.htm for the full letter.

Acknowledgments

The authors would like to thank Jay Livernois, editor, for allowing us to quote from *Orpheus or The Way to a Mask,* and for generously making this book available for electronic download. We also thank Jonathan Hart for patiently assisting us in editing and checking the information in this article.

Disclosure statement

No potential conflict of interest was reported by the authors.

References

Braggins, Sheila. 2012. *The Mystery behind the Voice: A Biography of Alfred Wolfsohn*. Kibworth Beauchamp, Leicestershire: Matador.

Cook, Orlanda. 2004. *Singing with Your Own Voice*. New York: Routledge.

Crawford, Kevin, and Bernadette Sweeney. forthcoming. *Roy Hart*. London: Routledge.

Janov, Arthur. 1970. *The Primal Scream*. New York: Putnam.

Kalo, Laura, George Whiteside, and David Midderigh. 1997. "The Roy Hart Theatre: Teaching the Totality of Self." In *The Vocal Vision*, edited by Marion Hampton and Barbara Acker, 185–202. New York: Applause.

Luchsinger, R., and C.L. Dublois. 1956. "Phonetische und stroboskopische Untersuchungen an einem Stimmphänomen." *Folia Phoniatrica* 8 (4): 201–210. doi:10.1159/000262743.

Magilton, Ian. 2018. *Roy Hart Theatre at Malerargues*. Thoiras: Magilton.

Pikes, Noah. 2019. *Dark Voices: The Genesis of Roy Hart Theatre*. 3rd ed. Zurich, Switzerland: Pikes.

Wolfsohn, Alfred. 1956. *Vox Humana: Alfred Wolfsohn's Experiments in Extension of Human Vocal Range*. New York: Smithsonian Folkways Records. https://folkways.si.edu/vox-humana-alfred-wolfsohns-experiments-in-extension-of-human-vocal-range/contemporary-electronic-science-nature-sounds/album/smithsonian.

Wolfsohn, Alfred. 2012. *Orpheus or the Way to a Mask* Translated by Marita Gunther. Woodstock, CT: Abraxas Publishing.

Zadek, Peter. 1998. *My Way: Eine Autobiographie*. Köln, German: Kiepenheuer & Witsch.

The Sharpe/Haydn Method

Edda Sharpe and Jan Haydn Rowles

ABSTRACT

Vocal Traditions is a series in the *Voice and Speech Review* that highlights historically important voice teachers and schools of thought in the world of vocal pedagogy. This essay explores the background of the Sharpe/Haydn Method, the central features of system, and the five key foundations.

Introduction and Background

Both of us (Edda and Jan) "got the accent bug" when we were children. But it was not until we trained as voice coaches on the voice studies course at the Royal Central School of Speech and Drama (Central) that we were first able to give structure to our explorations and purpose to our passion.

In the late 1990s, Edda was invited to teach the accents and dialects class to trainee-voice coaches on the prestigious master's program at Central. At the same time, we were both busy teaching accents to student actors in theatre schools across London. In this context, there was often very limited time to achieve useful results with groups of students that were of mixed skill level and with varying interests in this specific aspect of their acting training. It was in these teaching contexts that we began to identify a need for a simple way of teaching not just one accent at a time, but a structure that could apply to *all* accents. We wanted a method that *all* voice and acting students could understand and use, not just the ones that identified themselves as "good at accents" and especially not just those few that were able to readily grasp the International Phonetic Alphabet (IPA) and its applications. Of course, some students would also "get the accent bug" and be as engaged and excited as we were in the investigative, analytical, and "puzzle solving" aspect of accent study and acquisition, with its accompanying emphasis on IPA. Nevertheless, it was overwhelmingly evident to us that the vast majority of acting students felt alienated by phonetics.

Within the professional coaching world, the problem of how to teach accents accessibly and quickly without the use of the IPA was perhaps even more acute. In our experience, many professional actors seemed to have been alienated from the process of accent study by the way it had been approached phonetically in training. Some actors had an almost phobic response to phonetics, and many actors felt that phonetic analysis interfered with their acting process. This caused actors to avoid working on an accent in the belief that they were being more "intuitive," developing their own ways into the accent. But this intuitive approach also meant that the actor lacked a process that could support them. As coaches, we know that to inhabit an accent in a successful way requires actors to use both intuition *and* structure. So, we began to codify our ideas about accent coaching and training in an effort to solve this problem.

In designing and writing the material for our first book, *How To Do Accents*, it was our aim to provide a simple structure for breaking down and studying accents that was compatible with the actor's intuitive brain and the acting process (Sharpe and Rowles 2009). We wanted a process that liberated the nervous actor while giving them a much-needed structure to develop speech skills in a well-honed way. We wanted to create a system that was structured and rigorous enough to be of value, while being fully accessible and inclusive to those who found the overtly academic approach bewildering. We wanted to build a bridge between our world as accent coaches and their world as actors. So began the long process of creating the *How To Do Accents* system of accent breakdown, study, and practice.

Style

Our writing (and coaching) style is an extremely important part of our work. Our books are not academic, linguistic, or phonological textbooks. There are plenty of those available.[1] Rather, we write and speak to communicate with voice teachers, coaches, and actors. We want the words on the page to read like the spoken voice, not the written voice. We take the language of the linguist and phonetician and translate it into the language of the actor. We aim to distill the very detailed work of linguists and phoneticians and extract the elements relevant to the specific goals of the voice teacher and actor at work. We use solid know-how, clear practical steps, real-life examples, and the occasional dose of humor to work through the technical, cultural, and communicative layers in an accent, and we aim to give the insight, tools, and confidence to work with any accent.[2]

Key Features

There are three distinctive features of our system for breaking down and studying any accent. These three features are the philosophical pillars of our work:

Seeing Feeling Hearing

In our system, all three major senses (seeing, feeling, and hearing) are employed when exploring a new accent. Relying on having "a good ear" is arguably the biggest mistake a person can make, whether they are a student or coach. This point of view is a dead end for both coaches and actors. In our point of view, people who are "good at accents" experience them in a multi-sensory way. They feel the sounds, see the shapes and movements, and hear the results. The three connect. In all our work, we have exercises to encourage multisensory awareness and connection when learning the new accent.

Five Key Components

We have five main points of change from one accent to another. In our system we ensure that the student/actor/coach never feels overwhelmed by learning the accent, since any given accent can have a great deal of complex information for actors to process.[3] The accent is broken down into five key areas of study: The Foundations, The Two Planets, The Bite, The Shapes, and The Groove. These are outlined further below.

"You and the New"

Unless everyone has access to a standard accent of some kind, it seems of limited efficacy to teach and study an accent in comparison to a "standard." Why take two steps when one would seem more efficient and clearer to understand? Using the process and accompanying charts of "You and The New" students learn to track the changes in the new accent they are learning, instead of comparing themselves to a standard accent such as Received Pronunciation (RP) or any other "standard" accent. Rather, learners examine their own accent and the accent they are trying to acquire for a role. Our You and the New chart, which is found inside *How To Do Accents*, provides a useful accent breakdown and teaching tool.

The Five Key Components

The Foundations

There are four fundamental parts of our system that are needed to build an accent on a strong foundation. These foundations give an accent focus and hold it in place. They are:

(1) The Zone—Where the sound is placed.
(2) The Tone—The resonant quality of the accent.
(3) The Setting—The setting of the muscles of the face and mouth.
(4) The Direction—The direction in which the voice is set. (Sharpe and Rowles 2009)

Before we structured "The Foundations" in this way, in our experience most accent coaching material was based purely on learning the phonetic shifts from one accent to another. Stern (2017) was a notable exception to this historical precedent in his ground-breaking accent work in the late 1970s; *Acting in an Accent* included resonant focal points in his accent descriptions

In our system, there are seven zones, which can help the actor map out their mouth. This enables actors to visualize the sound hitting a point in the vocal track, feel it resonating there, and sustain this sound while speaking. The zones provide both a visual and kinesthetic anchor for an accent, and they stop it from "sliding out." These zones help actors build to tone, setting, and direction.

The Two Planets

The Two Planets refers to rhoticity. Understanding rhoticity and its implications is an essential skill for accent coaches. (Simply, rhotic is when the /r/ is always sounded in an accent, and non-rhotic is when the /r/ is only sounded before a vowel.) These are the two metaphorical planets. Which planet is your new accent on? Is it the same planet as yours? Or is it a "hybrid" in some process of migration from one planet to the other?

The Bite

As we taught and coached accents, we realized that there were several consonants that had a more powerful effect in accent change than others. These consonants really do have the power to "make or break" an accent. As with the two planets, there are patterns that can be learned, and these consonant patterns are essential to explore. The "bite," then, refers to the "impact that consonants can have on an accent and the significant ways in which consonants differ from region to region" (Sharpe and Rowles 2009, 56). There are five *Major Players*:

(1) /r/- tapping, bending, curling, or bunching
(2) /l/- light, dark, or not at all
(3) /h/- to drop or not to drop
(4) "ng"—are you "running, runnin', runn'n, or runningk" for the bus?
(5) "th"—are you "with it, wivvit, widdit, or wizzit"? (Sharpe and Rowles 2009, 56)

The Shapes

The shapes refer to vowel shapes. In our system, we use "The Kit List." This means of teaching vowels and accent was a tool that we had (perhaps surprisingly) not been exposed to as voice students. The list is based on "The Standard Lexical Sets for English" introduced by John C. Wells in *Accents of English*. Wells (1982) defined each lexical set on the basis of the pronunciation of words in two reference accents, which he calls Received Pronunciation (RP) and General American (GenAm). Although not completely failsafe, we found that these lexical sets or the "The Kit List" provide the most useful tool for organizing and labeling vowel shapes and comparing one accent to another. Being able to refer to something as a KIT vowel or a DRESS vowel and knowing which lexical set your words go into can be revelatory. This allows actors to see where some vowels have "jumped set" and where lexical sets have merged or divided from their own accent and a new accent. This way of thinking about accents also allows for accents to have an *inventory* (a list of vowels used by an accent) and a *distribution* (which vowels go with which words).

The Groove

The groove refers to the "music" played or to the intonation used when speaking in an accent. All accents have a unique music made of rhythms and tunes. Learning them is key to fully realizing the sounds of an accent. In this system, the groove has several simple steps:

(1) Frame it: Put the cultural historical, and geographical frame around your groove to understand where it comes from.
(2) Embody it: Get a feel for the new groove by using physical actions such as Laban effort actions[4] to anchor the physical dynamics of your voice.
(3) Identify the default tune: Explore the musical quality of an accent.
(4) Own it: Play the melodies to express actions, intention, and the emotional journey of your character. (Sharpe and Rowles 2009, 150)

Resources

The central text of the Sharpe/Haydn Method is *How To Do Accents*. But we also have written *How To Do Standard English Accents*, which offers more written detail on the varieties of RP or "Neutral Southern" accents of the United Kingdom using our method (Sharpe and Rowles 2012). The written resources also pair with our key digital resource— an app called *The Accent Kit*, co-created with Richard Ryder. This app offers practical examples and accent breakdowns from accents around the world, which uses The Five Key Components above as the framework for accent application. Accent enthusiasts are welcome to contribute their own accents for the app. More information is available at www.theaccentkit.com.

Notes

1. Some of our favorite resources include Collins and Mees (2013) as a formal phonetics textbook, Wells (1982) as an accent book that leans into IPA descriptions, and Turner (1950) as a book on voice and speech fundamentals for the stage. These resources have also strongly influenced our own method and approach to accent coaching and training.
2. Key individuals who have influenced our method include the accent coaches Jill McCullough (Meier and McCullough 2020) and Stern (2017).
3. We chose to have five key headings for accent work for a variety of reasons, but one key element is Miller's idea of "The Magical Number Seven, Plus or Minus Two." Miller (1956) argues that humans have a limit on our mental capacity and processing abilities. In short, most people can process seven ideas at once. Some can process nine, and some can only five. Thus, lists and theories that involve five or fewer concepts are the easiest to grasp and maintain.
4. Laban is a method and language for describing, visualizing, interpreting, and documenting human movement. See the Laban/Bartenieff Institute of Movement Studies for more information. https://labaninstitute.org/

Disclosure Statement

No potential conflict of interest was reported by the authors.

References

Collins, Beverley, and Inger M. Mees. 2013. *Practical Phonetics and Phonology: A Resource Book for Students*. 3rd ed. London: Routledge.

Meier, Paul, and Jill McCullough. 2020. "Episode 24: Jill McCullough." Podcast. *In a Manner of Speaking*. https://www.paulmeier.com/tag/jill-mccullough/

Miller, G.A. 1956. "The Magical Number Seven, Plus or Minus Two: Some Limits on Our Capacity for Processing Information." *Psychological Review* 63 (2): 81–97. doi:10.1037/h0043158.

Sharpe, Edda, and Jan Haydn Rowles. 2009. *How To Do Accents*. Revised 2nd ed. London: Oberon Books.

Sharpe, Edda, and Jan Haydn Rowles. 2012. *How To Standard English Accents*. London: Oberon Books.

Stern, David Alan. 2017. "David Alan Stern: My Journey to Now." *Voice and Speech Review* 11 (3): 348–361. doi:10.1080/23268263.2017.1401765.

Turner, J. Clifford. 1950. *Voice and Speech in the Theatre*. London: A&C Black.

Wells, J.C. 1982. *Accents of English*. Cambridge: Cambridge University Press.

Miller Voice Method

Scott Miller, John Patrick, Liam Joynt and Kristi Dana

ABSTRACT
Vocal Traditions is a series in the *Voice and Speech Review* that highlights historically important voice teachers and schools of thought in the world of vocal pedagogy. In this essay, Miller Voice Method (MVM) offers its overview, history, teaching style and philosophy, goals, and details on certification. The key features of MVM are explored including: active breath, the attention blueprint, athleticism, on-camera applications, and text transfusion. The essay discusses the importance of integration—how the methodology assists actors in bridging the gap between technique and application, and the vital connection between the philosophy of the work and the work itself. The essay also describes unique MVM offerings including a video series highlighting core exercises (found on its website), on-camera techniques for vocal diagnostic and development, personalized action plans, and perspectives that reprioritize the audience's experience as a vital component to actor training.

Overview

The Miller Voice Method (MVM) endeavors to solve the paradox of acting, namely inhabiting spontaneous recognizably human behavior *while* attempting to execute well-rehearsed moments under the duress and expectation of performance, which we then call "truthful"—a decidedly un-human human event.

Add to that the demands of making all the information in a given moment accessible to an audience, who often comes to the event expecting to be "done to" rather than engage in a quid pro quo relationship.

We model our exercises on how the brain works and how humans process thought and motor function: think and (re)act. Embedded in our approach to text analysis, memorization, and breath work are tools to keep the actor from fantasizing about how a scene should go or did go in a rehearsal last week. Rather, the actor has a method to connect exclusively with present information in the room and trust that the exhaustive exploration of the pre-rehearsal and rehearsal process will inform each moment without conscious thought about it.

We have developed a series of physical exercises and integrative techniques to create habits that use minimal effort for maximum efficiency in the production of sound. Upon this baseline, we develop each actor's full melodic range, placement, and tempo suppleness in order to deliver intonation that supports strong and clear points of view, which opens the gateway for the audience to see more of themselves.

History of MVM

About the Founder

While my (Scott Miller's) parent's drugs of choice were the more traditional ones for parents of the 60s and 70s, my muse was sports. It provided immediate and reliable feedback from the ball; it went where it was hit, passed, or thrown. Opportunity presented a neighborhood of older kids, which meant being the least skilled and last chosen for every game; improvement was a pre-requisite to survival. Home experiences taught that any delusions of superiority or safety resulted in vulnerability, which invariably led to a kind of emotional decimation. To feel superior was a luxury that encouraged a kind of falling asleep to present information, and that was literally very dangerous. In athletics, the transaction is dispassionately fair-minded. Work equals progress.

Withholding reliable boundaries for children ironically restricts the freedom of the child. Children spend attention developing their own boundary lines rather than in outright play. Not surprisingly, much of my adult exploration in the pursuit of knowledge comes through the portal of provocation, testing the lines. A passion in academia, which examines the holes and antiquated paradigms in the American Actor Training system, is squarely in-line.

A montage of life experience brought me to New York City after finishing law school to pursue "the actor's dream." It began with a few lessons from a very old Sanford Meisner, then Uta Hagen, and then Carol Rosenfeld for prolonged study. One of the most formative lessons Ms. Hagen bestowed upon me (and eventually MVM) was the basic concept of experiencing every choice full throttle, no matter the stage of development. "After all there was no other way to see if it was useful," she simply reminded.

Throughout training in the 90s, I remained a muddy speaker with a muffled voice, ironically born blue, strangled by the umbilical cord. The relationship between technique and ability to express it were light years apart. Finally, eight years in, the requisite pain and frustration had reached that threshold where the critical point of obviousness transformed choice into decision.

What would follow was a complete overhaul of an operating system, acting and otherwise. Two years of voice, speech, and Shakespeare work with Shane Ann Younts (now a colleague at NYU Grad Acting) began the journey. I later worked with her mentor, the late esteemed Robert Neff Williams from Juilliard, who developed a methodology in his own right but chose never to publish it. I also worked with two core energetic therapists and spent five years with two healers on theories of attention in the Catskills. This combined training grounded the work.

In training as an actor and in teaching in MFA programs, what became evident was that voice teachers were often expected to know about voice, and they were required to sensor their language about acting. Movement teachers were treated similarly. And acting teachers generally did not know much about the pedagogy of either voice or movement training.

"Could you imagine a more inefficient system if you tried?" I thought. Experience in professional sports and 40 years in training and coaching led to a bias toward integration. For example, pitching coaches are expected to know about hitting and speak of it adroitly. In American actor training, it seemed this cross application did not apply.

MVM began out of a desire to fill many of the holes in American actor training that failed to link breath, sound, movement, attention, and objective in a way that did not splinter apart the moment the actor stepped outside the safe haven of that discipline's studio and into the rigors of professional acting. The more practical challenge was not simply in opening an actor's capacity of expression; the challenge was to train actors in a way that they would survive the duress of live performance: integration.

Life in academia began in 2001, first in the undergraduate drama program at Tisch, and then a few years at Rutger's MFA program. By 2003, due to the Internet, it was clear this next generation of actors (with their entitlement to information and easy access to it) sought an integrative model free from silo approaches and ego-driven teachers. In January 2003, I was hired by Zelda Fichandler, the chair and visionary of the Graduate Acting Program at NYU. In my first faculty meeting, Zelda welcomed us all as "acting teachers." I knew I was home.

The fundamentals of the work came together over the next five years or so. The excellent tutelage in voice, speech, and Shakespeare; a sports background; Alexander Technique; a learned approach to breathing (which was pioneered by Carl Stough and passed on by the precise Jessica Wolf); and more extensive "character voice" exercises from provocative work with Lenard Petit and The Michael Chekhov Technique all led to an approach which seeks to teach the ability to integrate multiple disciplines and intentions efficiently.

The Creation of the MVM Studio: Enter John Patrick and Liam Joynt

The next seminal moment happened in 2007 when John Patrick, whom I had taught at the Rutger's MFA program, re-emerged. Zelda had encouraged all of us to source replacements in case of illness or professional conflicts. John was the obvious choice, a life-long teacher who came with more experiences in the various voice approaches than I did. With the permission of NYU Graduate Acting, for two years John trailed me and assisted me with the students.

Over the next 10 years, the work at Graduate Acting began to solidify, both in becoming a more permanent fixture on the floor, as well as in the methodology itself. With Mark Wing-Davey's arrival and support in 2009, the teacher training process became more formalized and recognized.

By 2010, John, along with the next two teachers in training, Liam Joynt and Rita Marchelya, pushed for the work to expand outside the narrow halls of Grad Acting. We met continuously for a year, and the foundations of MVM Studio were born. From the start, we always had a name dilemma. I was neither intrigued by having my name on it nor quite satisfied with the "Voice" in the name. Because at its heart, MVM is a method in integration through voice and breath, but it is primarily an acting and living model.

In the years to follow, Liam and John remained as pillars of the approach, while Rita moved on to pursue other goals. John is now head of voice and speech at UNC Chapel Hill's MFA Professional Actor Training Program, and Liam serves on the voice faculty at NYU in Graduate Acting. The academic synergy has allowed an expansion of the core exercises, which includes: the actor's relationship to the audience, the text and memorization, and the camera. John's work with the camera (as a diagnostic tool and its application to TV/Film work) has been groundbreaking. Liam has pioneered personalized assessments and action plans from both anatomical and neuroscience perspectives which offer students truly lasting habit change that can withstand the duress of performance. My area of concentration has focused on the audience: how, when, and why do humans pay attention, and what does the performer do or not do to maintain or break it? We embrace a constant re-evaluation of the work semester to semester, looking at the viability and efficacy of our current progressions and approaches.

Teaching Style and Philosophy of the Work

At the start of any new semester or workshop, we do a "circle talk" inspired by my years with Native American healers. In the MVM version, we sit in a circle; each participant then gets an equal amount of prescribed time to talk. Only the leader may chime in if there is an opportunity to share some edicts of the work in those early stages.

The purpose of the talking circle has many components. By giving the same allotment to each person, it begins to blur the illusion of status almost immediately. It provides a space solely devoted to the seeing of the other and, equally, to being seen. It allows for essential components of the work to reveal themselves as they begin to see the role of leadership as simply designed to provide boundaries and safety (i.e. direction and context).

Training can be hard work for actors; they are not generally trained like athletes, dancers, or musicians with the hours of repetitive habit breaking, which is then sculpted with curated work. In the beginning and by the end, it takes every ounce of the leader's passionate and performative self to keep learners compelled and focused on the artisan's work: building attention, focus, and curiosity.

In the work, we are fond of the phrase "falling" as a way to describe that experience of being completely dependent on present information, as opposed to the memory of a rehearsal or projected fantasy of the future. The exercises are designed to avoid breath holding and the organizational moments, which separate the student from present experience. We repeat (knowing nothing can ever really be repeated) in order to build the connections in the brain.

We seek transparency as much as humanly possible, even as transparency is clouded by confirmation bias. We seek to find ourselves incorrect or inaccurate, like any scientific method. The work posits that there is no such thing as knowledge, in so much as it means a fixed knowing. That knowledge evolves moment to moment influenced by the next new piece of information.

We devise exercises aimed at partnering with intuition over prediction. We understand prediction is a fundamental way our species survives. However, in the safe space of acting, intuition (not prediction) creates compelling moments.

We train our teachers to "fall" in the same way that they teach their students to rely on the information in the room, buoyed and frame worked by a prepared syllabus.

We train individuals to embrace rigor over preciousness and not to fear exceptionalism. We encourage integrity in the work over force, believing stamina and strength are inevitabilities when one is committed to integrity.

We believe life is a series of attempts, and then you die. There are no such realities as success or failure; these are merely angles.

Key Features

Centered in Integration

MVM was born out of a deep desire to bridge gaps between technique and application. The very gaps in how we as trainers communicate information. Imagine, I "observe" your experience, and I speak in "observational language." Now you must (hopefully) translate that language into "experiential language," for example. We understand that when the actor experiences *A* it most likely will produce *B* in the audience, not *A*. So we must (it seems) re-learn our very language of communication as trainers for the sake of efficiency and come to the performer rather than the old model of forcing the performer to come to us. This is the new model: everywhere and in everything, there is a curated individualized experience; this is the "new" universal.

The Active Breath

MVM employs a breathing pattern that we call the Active Breath (AB) as a fundamental technique that allows moment-to-moment acting to occur more readily. Essentially, the AB is a continuous flow of inhale and exhale without the pauses or holds at the top or bottom of the breath, which would normally occur in passive breathing states. The AB is more akin to an athletic or cardiovascular breath in its flow pattern, but AB does not have the speed of an athletic breath. The AB helps to stave off old habits. For instance, performers develop breathing habits throughout the memorization and rehearsal process. These habits can be rigid in their response to present moment impulses and invariably manifest in inefficient vocal use (an unbalanced use of intonation and airflow). The AB helps to both prevent and alert the actor to these covert habits. There is a musculature to the voice and the coordination of breathing that shifts when an actor is playing a projection of the scene ("idea") rather than being fully immersed in the moment-to-moment flow.

Beginning a scene with the Active Breath is the very manifestation of "trusting yourself." It is in this simple moment of presence that we have found encourages actors to "fall" into the scene and bravely work moment-to-moment. By engaging something simple, physical, and present as a scene begins, an actor does not rely on something dead (their historical preparation) or on something fantastical in anticipation (manipulating through tension). This is not in lieu of understanding what comes right before a scene or what the character wants from a scene; rather, this is how to actually launch from your known preparation into the unknown of present information.

The Attention Blueprint

We detail the Active Breath concept and physical technique in a lecture called "The Attention Blueprint." The Attention Blueprint is a drawing crafted in real time in front of students, so they can see a visual representation of these theories. In the blueprint, we posit that we can directly link hitches in breathing/speaking patterns to an audience's span of attention. The Attention Blueprint was born when MVM began to turn our primary attention away from the experience of the performer and became more interested in the experience of the audience. We are less interested in how something feels to the performer; instead, we are more interested in what information we get back from an audience in response to techniques an actor employs.

In this, we explored an exciting link between a performer's breathing habits and the way in which an audience unconsciously breathes in response. If a performer is holding their breath, so does the audience. If the performer is breathing in a predictable pattern, so will the audience. And if the audience falls into a mind-space where they can consistently predict what's going to happen, they will begin to lose attention. This is the difference between a 90-minute play feeling like it lasts four hours vs. 10 minutes. In film and television, the editor can completely control the audience's empathetic tendencies in this manner and can keep us hanging by a thread in great anticipation and suspense. For the theatrical actor, our breathing and vocal rhythms *are* the editors. How empowering. How terrifying.

The blueprint also details the importance of the audience being satiated with an abundance of information. This means if the audience does not have enough to be beautifully baffled by, then they will again lose interest. This "information" can be broken down into "intellectual" information and "visceral" information. Intellectual information consists of elements like interesting plot lines, characters, and language that is intelligible and understandable. Visceral information is the emotional and psychological experience shared through the quality of vocal/physical expression: a kind of uninhibited resonance that vibrates the room and results in the audience feeling surrounded and invited by the performer. If we keep the audience occupied with abundant information to process both intellectually and viscerally, then we keep them in a sustained state of suspense where their attention is rapt, so they can truly receive the dilemma of the play as perhaps a personal dilemma.

Acting is an Athletic Event

Another integration gap we observe surrounds the emphasis of "release and relaxation" in actor training. Quite simply, we do not understand what is relaxed about playing through heightened circumstances live in front of 500 people or on a film set with 50 million dollars at stake. Of course, shifting attention away from performance anxiety to the simple reality of doing is essential for success, but how in the world do we do this with everyone watching us? It is quite easy to find this deep state of relaxation in the vacuum of the studio or rehearsal hall where you build trust over several weeks, months, or years. But how does this relate to the intense audition room or the critic-filled opening night?

In response to the above phenomenon, we theorize that acting can be viewed more accurately as an athletic event. The correlations between the two arenas are staggering: big crowds looking on, athletes/performers required to be in the moment, and huge stakes of circumstance. Moreover, actors and athletes are instantly replaceable due to the high supply of talent, minimal opportunities, and constant states of free agency.

Any athlete that has attempted to produce at a high level understands that there is nothing natural or normal about that circumstance. Therefore, there can be nothing natural or normal about the way they breathe and focus. The breath must encourage the body and focus to be super-sensitized and ready for anything. And all this happens *before* attention is put on a partner or the task at hand, just like the pitcher or quarterback. Actors/athletes get their body at the ready, look up, see the target, and *then* go, working to maintain this state of flow as obstacles emerge.

On-camera Integration

MVM utilizes the camera to make voice and acting training as objective as possible. Starting with diagnostic work in the earlier days of training through modules involving vocal resonance and dialects, we are able to *show* a student the physical habits that are possibly inhibiting the work rather than only relying on verbal and physical feedback. Learning becomes exponentially more efficient when an actor sees their habits shift on screen at the exact moment when their classmates erupt in positive support of the moment. This inclusive approach to voice work utilizes the technology available to us as well as acknowledges technology's pervasive presence in the field. Students by the end of training should be as comfortable with a camera in their workspace as the props they utilize for scene work.

Text Analysis and Memorization: "Text Transfusion"

Another integration gap we observe is how actors memorize lines. How is it that a universal task that actors engage in is not discussed by any major acting technique with prescriptive best practice for memorization? If the goal were to simply memorize the material, then the "how" does not matter. Just get it done.

Instead, the goal for us was to replicate the way the brain remembers things in unscripted conversations, and certainly, it was not by blandly saying things over and over. We registered feedback from actors that no matter how well memorized a piece of text was, when it was uttered in acting it felt slightly different in experience than when talking in life. Why?

Human memory is made up of multiple quadrants taking in multiple types of information at once (visual, auditory, sensory), and when it fires during recall, all these areas "light up." Every word we speak to further our intention in life engages our memory and all its quadrants. Imagine now how unfulfilled our memory is from simply staring at a page saying words over and over. Associations, on every informational level, are associative to the memory, and they come along for the ride as they stir recall. Could even the actor's fear and desperation to get "off book" be part of the memory? Why not?

The final piece to come together was the notion that activity in the thought area of the brain preempts motor function (speaking/moving). That is, we "have thought, recall, move," which are all inspired by stimuli from the outside world or from our inside world (i.e. a trigger). There is a common fear that if actors memorize their lines too early then they could become inflexible. We found that actors become less flexible as a result of *how* they get off-book, not how *early* they get off-book.

Our systematic approach called "Text Transfusion" was designed to address the missing pieces in an actor's process toward verbatim recall, allowing the brain many more pieces of experience on its journey toward speech. Remember, every physical experience in life contacts the memory before execution.

Goals of the Organization

The MVM approach continues to grow, and we share the work with people in a variety of occupations where the clarity of expression is vital: actors; singers; voice, speech, acting, and movement teachers; and those in the non-performance world like business leaders, newscasters, athletes, politicians, lawyers, doctors, religious leaders, and more. Those who find their way to the MVM are people who seek a training system founded in compassion, transparency, frankness, and curiosity.

In theatre programs, we strive to assist students not only with a fundamentally sound vocal technique but also with an integrative model that blends the fabric of all their work into the tapestry of a compelling performance. We believe that the actor's use of breath can no longer be secondary or an afterthought or something that the actor "hopes" will happen in the acting class if they release tension. We seek to help teachers understand how to integrate this work as a basic component of acting training, where training the breath takes on just as much importance as any other component of the acting work. To that end, we aim to break the mold of what a "voice teacher" does or what they have traditionally done. No longer is it enough to help produce a healthy, flexible, resonant voice and then hope for the best under the duress of performance.

We desire a world where parents, spouses, and intercultural participants have vast access to MVM training to increase capacities of patience, compassion, effective listening, and conflict management. We seek to bring the work into grammar schools where access to free flow of breath and voice may already be stunted.

Current MVM collaborations are underway with top MBA business programs that specialize in global communication strategies and conflict/mediation resolution, as well as LGBTQ centers with members who feel their voice is marginalized or literally redeveloping as they coordinate their voice after gender transition surgery and/or hormone therapy.

To summarize, we continue on the path of:

- Integrating intention with breath, building a flexible, responsive, and resilient voice through extended and received movement, thought, emotional life, and point of view—in short, a way to transform competent into compelling.
- Developing actors and other communicators who work with the Active Breath as a tool to both receive present information and reveal maximum information in their sound while maintaining dynamic performance/presentation work.
- Training teachers who are curious, compassionate, frank, and transparent, and who are interested in modeling these qualities and fostering them in their students.
- Sharing the work globally via our web-based tutorial video series and through trainers who travel, live, or work outside the U.S.
- Continuously evolving the method with the aid of science, experience, and up-to-date knowledge as a baseline, valuing rigor over preciousness by discarding what becomes ineffective or irrelevant to the needs of the twenty-first century communicator by treating the studio like a laboratory.

Certification Process

Historically, our teacher training model first required a person to have experience in the work as a student, so they might develop a psychophysical understanding of the work and an appreciation for the challenges and revelations that arise in the training. Then, after a time, they could move into the role of apprentice, typically for a two-year period. The apprenticeship allowed for hands-on work with the students, a key component to our work. Once the apprenticeship had ended, teachers-in-training would return for various workshops, continued education opportunities and receive mentorship.

After nearly 20 years of research in the field with our teacher trainees, we are now prepared to share our findings and experiences with those that wish to become certified in our comprehensive approach. Our hope is that the number of instructors teaching the approach in academic programs across the United States and the world continues to grow. Equally, as our focus expands beyond actors, the need for trainers schooled in our approach is growing.

We see great value in sharing tools with anyone who desires to better align their intended expression with what is actually communicated. To that end, we are launching our Teacher Certification Program in the summer of 2018. The diversity of our offerings will include:

- Philosophies of teaching
- Our "Attention Blueprint"
- Core MVM exercise progressions and hands-on work
- Acting integration work
- Text transfusion: MVM's script analysis and memorization process
- Scene integration process
- Character voice work
- On-camera work
- Teacher feedback from lead teachers
- Mentoring and guidance throughout the training and after
- MVM Video Series with lifetime access to curated workouts, how-to videos, and the full video library

Contact Information

Please visit our website to learn more about the MVM Video Series, read about our teachers, and learn more about our upcoming Teacher Certification Program: https://www.millervoicemethod.com/.

If you have questions or want to discuss the work please email us at info@ MillerVoiceMethod.com. Social media communication is on Facebook by visiting "Miller Voice Method Studio" and on Twitter: @MVMStudio. The Miller Voice Method team is incredibly excited to share the work. We would love to hear from and learn from you.

Disclosure statement

No potential conflict of interest was reported by the authors.

A Voice Pedagogy Based in Middendorf Breathwork

Jeff Crockett

ABSTRACT

Vocal Traditions is a series in the Voice and Speech Review that highlights historically important voice teachers and schools of thought in the world of vocal pedagogy. In this essay, the author offers a voice pedagogy based on Middendorf Breathwork including an overview, history, teaching style and philosophy, exercises, and next steps in training.

Introduction

Middendorf Breathwork, also called *Breathexperience*, is known among performing artists and psychotherapists in Germany, Switzerland, Holland, and Italy. Although Ilse Middendorf taught performers at the Berlin University of the Arts (Universität der Künste Berlin), she was considered a breath therapist. She called her work, Der Erfahrbare Atem, which means the breath that is experienced. This title captures the essence and meaning of her work: through experiencing the breath, we access its power for integration toward wholeness and connection to our resources of power and creativity.

Ilse Middendorf was searching for the essence of the person in movement and found breath to be the bridge connecting the body with this essence of Self. The scope of her work involved the path of individuation and authentic expression. The Middendorf institutes that certify practitioners and teach the entire body of her work offer a path for integrating emotional, physical, and spiritual aspects of being. It is an educational process with therapeutic benefits.

This article is not a treatise on Middendorf Breathwork per se, but rather a description of a voice pedagogy that employs the principles she discovered, her overall approach, and philosophical framework. There are common guiding principles that unify a pedagogy based in Middendorf Breathwork and are shared by teachers working with voice, movement, and acting in Europe, Canada, Australia, and the USA.

This voice pedagogy is a system that operates in a paradigm of wholeness and does not treat any component separate from its relationship with the whole. It is informed by the individual who is practicing, as they engage with the principles Middendorf discovered and organized to reflect the integrity of wholeness, which is the central feature. The approach recognizes our personal relationship with the body, breath, and voice, and it incorporates the unique lived experience of each person. It is not a predictable routine of exercises or a method to breathe correctly. Rather, it is a distinct approach to working with the voice that integrates the elements of the whole person and their authentic and dynamic expression. The aim of this article is to introduce this work to the community of voice professionals and their colleagues to further the collaboration and innovation within the field of voice teaching.

Ilse Middendorf said, "This work lives in the experience of wholeness." She believed that all elements reflect the whole, and her teaching style demonstrated this idea. When she wrote her book, *The Perceptible Breath*, she made a bold choice to omit a typical table of contents, because a linear table of contents would be counter to the way the work operates. Instead, she painted a mandala. The mandala captures the discernible elements of the work, relating to the other parts, and with the whole, without losing its integrity and relational properties. She instructs the reader to contemplate the mandala and notice where their attention is drawn, and then refer to the corresponding chart which will tell them the page number to begin reading. This might seem like an exercise in eccentricity, but when you look at the invitation she is offering the reader, or student, you see that she embodied the work in everything she did.

The way we engage with the work, how we choose the exercises we use, in what order, and for how long, is like a dialogue or a conversation between the person and their breath. This metaphor of a dialogue describes the method of engagement that is distinctive of this work.

History

Ilse Middendorf was born in 1910 in Frankenberg, Germany (Johnson 1995). As a young woman in her twenties, she felt that breathing was not stressed enough. She felt that breath movement had a different shape than what was being taught and that some of the movements went "against the natural movement of breath" (Johnson 1995, 68). She also studied and taught the Mastanang Method, which is a "work where body state and mind are inter-related on Tibetan movements" (Johnson 1995, 68). She was looking for something more direct and more involved with human reality. At this time, she began a lifelong practice of spending the early morning hours every day experimenting and conducting systematic research into the nature of breath. She began to teach breathing therapy based on her discoveries in 1935. In 1938 she met Cornelius Veening, a Jungian depth psychologist and respiratory therapist, who became her teacher and mentor. She worked with him for almost 30 years. As a Jungian, she viewed the unconscious as an intelligent source for healing and personal transformation, as well as a rich source of archetypal experiences, giving meaning and importance for the individual and the world. She would say, "Jung worked with dreams; I work with the breath." She died in May of 2009.

Fascination with the emotional and personal experiences during my actor training pulled me into a lifelong curiosity about the nature of consciousness and the connection with the body, breath, and voice. My training at The Central School, particularly the teachings of David Carey and Cicely Berry, gave me invaluable keys that unlocked doors within myself and my teaching, leading me to discover the power of the body to connect the person with the expression of thought and voice. The discoveries I made also brought doubts and confusion. A door would open in my teaching only to lead me down pathways that felt like a never-ending maze. The influence of the body/mind connection with voice was my focus. I was taking regular Alexander Technique lessons, and my appreciation for the mysteries of presence and communication was expanding. I decided to enroll in the Alexander Technique teacher training, thinking the technique would anchor me and bring clarity. This was an important step in many ways, but my instincts became removed and distant. I could see more clearly, but I became more self-conscious. Shortly after I finished my training, I was hired to be the voice teacher at the American Conservatory Theater (ACT) in San Francisco. This was a dream job, yet I felt a crisis of confidence. The spontaneity in my teaching had dried up, and I was seriously doubting the health and value of the emotional component in the voice work that was being promoted at the time. I wanted to work deeply with people, but in healthy and productive ways, and I wanted to find security within my body. I happened to receive a book called *Bone, Breath, and Gesture* (Johnson 1995). I immediately lit up when I read an interview with Ilse Middendorf, who spoke about the breath in ways that felt true to me. I had an immediate sense that I needed to study her work. I was stunned when I read at the end of the article that the only institute for her work in the US was in San Francisco! I attended a weekend retreat days later. This was exactly 25 years ago.

The first time I worked with Ilse was in 2000 and the last was in Berlin in 2008. She was exacting and precise in her teaching. She often arrived early and would simply sit on her stool waiting for us. Her presence was arresting and inviting, at times intimidating. Her intelligence and deep wisdom were delivered with humor. She was elegant and charming in her personal style, often wearing pearls when she taught. At the end of a workshop, there was always a champagne toast and an atmosphere of celebration.

Her work was an integrating force that gave me the tools to stay in my direct experience, trusting the unfolding of my work, preserving the profundity of human experience while finding cohesion, balance, efficiency, and immediacy in my teaching and my life. The brilliance in her teaching was her ability to organize the complex mystery from the experience of breath without diminishing its profound nature. Everything she did in her teaching reflected the nature of what she was teaching.

Overview

A voice pedagogy based in Middendorf Breathwork unfolds through sensing the movement of breath that comes and goes on its own (Middendorf 1990). The uncontrolled movement of breath is in communication with our wholeness and moves in a direction that brings balance to all levels of being. A process of integration is activated and enhanced by our conscious consent to allow the movement and to sense it directly with our presence. Aspects that are out of alignment with our wholeness are integrated. The entire person is involved, including the implicit memories in the body and their individual psychological and emotional tendencies. The process of transformation occurs through the subjective sensation of breath movement rather than psychological approaches, strategies to change habits, or expectations and standards from an external source.

Each person is centered in their direct experience of sensation rather than a mental observation of it (Middendorf 1990). This bypasses the problems that arise from self-consciously listening to the voice and watching the body with an eye to correct it. The influence on the embodiment of voice and the authentic expression of vocal communication occurs indirectly and holistically because we maintain the link to our whole being as we work. Thought and breath are never separated, and breath is always in a responsive state. Thoughts, feelings, and the entire lived experience of the person are reflected in the breath movement and perceived in the voice. As spontaneity is developed from practicing with breath that is free to shift its rhythm authentically, the unique essence of the person emerges (Middendorf 1990). Connection between people is felt and experienced through breath movement. Breath movement and the experience of deep listening become the same. Listening and speaking are brought together as whole communication.

Principles and Key Features

Three Ways of Breathing

The unconscious breath: This is breath that comes and goes on its own and without our awareness; it is in communication with the unconscious and controlled by the autonomic nervous system. In her book, *The Perceptible Breath*, she writes:

> Breathing always includes the "whole" of a person, even if we are not ready to experience that [...] It flows through our body in accordance with all our developments, whether spiritual, mental, or corporal.
>
> (Middendorf 1990, 18–19)

The controlled breath: When the breath is controlled or directed, it loses its sophisticated nature, its self-regulating properties, and its communication with the whole of the person (Middendorf 1990). When it is used to stimulate cathartic experiences, there is a danger of diminishing personal autonomy. Often the experience does not integrate and make lasting change.

The perceptible breath, or the experienced breath: This way of breathing is centered in the developments that arise from engaging with the unconscious breath while it is sensed consciously (Middendorf 1990). We bring our presence to the sensation of its movement and allow it to come and go without interfering or directing it. We are consciously choosing to sense it and receive the felt experience of its movement that we also choose consciously to allow. The perceptible breath is not a mental observation of breath, but a direct experience of it through sensing. A powerful dynamic is established between the unconscious and our conscious awareness.

Ilse referred to the perceptible breath as "the guiderope [*sic*] which will never betray throughout the adventure called life" (Middendorf 1990, 28). She taught the importance of patience until clarity of consciousness could develop out of understanding the unconscious. She writes in her book, *The Perceptible Breath*:

> Breath is a connecting force. It creates a bodily equilibrium and balance and helps us to make inner and outer impressions interchangeable. It connects the human being with the outside world, and the outside world with his inner world. Breathing is an original unceasing movement and therefore, actual life. The ineffable has given nature various autonomous laws which have still to come to fruition. Experiencing the breath means to start to live a new life in a new way.
>
> (Middendorf 1990, 12)

Foundational Principle

The trinity of sensation, presence, and breath that comes and goes on its own are interrelated, inseparable, and in communication (Middendorf 1990, 20). Anytime we improve one of these elements, the other two are enhanced. Everything grows out of this principle. This was Ilse's initial discovery, and it became the foundational principle for all her work.

This foundational principle makes clear the primary principle: Breath moves with intelligence toward balancing the parts in relationship with the whole (Middendorf 1990, 25). This intelligence is sometimes referred to as somatic intelligence, but it is also experienced as coherence that is perceived in our outer environment as well as within the body. It is our life force and the movement that is experienced as our authentic rhythm. When we use the word "breath," we are referring to the bodily movement that is sensed. For us, exhalation is a movement in the body, not the release of air. Breath is a movement that happens without our doing it. We rarely use the verb *breathe* but rather the noun *breath*.

Breath creates a space in the body, growing wide and swinging back (Middendorf 1990). It chooses the space it needs and is experienced dimensionally in any area of the body. If you only think of breath as lungs, diaphragm, and air, the movement of breath will not make sense to you. If you think the breath should always be low, you will inhibit many important breath experiences. Breath is much more than a fuel for voice.

Breath Spaces

Breath moves in three main breath spaces in the body (Middendorf 1990, 31–39). The movement of breath develops space and claims the space it needs. Each space has an archetypal experience that is felt personally:

- The lower space: the feet, legs, pelvis, lower abdomen below the navel and the lower back. This space is the seat of vitality, instinctual impulses, driving life force, personal privacy, and security in being.
- The middle space: the area of the torso above the navel and below the sternum, including the lower ribs and middle back. Here we have conscious recognition that I am me, the development of the self through encountering the persona and the ego, and the relational dynamics with others.
- The upper space: the head, neck, shoulders, arms, hands, upper ribs, including the upper back. Here we experience our unique expression in the world, the unfolding and evolving, soulful longing to become, and the connection to spiritual experiences.

There are laws that reflect the direction of breath movement (Middendorf 1990). The direction carries meaning, felt experiences, and a statement or expression. These directions carry common archetypal experiences, feelings, and physical effects. Each person, as they practice, will also face issues from within themselves concerning these spaces.

Breath that is received in the lower space will tend to rise on exhale (Middendorf 1990, 32). This uprising exhale supports the vertical dimension, giving form to our standpoint in the world and our experience of autonomy. Breath that is received in the upper space will descend, called the down-flowing breath. It is the compliment to the uprising breath, supporting the vertical dimension in the experience of soft grounding. Breath from the middle space will move horizontally, toward the inner core, or toward the outer space. It is the bridge between the self, the environment, and the breath of others (Middendorf 1990, 38–42).

The Breath Cycle

The breath cycle is whole. Every element of the cycle influences and is influenced by the others. The cycle consists of the impulse of inhalation, the inhalation, the transition to exhalation, the exhalation, the transition to the pause, and the pause. From this point of view, we would never say that exhalation is more important than inhalation.

Generally, the inhalation claims space, and the exhalation moves with direction. As a Jungian, Ilse often referred to the masculine and feminine principles in her work (Middendorf 1990, 103). She referred to the inhalation as the feminine principle and the exhalation as the masculine. Not everyone responds to this binary framework. If I were to use this language, I would label them the opposite; the inhalation would be masculine because it claims space, sometimes all over and at once, and the exhalation would be feminine because it moves with direction that unites, relates, and connects—sometimes with voice.

The transitions in the cycle carry importance. The impulse of inhalation is the potential that is felt as a spark, like an ignition. The transition into exhalation calls our presence strongly, providing an opportunity for transformation. The end of exhalation brings healing properties that integrate in the transition into the pause, sometimes called the silence.

Our dialogue with the breath leads the process of balancing the cycle and developing the relationship between the three breath spaces. Breath claims the space that brings the body into balance (Middendorf 1990, 80–81). It is the breath that improves posture, not the other way around. What was too narrow in the body begins to widen, and what was too wide begins to swing back. Breath movement itself improves the tonus[1] and posture of the body and influences the way we relate to gravity (Middendorf 1990, 32).

There are three ways of relating to gravity, and each are as psychological as they are physical:

- Dropping
- Pulling up
- Being carried

Dropping is a surrender into the downward pull from gravity (Middendorf 1990, 32). It diminishes breath space in the upper and promotes a lack of personal responsibility. Pulling up diminishes breath space in the lower and reflects a hyper sense of self concern and control. Being carried is a condition where we choose to allow the ground to come up and to hold us. It reflects a state of trust and responsiveness.

Teaching/Learning the Work

Breath follows principles. The teacher's embodiment of these principles is the foundation of the teaching. The teacher invites an environment in which students experience these principles in a deeply personal way. This requires the student to feel safe enough to encounter themselves. Choice invites safety, and it invites the quality of engagement, which was a primary focus for Ilse: personal responsibility (Middendorf 1990).

Today we have information from Stephen Porges and his Polyvagal Theory (Porges 2011; Cazden 2017), and other experts who work with trauma and the body. Understanding the nature of a felt sense of safety, the autonomic nervous system, and the body's response to trauma is critical for teaching this work responsibly.

In a typical class, there are stools arranged in a circle. A group is sitting—letting themselves receive the support from the floor and the stool. They are consciously choosing to let themselves be carried and to shift their orientation away from thoughts by tuning in to the sensation of the body and the movement of breath.

The metaphor of a dialogue informs the structure of the class, which is practiced in three modes: working, resonating, and resting (Middendorf 1990). Each phase represents an element of the *conversation*. This metaphor clarifies how the teacher engages with the students, and how the students engage with the work. Using the metaphor, the working phase—the exercises—are questions we ask the body. The choice of exercise is determined in the moment and from the dialogue the teacher is having with their breath and the felt sense of the group. The dialogue begins with the teacher offering an exercise and demonstrating it, embodying their authentic experience. This invites the students into their singular experience of the exercise. This metaphor of a dialogue helps the student enter the work and clarifies their relationships with their practice. The exercises are employed in ways unlike many other systems. They are not a means to an end, but a conversation, and a conversation is different from giving marching orders or following a routine.

The next phase we call resonating (Middendorf 1990). This is when we listen for the response from the breath. We do not analyze how the breath is responding; we let ourselves be carried, and we let go of any expectation. We simply receive the ongoing sensory experience of the breath.

Resting is the phase where we relax our focus after we resonate (Middendorf 1990). It is the pause in the dialogue when we reflect on the meaning or the effect of the entire conversation. We respect the intimacy of our experience, while being aware of the others in the group, who are engaged in their personal experience. The group, the individuals in the group, and you are all in a dialogue that has many layers. Sensing the atmosphere this creates is a skill that supports somatic listening and our responsiveness to others. If a student feels moved to speak about their experience, this is the time to share with the group using their own words—in their own way. When they share their experience, not only are they contributing to the group, they are also embodying their experience, supporting their autonomy, and developing their voice.

The Exercises

We teach principles, and we use the exercises to invite an *experience* of the principles. Each student works with the same exercise but receives from the breath the experience they need. An atmosphere of acceptance and curiosity supports the student to allow this process to unfold. Comparison, expectation, and goal-seeking block it. The teacher is engaged in the dialogue through choosing an exercise, as though they are asking what might invite the experience with these particular people now. There are some exercises that Ilse developed many years ago, some I learned from other teachers, and some I invented or were inspired by watching my students explore. It is a dynamic and alive work, like a really good conversation.

There are basic categories of exercises that are organized based on the laws and principles that the breath follows. Stretching, pressing, tapping, and circling are examples. There are also basic offers made with the exercises. For example, a teacher might offer an exercise to invite breath space to develop, or they might offer a stimulation exercise to assist the breath in finding its authentic rhythm.

We have methods for working with voice. The vowels stimulate distinct breath spaces and shapes in the body, and each consonant stimulates a specific breath response in the body. If a teacher wanted to work with the vowel-breath-space work, they would offer an exercise that would invite breath space to develop (Middendorf 1990). If I receive my breath without pulling on it while silently sounding a vowel, the breath will be attracted to a particular breath space in my body. As I sound on exhale, without manipulating the exhale, the voice becomes embodied. We typically work silently for quite a while as we sense the breath space developing without manipulating it. When the exhale is sounded, we want to remain in contact with the experience of ourselves in the breath space. This allows the voice to communicate the inner life of the person.

We work with all the vowels including the umlauts[2] (Middendorf 1990). They each evoke a specific breath experience, as do the consonants. When I work with the vowels and consonants, I experience an immediacy in my voice. I sense a unity with myself, my body, and my expression. I can use the vowels to develop inner tonus, and I can also use the consonants to develop breath flexibility. Ultimately, the link between thought and breath remains intact, and the link to speaking is quite simple.

Training

As teachers embody the work, their essence, including their personal style, informs the way they facilitate the work. If the teacher is embodying the integrity of the work, they are in their own creativity in how they teach. Who the students are and the relationship among and between them informs the way they work. No two voice teachers who are rooted in Middendorf principles are the same, but we all share a foundation in these principles and approach.

There are Middendorf practitioners who have evolved their own voice pedagogy using a strong foundation in Middendorf Breathwork. Maria Höller-Zangenfeind (b. 1952- d. 2011) was a Middendorf practitioner who taught alongside Ilse at the institute in Berlin. Maria combined pressing and resistance with the vowel breath-space work that Ilse had originated. In response to the work Maria was developing, Ilse asked her to stop calling her work Middendorf. Maria then called her work Atem-Tonus-Ton. Maria was a guest teacher in my first year of training for certification. She mentioned to me that she was instructed to teach pure Middendorf with us and not her work. She then shrugged her shoulders and said, "It all feels like Middendorf to me."

If Ilse were alive today, I have a feeling she would say something similar to me. I am calling the work I teach Breath Embodiment, but every day I feel the impact of her work on my teaching and my life, and I am deeply grateful for her. I am in private practice in Santa Monica, California.[3]

There are several people who have trained with me in these principles and make use of them in their own teaching, in their own way. They are Dawn-Elin Fraser, Raife Baker, Miles Borrero, Emily Jeanne Brown, Tovah Close, Christin Davis, Alexa Erbach, Diana Gonzalez- Morett, Natalie Hegg, Stephanie Hunt, Stacey Jensen, Emily Kitchens, Nancy Ma, Lakisha May, Lisa Porter, Lauren Roth, Elyyse Shafarman, Julian Stetkevych, and Steven Strobel.

Notes

1. The constant low-level activity of a body tissue, especially muscle tone.
2. In linguistics, an umlaut is a sound change in which a vowel is pronounced more like a following vowel or semivowel.
3. See https://breathembodiment.com.

Disclosure statement

No potential conflict of interest was reported by the author.

References

Cazden, J. 2017. "Stalking the Calm Buzz: How the Polyvagal Theory Links Stage Presence, Mammal Evolution, and the Root of the Vocal Nerve." *Voice and Speech Review* 11 (2): 132–153. doi:10.1080/23268263.2017.1390036.

Johnson, D. 1995. *Bone, Breath, and Gesture: Practices of Embodiment Volume 1*. Berkeley, CA: North Atlantic Books.

Middendorf, I. 1990. *The Perceptible Breath: A Breathing Science Paderborn*. West-Germany: Juntermann-Verlag.

Porges, S. 2011. *The Polyvagal Theory: Neurophysiological Foundations of Emotions, Attachment, Communication, and Self-Regulation*. New York: W.W. Norton & Company.

Vocal Combat Technique

D'Arcy Smith and Chaslee Schweitzer

ABSTRACT
Vocal Traditions is a series in the *Voice and Speech Review* that high-lights both historically important and contemporary voice teachers and schools of thought in the world of vocal pedagogy. This essay explores the background of the Vocal Combat Technique, the central features of the system, and the pillars of the technique.

Overview

Vocal Combat Technique (VCT) was created to train performers to go to vocal extremes in the healthiest way possible. Vocal extremes include sounds such as screams, grunts, growls, creature voices, and simulation of victimization sounds (getting shot or stabbed, choking, being poisoned, electrocuted, thrown out of a plane, set on fire, hit with blunt objects, etc). VCT uses evidenced based practices to meet industry standards and ensure that the performer is vocally fit, knows how to reset and recover from vocally stress-ful events, and understands the industry requirements for vocally stressful work. This technique is a voice, movement, and body technique that integrates vocalization and physicality to create believable and aggressive sounds related to the situation and action in the body.

Performers are trained, in person and/or virtually, by both the founder and indus-try experts to ensure that the training stays relevant to the professional artist. While VCT was primarily designed with performers, stage combatants, and voice over actors in mind, it has found application outside of performance with fitness instructors and drill instructors. It should be noted that VCT is not a complete voice system designed to fully train the actor for general performance situations. It is advanced training created to fill a void in current voice pedagogy and address the needs of performers to go to vocal extremes. Since 2015, the focus has shifted to training not only stage combat actors, but also actors for voice over and video games.

History

The founder, D'Arcy Smith, studied with several master voice teachers and has incorpo-rated particular elements from a variety of different methods. An important element of VCT is that there are various approaches to find the sound needed, since performers who seek this training come from a variety of training backgrounds (Smith 2007). For this reason, VCT training seeks to be flexible enough for each individual performer regardless of their previous voice training.

Major influences on the methodology include, Lessac, Linklater, Fitzmaurice, Estill, Stough, Roy Hart, Laban, and draws in a large part from voice health practices including semi occluded vocal tract (SOVT). It includes specific teachers, but is not limited to, Katelyn Reid, Rocco Dal Vera, David Smukler, Catherine Fitzmaurice, Barry Kurr, Kerrie Obert, Paul Farrington, Richard Armstrong, Ingo Titze, Eric Armstrong, Dale Genge, Gayle Murphy, and more.

Smith first began teaching VCT at Wright State University in 2006 to BFA acting students after realizing that traditional methods were not preparing them for extremes. The work at that time focused on breath support, creating an open channel, and adding growls and grunts or screaming, as needed for stage combat scenes. Smith states:

> Very early in my career as a voice coach, I was coaching a production of *West Side Story*. While most of my work focused on the dialects, I was also responsible for the actors' voices and assisted the musical director. One of the actors I had trained in voice production was in the show. Early in the show, he is grabbed, dragged upstage, thrown against a fence, and pinned there as he shouts, "Jets!" The sound that came out of his body was one of the most clean, open, and supported sounds I have heard. I knew that I had a role in that moment, because that was what I had trained him to do. I also knew that I had failed that actor, because at that moment I did not believe that a character in that situation would make that kind of sound. I never trained him for what to do in those situations. From that time, I have studied with a number of master voice teachers. I am a big believer in finding what works and what is healthy for the individual actor. I owe much of my knowledge to those I have studied with, but just as much to those who I have coached and trained – if not more.

In 2009 while head of voice at Toi Whakaari: New Zealand Drama School, Smith was invited to work and train with *kapa haka* teacher Teina Moetara.[1] During this time, he learned about their methods for vocal extremes and how VCT might be able to help. The *haka* has a long and sacred tradition which includes making aggressive sounds. When performing in three productions a day, the Māori performers asked for help making their traditional sounds sustainable. By observing the *kapa haka* and working with the Māori, Smith gained insight into how the Māori traditionally produce aggressive sounds while offering tools such as breath support and "anchoring" to support the performers.

Between 2011 and 2015 Smith used the technique in specific productions while working as resident voice coach at the Guthrie Theatre in Minneapolis, MN. Later the technique was also used to train all of the actors for four years at the Actors Theatre of Louisville extensively preparing the cast for their production of *Dracula*.

VCT underwent a pedagogical shift in 2015 from working primarily with stage combat to focusing on further vocal extremes for video games. Smith was teaching a Vocal Combat Class at Rapier Wit, a stage combat school in Toronto, Canada, run by Daniel Levinson. During this workshop, he was approached by Ivan Sherry, John Nelles, and later Kim Hurdon, who wanted to know if the voice work could be used to help video game actors. Smith remarked, "While I was already training actors to do vocally extreme work, this was next level." The challenge was not only being able to create the sounds in the healthiest way possible, but also to make sure the sounds were extreme and believable; it was also important that the actor could sustain their voice through the two-hour session and then recover well enough to record the next day.

Smith and Katelyn Reid, who is a speech language pathologist (SLP) with the University of Cincinnati (UC Health), updated the vocal methodology to help performers create these sounds. In 2018, an unpublished pilot study was conducted with the otolaryngology department at The University of Cincinnati, the technique was tested and found it reduced fatigue by 50% and improved recovery time by 60%.

The study, with the help of Kim Hurdon and Chris Hidalgo from Ubisoft Montreal, was an intensive simulation that included 100 barks, and 120 "Reaxs" or "Onos" that included the most aggressive sounds a performer would need to make during a session (screaming, set on fire, stabbed in a variety of places, electrocuted, etc.). Five participants went through this simulation and measured them before and after the simulation. A week later, they were then trained in VCT in a 3-hour group session, and then put them through the simulation again. The results were significant. The study suggests that VCT teaches actors to survive vocal extremes and improves their recovery time and ability to return to work.

A randomized controlled study was conducted in 2020 and analysis is still being completed on the collected data.

VCT has been used to train actors for video games for Ubisoft, Riot Games, Ninja Theory, and other productions. As of this article's publication, workshops are run on a semi-regular basis online due to the COVID-19 pandemic. Plans are currently underway to certify voice coaches in VCT and create training workshops for directors.

About the Founder

D'Arcy Smith is a Professor of Voice, Speech and Dialects in the CCM-Acting department at the University of Cincinnati. He has trained actors in voice production, dialects, voice-over and acting Shakespeare for over 15 years. Before coming to CCM, he was the resident voice and dialect coach at the Guthrie Theater and worked at numerous professional theaters. He has taught in Canada, the United Kingdom, and New Zealand. For the past 10 years, he has been training and coaching actors in how to go to vocal extremes. He created Vocal Combat Technique to train and help performers create these sounds in the healthiest way possible for the stage and for stage combat situations.

He has a master's degree in theatre specializing in voice/dialect training and has studied with numerous master teachers in a variety of voice/dialect methodologies. Before this he was an actor and worked professionally for 7 years. His time coaching, researching, and learning in other countries (and languages) has given him a great deal of knowledge in the training of actors. He has trained and coached countless actors from many backgrounds and cultures in just about every accent and adapted voice techniques to those he teaches.

Consultants

Katelyn Reid, BFA, MA, CCC-SLP, practices as a voice pathologist for UC Health's nationally ranked ears, nose, and throat (ENT) department, as well continuing to teach as adjunct faculty member at the University of Cincinnati: College Conservatory of Music (CCM)—often working to help students overcome vocal impediments in the process. Katelyn is a graduate of the CCM dramatic performance program. During her time as an undergraduate student, she developed a deep interest and passion for all things voice and speech. Upon graduation, she was offered a position as adjunct faculty teaching voice and speech for CCM's nationally ranked musical theater program, where she discovered not only a passion for teaching in general, but also an aptitude for vocal and dialect coaching.

Kim Hurdon is both a casting and voice director with over 30 years of experience. She has been dubbed "The Queen of Voice" by the Alliance of Canadian Cinema, Television and Radio Artists (ACTRA) and has appeared as a voice-specialist on TV, radio, Clubhouse, online panels, and in print. Her most recent work includes *Rusty Rivets, D.N. Ace, Molly of Denali, The Magic School Bus Rides Again, Blue's Clues and You*, and *Max and Ruby*. For gaming, her work includes *Far Cry 5, 6, Watch Dogs: Legion, Hyperscape, Ghost Recon*, and *Assassin's Creed Syndicate*.

Key Features

Arguably, voice training has traditionally worked from what is aesthetically pleasing and from a health vocal production standpoint. In the case of vocal extremes, that kind of training is ineffective, as it does not prepare actors for the real-world demands. Rather than starting from what is healthy, VCT starts from what is *required* and then works to make the sounds healthy and sustainable.

Vocal Fitness

Before undertaking this work, the performers are given vocal health information directly from or based on the consultations from Katelyn Reid, SLP. During the class or workshop, Smith goes through Vocal Fitness exercises with performers to build sustainable habits and to assess the vocal aptitude of performers. The Vocal Fitness section of VCT not only helps to build skills needed for the coming vocal extremes but also helps Smith to identify performers who may not be in strong vocal health and need monitoring during the workshop.

Vocal Mechanics/Effects

Once the performer has the vocal fitness and agility needed, exercises are introduced to train them how to perform the "effects" in isolation in order to give the perception of aggression without harm. This includes the sound needed for screams, growls, shouting, sobbing, choking, getting stabbed, grunting, etc. These sounds are taught in a sequential fashion, building on the vocal foundations of the previous session before adding on the desired effect.

Target Practice

This final element is a crucial part of the VCT. Until this point the performers have been using vocal techniques in isolation, this is the point in the training where further body integration and application to performance are introduced. Whether its staged combat, in the voice over booth, or performing motion capture, performers must be in a physical position that matches the action of the story. The Target Practice section of the VCT training includes exercises specifically developed to help the performer integrate the training into performance for a fight or voice over session. For example, creating the sound of getting stabbed in the throat within the situation of the fight. Actors need to be able to use the technique in performance and be ready to deliver extremes on demand in a way that meets the expectations of the production.

Discussion of Teaching Style

When instructing VCT in an academic setting over 10 weeks, Smith spends weeks one to two on Vocal Fitness, weeks three to five on Vocal Mechanics and fitness, weeks five through eight introducing Vocal Effects, and the final two weeks on Target Practice. The shorter courses and workshops follow a similar structure of Vocal Fitness and assessment, Vocal Mechanics, Vocal Effects, and Target Practice covering specific target sounds like screams and gunshots.

VCT has a set of pillars that exemplify the philosophy behind Smith's instruction of the technique.

Pillars of Vocal Combat Technique This Is Not an Emotional Technique

Many actors will put themselves psychologically into the extreme situation to find an extreme sound because they do not know how to make the sound. All they can rely on is mentally putting themselves into something like the state of being on fire and see what sounds come out. This situation is both physically and mentally taxing on the performer. VCT works from the sound back to the action. Actors can make a sound that is terrifying to the listener without an emotional context. Training in VCT not only protects the actor physically but also has the added advantage of protecting the actor's mental wellbeing, by giving them a physical tool allowing them to scream like they are on fire without leaving a session both emotionally and physically drained.

Consent. You Can Stop at Any Time

The point of taking a Vocal Combat workshop is that there is no pressure to immediately deliver results, as opposed to when you are in the booth or ona job where there is an implied pressure to continue on. Participants can stop at any time and are encouraged to listen to their limits. Smith tells clients, "You can stop at any time without any judgment from me. In fact, I'll applaud you for saying 'I'm done,' or 'I'll take a break' or 'I'll practice this later on.'" Part of VCT is that participants learn their limits and to advocate for their own vocal health.

Empowering the Performer. They are the Expert

When working with a performer, Smith will ask them questions such as "How does that feel?" and "Does that feel sustainable?" If a sound does not sound and feel repeatable, then they will be asked to do it again and then reassess. The aim is to be able to not only create extreme vocal sounds like barks or screams, but also repeat those sounds potentially hundreds of times in different takes. Smith may question an actor's assessment if he hears something that sounds unsustainable, but ultimately the actor is the expert and needs to be able to reflect on how something feels to learn when they hit the target and when they do not. VCT helps to hone this awareness.

The Approach Is Holistic

VCT's tools of Vocal Fitness, Vocal Mechanics and Effects, and Target Practice have been shown to create less fatigue. The sequence helps to ensure that they are strong enough to perform the tasks before learning the vocal effects. Target Practice is a large part of the injury prevention model. If they do not know what sound is required, performers will experiment with many different sounds, which could be a quick path to fatigue. VCT educates performers, so they know what the target sound is and how to safely execute the vocal effect using their vocal fitness. Pre and post warm up and recovery are other tools that are taught to encourage sustainability in performance. The recovery, warm ups, and vocal fitness are the foundation that supports a performer's sustainable career

Just Because It Sounds Terrible, Does Not Mean That It Hurts

If a sound feels "wrong" to the actor, as in it hurts or does not feel sustainable, then we need to continue to find a way to tell the story without taxing their voice. However, some of these sounds may be just unfamiliar to the actor. In VCT, performers may be asked to make sounds that they may have never made before or sounds that are perceived as ugly. Performers are not always accustomed to making ugly, shocking, or terrifying sounds. VCT helps performers distinguish between a sound that is painful and costly, and a sound that feels unfamiliar or "foreign" to a performer. This opens up the variety of voice effects they can create without sacrificing sustainability.

There Is No Perfect Scream, Just the One that Tells the Story

There are many different kinds of screams. Just like each actor's vocal instrument and ability is different. Performers will be coached into and given examples of a variety of choices for screams during training. VCT focuses on finding the scream for the performer that is their scream, tells the story, is sustainable, and one that the actor enjoys.

Do Not Just Create Sounds, Tell the Story

The voice effects are used in service of telling the story of the action. Physical postures are used in combination with the voice effects to target the specific sound depending on the position of the character in the game. It takes both the voice and the body to effectively tell the story of the action. At times the performer may be creating a sound that is too aggressive and costing their voice. Training performers to only do the amount needed helps reduce their vocal load and risk of injury.

Use Multiple Approaches

To effectively teach vocal extremes, multiple modalities are used to help a performer achieve the desired sound. A teacher must be able to not only model the sound repeatedly, but also understand the target and steps to create the sound. Instruction includes describing the anatomy cues of what is occurring in the body and voice. Images or animal examples are used to help the actor target the sound. The approaches used include combinations of call and response, physical anatomy cues, and images/animals, depending on what works best for each actor.

Goals of the Organization

The goals of the organization are to:

- Advocate for vocal health of performers,
- Conduct research and best practices for vocal extremes,
- Conduct training workshops to help actors, directors, and teachers improve vocal extreme training for performers.

The real-world working situations for video game performers can challenge the holistic approach VCT supports. Therefore, advocacy for video game performers is a particularly large part of the work VCT does within the industry. Smith is in conversation with unions, producers, and industry professionals to educate and promote change surrounding safe practices for voice over artists. The training also addresses with performers how to address situations in sessions that may try to push performers past their vocal limits.

Recently, Smith was asked by ACTRA Toronto, the union that represents actors in Toronto, Canada, to write a document for Best Practices for Vocal Extremes, entitled "Vocal Health for Extreme Voice Performance" (Smith 2021).

Following the pillar of being a holistic training, VCT is currently working with unions to advocate for vocal health and sustainable practices for video game voice over performers. There has historically been a lack of protection and training in the industry for video game actors. During the 2016 voice actor strike, some of the concerns brought to SAG-AFTRA[2] were safety concerns. While this gap has been acknowledged, there is still advocacy work to be done throughout the industry. The safety of the industry voice actors enter into is important. No matter how trained an actor is, the training becomes irrelevant if they are faced with situations where they are pushed beyond sustainable limits. Thus, educating the industry and advocating for performers is part of VCT's work. VCT is committed to researching best practices for vocal extremes and has completed two studies to test the efficacy of the technique. The outcomes of these suggest positive results for the participants when using VCT. The Vocal Fitness portion of the training was created in collaboration with SLP, Katelyn Reid, to ensure VCT's best practices were supported by speech science.

VCT workshops are offered throughout the calendar year both virtually and in person. A unique component of the workshop is that participants are not only trained in the technique but they also can practice application with an industry professional to ensure that their skills meet the current expectations of the professional video game industry.

Certification Process

There are plans for future teacher training and certification in Vocal Combat Technique. The current focus is on training voice actors, research, and advocating for sustainable industry practices. Through VCT participants can receive intensive training in:

- Voice Health and Fitness
- Voice Mechanics
- Recovery Techniques
- Reset Techniques
- Video Game Sounds/Efforts

Contact Information and How to Get Involved

Here is the list of connection resources:

- Website: www.vocalcombat.com
- E-Mail: vocalcombat@gmail.com
- Social media: https://www.facebook.com/vocalcombattechnique/

Notes

1. For more information on the *kapa haka*, see (Tourism New Zealand 2021).
2. SAG-AFTRA is the Screen Actors Guild—American Federation of Television and Radio Artists, which is based in the United States.

Disclosure statement

No potential conflict of interest was disclosed by the authors.

References

Smith, D'Arcy. 2007. "The Issue of Vocal Practice: Finding a Vocabulary for Our Blocks and Resistances." *Voice and Speech Review* 5 (1): 128–131. doi:10.1080/23268263.2007.10769748.

Smith, D'Arcy. 2021. "Vocal Health for Extreme Voice Performance." *Alliance of Canadian Cinema, Television and Radio Artists*, October 9, 2021. https://www.actratoronto.com/vocal-health/

Tourism New Zealand. 2021. "Kapa Haka: Māori Performing Arts." *Tourism New Zealand*, September 1, 2021. https://www.newzealand.com/us/feature/kapa-haka-maori-performance/

Somatic Voicework™ The LoVetri Method

Andrew R. White

ABSTRACT
This article attempts to acquaint the reader with some of the basic precepts of Somatic Voicework™ The LoVetri Method and its creator Jeannette LoVetri. Although mastery of its practice takes years to develop, one can start down the road towards mastery by taking the summer workshops now held annually at Baldwin Wallace University in July. Participants report significant improvement in their teaching effectiveness resulting from these workshops. The method does not prescribe specific exercises per se, but rather provides the teacher with an understanding of how to construct exercises of his or her own to serve the immediate needs of the student moment by moment in a lesson.

Overview

The term "somatic" comes from the Greek word *soma,* and means that which pertains to the body. *Somatic Voicework™ The LoVetri Method* is a body-based method of voice cultivation developed by singer, teacher, researcher, and author Jeannette LoVetri, largely to address the conflicting requirements of the wide array of musical styles with which today's singers, and their teachers, must contend.

It is based in both traditional vocal pedagogy and current voice science, and embraces the concept of vocal registers, apart from resonance or any other factor, as its central tenant, and assumes that they can come under the singer's volitional control. A command of registration is key to the mastery of varied vocal styles. This focus on laryngeal function distinguishes the method from other modern pedagogies in which acoustics, breath management, or conscious anatomical manipulation of the structures within the throat are the primary focus.

The term "function" figures largely in the work, as teachers are called upon to "listen functionally" and base decisions on "functional awareness." This is because an understanding of how the voice is working is what governs the choice of vocal exercises deemed appropriate to the student's needs in the moment, moment by moment, throughout the duration of a lesson and/or course of study. This tailored approach to voice teaching, while certainly best mastered with time and experience, is nevertheless made approachable for the novice by a fairly simple set of variables, and a written set of guidelines called the "Solution Sequence®," found in the course materials and abbreviated on laminated cards for easy reference in the studio (LoVetri 2017, II, 57–79).

In addition to the somatic aspect, "psyche" also figures prominently in this work. A wholistic/humanistic outlook fosters respect for the connection with the inner self, or the mental and emotional landscape of the singer, and the necessity of both singers and teachers to stay connected to honest and authentic vocal expression while singing.

A strong sense of community is established in her workshops that extends beyond the course participants themselves by inviting those who wish to do so to become part of the Somatic Voicework™ Teachers Association, which holds regular teacher support sessions and hosts an Internet chat room where members from around the world share expertise on topics arising in the voice studio. The "Pianoside Manner®," and the 12 tenants of "Useful Somatic Voicework™ Protocol" inform teachers in how to consider the whole student, not just the voice.

History

Jeannette LoVetri ("Jeanie," as she prefers to be called) grew up in Connecticut where, as a teenager, she worked as a church organist and vocal soloist. She was cast in various musical theatre productions, and worked as a musical director for several productions before moving to New York, where she studied at The Manhattan School of Music and with Maestro Vincent La Selva at the Extension Division of The Julliard School. She continued her studies with a variety of well-known New York City voice teachers for some 15 years until, in a state of vocal confusion, she found it best to discontinue formal singing training with private teachers. She was by then 29 and had had nearly 15 years of high-level training in singing, but felt she was still in some ways an unfinished product.

All of her voice teachers were classically oriented, and she found herself repeatedly up against the attitude that singing musical theatre, particularly in a "belt" style, which was frequently requested, would ruin her voice. This made no sense to her as she had been singing both classical music (as a lyric coloratura soprano) and musical theatre (including belt repertoire) for the better part of her life. She became determined to debunk the myths surrounding musical theatre singing and its impact on vocal health, and to demystify the modalities that made it possible for her to transition between styles successfully without vocal damage.

At that time she began what subsequently became annual attendance at The Voice Foundation *Symposium: Care Of The Professional Voice*, first held at The Julliard School in New York City, then later in Denver, Colorado, and currently in Philadelphia, Pennsylvania, and there came into contact with many of the world's foremost voice scientists, medical doctors, and speech language pathologists, as well as other singing teachers. She was able to study informally by observing and occasionally working with such giants in the field as doctors Robert Sataloff, Ingo Titze, Johan Sundberg, and Peak Woo, and eventually participated in voice research studies, ultimately conducting research of her own. She has authored or coauthored over 20 articles published in peer-reviewed journals, four book chapters, and has been widely acclaimed nationally and internationally as a workshop clinician, particularly in music theater and related styles.

In 2000, she introduced the term "Contemporary Commercial Music" (CCM) at a conference sponsored by the New York Singing Teacher's Association (NYSTA) as a replacement for the then prevalent term "non-classical" to identify music of a more "popular" orientation. This previously unused and untainted term had no prior connotations or specific meaning and was, for that reason, a good choice to describe musical styles arising from a tradition other than that of European classical music. CCM was offered as a complimentary but contrasting term to "classical," which also describes many related styles that have similar origins. Both terms, as generic descriptions, encompass many different eras and types of music that seemed equal in importance but different in origin. It was her feeling that the term "non-classical" was belittling, forcing music other than classical to be considered as "non" or not important in comparison to classical styles, and therefore implied that they were of inferior status to classical styles. The term "CCM" has since been widely embraced by the academic, scientific, medical, and singing communities, and is now the term predominantly used in these communities. This new generic term, "Contemporary Commercial Music," has helped the multiple voice-related disciplines see the relationship between these seemingly diverse styles, most of which were born in the United States of common people, and helped eliminate the condescension which had been perpetuated in academic institutions for nearly 100 years.

In 2002, LoVetri was invited by Shenandoah University to establish there a course for teachers of singing. This annual summer course became the Contemporary Commercial Vocal Pedagogy Institute in 2003. The Institute was founded for her by then Dean Dr. Charlotte Collins in order for her to teach her method, *Somatic Voicework*™ under the protection of a university institute, existing as a separate entity within the school. While at the Institute she codified her method into what it is today, establishing a three-level course structure taught over a nine-day period. Separate levels have subsequently been given at The University of Massachusetts, Dartmouth; Albion College, MI; University of Central Oklahoma; University of Michigan Ann Arbor in the Medical Center; The City College of New York; Douglas College, Vancouver; and the University of Illinois, Chicago at the Chicago Institute for Voice Care. The LoVetri Institute for Somatic Voicework™ continues at Baldwin Wallace University Conservatory of Music in Berea, OH. It was also offered for the first time in 2017 in São Paulo, Brazil and in Australia at Artsworx University in Toowoomba.

Initially, the course was targeted toward classically oriented voice teachers, especially college professors from classical vocal departments at universities newly offering musical theatre degree programs. Some instructors with no training in CCM whatsoever found themselves called upon to address the needs of students who were being asked to perform CCM repertoire. The early emphasis on her course materials included a large component of comparison/contrast teaching between requirements of traditional classical vocal training and that which is required by CCM styles, including musical theatre. Over time, however, teachers of CCM styles have been drawn to the courses, and at this time, it is not uncommon to find knowledgeable and highly skilled voice teachers with no classical training whatsoever among the participants. Such teachers are increasingly in demand for positions at schools with musical theatre, jazz, and commercial music programs. They have commented that LoVetri's program provided pedagogical, health and functional information they had not been able to find elsewhere.

About the founder

Jeannette LoVetri was a Van Lawrence Fellowship recipient in 1999, is a past-President of NYSTA, Secretary of the American Academy of Teachers of Singing (AATS), Advisory Board member of the Voice Foundation, and twice Master Teacher for the National Association of

Teachers of Singing (NATS) Internship Program. Her master class presentations have taken her all over the country and abroad to such far-flung places as São Paulo, Brazil; Sidney, Australia; and Stockholm, Sweden to name just a few. In addition to her master classes, residencies, and publications she has given over a dozen peer-reviewed presentations at conferences such as the Pan-European Voice Conference, Physiology and Acoustics of the Singing Voice, The Fall Voice Conference and The Rehabilitation of the Professional Voice. She has served as a consultant for such medical institutions as the Grabscheidt Voice Center at Mount Sinai Medical Center, NY; the New York Eye and Ear Infirmary, and Blue Cross Blue Shield of Greater New York, and is lecturer, at the appointment of Dr. Robert T. Sataloff, at Drexel University College of Medicine, Department of Head and Neck Surgery. She accepts referrals from Doctor Sataloff, as well as Drs. Peak Woo, and Gwen Korovin, as well as Speech Language Pathologists throughout the U.S.A. LoVetri's students include such notables as Kate McGarry, Luciana Souza and Theo Bleckmann, (Grammy-nominated jazz vocalists) Brian D'Arcy James, and Daniel Evans (Tony-nominated Broadway stars), Trey Anastasio (of the rock band Phish) and Meredith Monk, a multi-disciplinary modern singer, choreographer, filmmaker, US Medal of Honor, and MacArthur "Genius" award winner, who has worked with Ms. LoVetri for over 30 years. LoVetri's students have appeared in over 25 Broadway productions, 7 national, and 2 European tours, as well as well as television and concert appearances in such prestigious venues as Carnegie Hall, Avery Fisher (now Geffen) Hall, The Hollywood Bowl, and London's Albert Hall.

Key features

"Functional Training" manifests itself primarily in registration and vowel sound purity, facilitated by the release of constriction. Resonance is seen as a byproduct of vowel production, whereas registration addresses the sound as it arises from the source as tonal texture. Many modern vocal pedagogies seek to control the larynx by controlling the breath ("breath control" or "breath management systems"), but Somatic Voicework™ The LoVetri Method asserts that it is the vocal folds in the larynx that control the breath and not the other way around. LoVetri often says, "The vocal folds control the airflow." Since registration governs vocal fold function, registration impacts breath flow, as well as "closed quotient" (CQ: the ratio of durations of the closed and open phases of the phonation cycle), vertical laryngeal position within the throat, and the resulting acoustic envelope. Therefore, from a purely anatomical and physiologic standpoint, registration is the central topic, while from a practical standpoint, mastery of the three types of registration called "head," "mix," and "chest" (industry terms) is the standard for professional musical theatre and almost all other CCM styles.

Mastery of registration requires the achievement of a balance of strength between "head" register (cricothyroid dominant, or CTD, "loft," "falsetto") and "chest" register (thyroarytenoid dominant or TAD, "modal," "ordinario"), and a coordination between the two across the *passaggio* (the pitch level at which there is a natural inclination to switch from one register to the other) that allows the third register, called "mix," to emerge. To achieve this balance it is necessary to isolate the head and chest registers, cultivate each of them separately, and extend the overlap between them (the number of pitches that can, by the singer's volition, be sung in either register). It is this capacity to mix the registers, and the extension of the overlap, that gives access to a healthy "belt" sound.

"Belt" (also an industry term) means to carry the chest voice above the *passaggio* in a loud, bright sound. It is the predominant sound used in musical theater and many other CCM styles. It can be unhealthy if the voice is imbalanced, because the underdeveloped head register allows an over-thickening of the vocal folds, resulting in a high degree of laryngeal elevation and constriction that medical professionals refer to as "hyperfunction." The state of hyperfunction typically limits the upper range of the belt, and results in a "hole in the voice," an area in the lower part of the head voice that is extremely weak and in some cases will not phonate at all. It is imperative that CCM singers achieve and maintain register balance to prevent their belt sounds from becoming hyperfunctional (Lawrence 1979, 26–29).

While registration is central, posture and breathing are not ignored or treated as an afterthought. In fact, posture and alignment are discussed anatomically, but are also addressed through body awareness exercises, and through reference to various forms of body work such as yoga, Pilates, Feldenkreis, Alexander Technique, etc. The idea is that posture is affected by heightened kinesthetic awareness, gained over time, and deepened through subjective experience.

The promotion of heightened kinesthetic and auditory awareness permeates all aspects of the work. The posture advocated embraces traditional values such as a level head, slightly lifted rib cage, a lengthened spine, a level pelvis, with feet positioned for good balance directly under the torso. With increased awareness of balance, movement, and coordination, for example, it becomes possible to notice and then eliminate "blocks" in the body (areas where proprioception is shut down). That, in turn, amplifies both strength in the body and freedom in the throat. This is a distinguishing aspect of Somatic Voicework™, setting it apart from other approaches in which posture is imposed peripherally.

The approach to breathing acknowledges research that indicates breath strategies among professional singers vary greatly, and can be equally successful even when those approaches seem diametrically opposed to one another (Leanderson and Sundberg 1988, 2–12). It is not necessary or even desirable for CCM singers to generate the level of subglottic pressure classical singing requires, and there is a great variation in breath pressure requirements among different CCM styles, and between different individual singers within any style.

The rib cage must be trained to stay in a comfortably expanded position during both phases of the breath cycle. This is learned slowly, and is most easily accomplished when the student is able to sing at a comfortable *mezzo forte* on /a/. Once this basic skill is mastered attention must be paid to extending the breath phrase. As the singer passes the tidal point of the breath phrase (the point at which the body's natural response transitions from exhalation to breath renewal) the abdominal muscles must be trained to pull up and in. This abdominal response must also occur at moments of increased power and high range. These are deliberate actions that must be trained because they are beyond that which happens naturally in speech, but should not be conflated with any sort of *appoggio* pedagogy in which a deliberate antagonism between inhalatory and exhalatory muscles is elicited and maintained throughout the phrase. To dictate a single approach to "breath support" is simply not operable in the twenty-first-century voice studio. Somatic Voicework™ allows for individual students to find what is operable for them.

Purity of vowel is both a goal and a tool. A constricted voice will not be capable of a truly pure vowel, but working towards purity of vowel will help to release constriction. Constriction occurs when the neck and throat muscles engage while singing. The primary function of these muscles is to assist in swallowing and/or to protect against choking. They can cause the voice to sound swallowed, muffled, nasal, pinched, or behave oddly in a number of affectations. Generally, the elimination and/or reduction of constriction results in a freer, more natural sounding vocal production, and allows for greater emotionally based expression while singing. Acknowledging that some CCM styles such as Rock, Rhythm and Blues, Gospel or Broadway belting will engender a certain amount of constriction in order to get an "authentic" sound, Somatic Voicework™ seeks to eliminate any extra vocal effort in these styles, minimizing constriction rather than encouraging it.

Balanced registration also facilitates keeping vowel sounds true to their natural pronunciation, and lets the singer consciously choose to stay close to spoken sound production or modify the vowels for acoustic or expressive purposes. This is necessary in music as it allows the singing to remain true to the vocalist's intentions and artistic choices.

Terminology

LoVetri has not created any new terms to describe vocal function or output. In this, she is quite unusual. She draws her terminology from the music industry (primarily Musical Theater), from traditional classical vocal pedagogy as accepted over the past 200 years, and from voice medicine, health and science, using all words as accurately as possible. Many teachers make up terms that apply only to their own work, forcing those who are not disciples of that method to seek special "translation" of both the terms and what they represent in order to communicate about them. LoVetri's method allows anyone who is trained in traditional methods to discuss function in nearly universally understood terms. It also allows *Somatic Voicework™* practitioners to read voice science research and understand the information in a basic way without becoming voice scientists themselves. This facilitates inter-disciplinary communication, inter-personal interaction, and helps eliminate friction in both.

Example exercises and discussion of teaching style

The vocal exercises found in *Somatic Voicework™ The LoVetri Method* are themselves typically simple: pitch slides, scales, and arpeggios of varying lengths that may be done at varying tempi and performed either staccato or legato. It is the manner in which the exercises are performed, however, that is of utmost importance. LoVetri believes that the intention for the exercise is more important than the pitches, syllables and vowels that make up the exercise. It is the *how,* not the *what,* that she seeks to clarify.

Because there are a limited number of combinations of pitches, vowels, syllables, and volume levels within a singer's normal sung vocal range, if any specific vocal exercise does not produce a rapid change in a student's vocal production, many teachers run out of exercise options and turn to other things such as "resonance" or "breath management" to produce vocal changes. *Somatic Voicework™* always strives to help the singer find efficient vocal production with as little excess effort as possible. When using the sung vocal exercise as a stimulus, it can take quite some time to arrive at the best possible coordination and have it be available consistently. During this time of patiently seeking a new coordination, students are asked to "wait for the bus." The phrase connotes repeating the same exercise on different pitches for 30–60 seconds, allowing the throat to respond slowly and the singer to notice how things sound and feel during the wait. Each vocal response gives a glimpse of what is taking place in the throat and body as the sound is being made. The teacher learns to listen for subtle changes in the sound, notice adjustments in the body, and use these perceptions to help select subsequent exercises. When the desired sound finally arises spontaneously, the chosen exercise has done its job. Sometimes in these circumstances singers are startled to hear what emerges from their own throats. This is a powerful and unique aspect of *Somatic Voicework*™.

Based on the belief that a singer has very little ability to control directly any of the vocal anatomy from about the middle of the mouth back, exercises to encourage specific new behaviors in this area must do so indirectly, by varying three basic factors: vowel, volume, and pitch. Because both registration and vowel sound shaping respond to the imagination of the singer, over time, singers can learn to call upon the three registers directly (which is not the case in other pedagogies in which resonance strategies are employed to effect registration indirectly, or registration is ignored entirely) and make a specific type of vowel at the same time. Register balance facilitates vowel sound control, and connection to efficient coordination of pressure from the activity of the abdominal muscles. This is also unique to *Somatic Voicework*™ but is important because in the music marketplace, being able to sing with these tools is required for making appropriate sounds.

In using registration as a tool to balance function, for example, it is possible to teach a belter who, through prolonged overuse of the chest register has a weak and limited head register. She might be asked to sing close vowels (/i/ and /u/) at soft volume moderately high in her range on short, staccato scales in a "baby-like" or "cooing" tone (It is expected that the teacher will demonstrate exactly what he or she is asking the student to do for every exercise.); whereas, a classical soprano who, from years of singing head voice dominant literature, now has a chest register in a state of atrophy, might be asked to sing open vowels (/a/ and /ɔ/) at moderately loud volume in the lower middle range on long single pitches or two-note slides in a "foggy," or "Santa Claus" sound. "Waiting for the bus," as described above, is Jeanie's beloved admonishment to give each exercise enough time to allow the voice to adjust to it. The vowel /æ/ on pitch slides across the *passaggio* performed with control over volume while rising is particularly useful for eliciting mixed registration.

Semi-occluded vocal tract exercises (SOVTEs, these can include various hums, lip and tongue trills, use of straws and "bubblers") are approached cautiously in this method. It is understood they may be valuable for regulating breath flow, and inducing "flow phonation" (as opposed to "breathy" or "pressed"), but can generate unwanted muscular tension in the throat that later must be released. It is also impossible for such exercises to generate a true "open-throated" sound in any style, therefore they are not seen as an all-purpose panecea as they are in some other approaches.

There is a class of exercises called "extended behaviors" that may include singing with the head tilted back, the tongue protruded, the tongue placed over a straw, the use of various sizes of corks held between the teeth, exaggerated facial positioning such as pursed lips or smiling, use of character voices like "monster" or "chipmunks" sounds, singing in altered postures such as with arms over head, bending over, or in the supine position. Each of these exercises deliberately takes a student outside typical vocal use and changes the patterns of muscle response thereby shifting awareness of both sound and feeling. They break up "muscle memory" (familiar physical responses) to allow new ones to arise. Each exercise has a specific purpose, and will be selected for the student based on the teacher's analysis of the student's needs, and will be adjusted lesson-by-lesson.

As important as the exercise and its execution, the manner in which the teacher instructs the student to do them is equally significant. The student is never to be made to feel under attack, or put on the defensive; rather, if the exercise needs to be corrected it is the anatomical structure that is not cooperating, and the body or throat, that needs encouragement, not the student. The *Somatic Voicework*™ philosophy is to always question the student about how he or she experiences the exercises, and accept whatever answer is given. The teachers do not dictate what the student *should* be feeling; rather, they ask what the student *is* feeling (or hearing, or both.) It is the teacher's responsibility to coax the desired sounds from the student, and if the student's voice does not respond it is the teacher's failure, and not the student's.

One of the most vocally inhibitive emotions is shame. The singer's voice must be a window to the soul, so any emotionally abusive behavior on the part of the teacher is not only objectionable, but also inherently at cross purposes with vocal study. A goodly portion of the materials address the concept of a teacher's "Pianoside Manner®," a reference to what is called "bed-side manner" in the medical profession. This, along with the famous tenant of the Hippocratic Oath "first do no harm," are primary values in this work.

Goals of the organization

At its foundation, *SVW*™ *The LoVetri Method* holds the belief that the art of singing has healing properties for both the singer and the listener. All people have the capacity to sing, and civilization is advanced by the thoughtful pursuit of this art both individually and collectively. The goals of the organization are to make the best information available to the widest number of people so that singers and audiences alike may be uplifted regardless of voice type or musical style.

Certification process

There are three levels of certification. All three levels are offered annually at Baldwin Wallace University in July. Level I is frequently available elsewhere; however, at this time, Baldwin Wallace is the only place offering the full three-level course.

Level I lays the groundwork for the method. Much information is disseminated about voice science, principles of functional training, vocal health, voice categories, ages, and individual student parameters, and types of dysfunction. Vocal exercises are introduced, and "practice modules" are presented which detail how a lesson or practice session might progress. These practice modules model a structure that will serve as a framework for the more advanced work in Level II.

Level II focuses much more on listening and diagnostic skills. Here, one learns to perceive vocal imbalances, types of constriction, "blocks" in the body, and problems specific to various musical styles, in addition to emotional/psychological dynamics, and how they can be honored and channeled productively in a lesson. This ability to read the student physically, vocally, and psychologically is then brought to bear on the "Solution Sequence®," in which specific solutions to perceived problems are graphed systematically.

Level III offers more advanced listening and problem-solving skills. Specific problems arising from different styles, and complex problems are more thoroughly addressed. This is where Jeanie presents her approach to dealing with "amusia" ("tone-deafness"), and other vexing problems with which voice teachers must contend periodically. A discussion of the element of communication in singing is presented here, as well as how the voice teacher fits into the voice care team in communicating with otolaryngologists and speech language pathologists. This is also the portion of the course in which guest lecturers are invited to offer lectures or master class presentations on a variety of related subjects.

Most sessions are initiated and/or closed with bodywork exercises by noted practitioners. These help release tension and open the mind, as well as introduce those who may not have had body work to some of those experiences.

Contact information, resources, and how to get involved

Taking any of the levels grants one access to the chat room in which members from all over the world post on a wide variety of topics related to singing and vocal pedagogy. For a nominal annual fee, one can also become a member of the SVW™ The LoVetri Method Teachers Association, which includes a listing on the website, and access to members-only materials available on the site. For more information, one can refer to the Voice Workshop website: www.thevoiceworkshop.com, and also the Teachers Association website: www.somaticvoicework.com.

Disclosure statement

No potential conflict of interest was reported by the author.

References

Lawrence, Van. 1979. "Laryngological Observations on 'Belting.'" *Journal of Research in Singing* 2 (1): 26–29.
Leanderson, R., and J. Sundberg. 1988. "Breathing for Singing." *Journal of Voice* 2 (1): 2–12.
LoVetri, J. 2017. *Somatic Voicework™ The LoVetri Method: Course Materials, Levels I, II, and III*. New York: The Voice Workshop.

Breathwork Africa

Marj Murray and Ela Manga

ABSTRACT
Vocal Traditions is a series in the *Voice and Speech Review* that high-lights historically important voice teachers and schools of thought in the world of vocal pedagogy. This essay explores the background of Breathwork Africa, the philosophical overview, and the key features.

Introduction

Changing the way you breathe can change the way you feel, think, act, modulate, and express. Breath affects, and is affected, by everything we do, think, and feel. Breath is a language. It supports our communication, the energy in a room, and our physical presence. It reflects our emotional and physical states, and by changing our breathing, we can change these states.

Common medical knowledge states that we unconsciously breathe about 22,000 breaths a day. I say unconsciously because we often do not pay much attention to our breath except when we cannot access it. Breathing is an automatic function—it happens without us having to think about it. It can also be a conscious function; we can override the way we are breathing to serve a particular purpose or outcome. So, if we need to relax, we can breathe in a certain way; if we need to increase our energy, there is a technique for that as well.

What Is Breathwork?

"Breathwork is the use of Breath Awareness and Conscious Breathing for healing and growth, personal awakening and transformation in spirit, mind and body" (Brulé 2017, 65). Living and working with conscious breathing is about embracing the gift of life. To open to the spirit of the breath means to commit to living your fullest potential, taking responsibility for your health and your choices. Making conscious breathing part of your life means that you have gained a lifelong tool that will support health and anchor you to your most authentic self.

In this time of chaos and uncertainty, we are being called on to shift the space from which we are operating and create a new mind-body architecture that supports deeper awareness and consciousness. Emotional intelligence, the ability to listen, communicate effectively, focus, and to make healthy choices requires that we live more consciously.

The ability to manage our energy requires the ability to live and work with more awareness. Thus, the role of breathwork has become even more relevant and urgent. When our breathing patterns become locked or fixed, either from an acute traumatic event or over time, it loses its adaptability and fluidity and leads to the development of sub-optimal breathing habits and patterns.

My observations have shown that these suboptimal patterns have been the underlying cause of many of the mental, emotional, and physical symptoms we experience. Our breathing system is the only system in the body that is both voluntary and automatic, both conscious and unconscious. That is not an accident; it is an opportunity to take part in our own evolution and to determine our own nature. We can look at breathing as an untapped resource. Most people do not know the power and potential that it holds. The breath can be used as a tool to transform, change, strengthen, support, and enhance various aspects of ourselves.

Sub-optimal breathing results in premature aging and inefficient metabolism, setting up a cycle of inflammation and toxic build up. When cellular function is not optimized, it impacts our sleep, mood, energy, and general state of health (Perez-Chada et al. 2007). In my experience, we have unnatural cravings; we suffer a poor quality of life, and we may increase the likelihood of many diseases and illnesses. Breathing optimally gets us to shift out of inflammatory states, activating and supporting the body's innate wisdom by generating authentic energy vs adrenalized energy. Optimal breathing supports the body's natural ability to heal, repair and recover (Benchetrit 2000). As I have seen, many people have learned to apply remedial breathing for asthma, anxiety, pain management, chronic fatigue, high blood pressure-low blood pressure, weight loss, headaches, insomnia, depression, allergies, and auto-immune diseases. Optimum breathing may support peak performance and clarity of thinking and feeling.

The Birth of Breathwork Africa

Breathwork Africa is a social enterprise and community network officially started in 2018 to formalize breathwork training on the African continent. It was operating informally for about three years prior to 2018. Our focus was on in-person training, groups, and one-on one sessions. With the advent of COVID-19, we realized the need to support people with online breathing sessions, so BreathCafe was birthed. This is an online platform where people could tap into six breathwork sessions a week and a monthly Breathwork Masterclass. With the world opening after the pandemic, we have responded to the need and now BreathCafe encompasses online and in-person sessions as well as Breath @ Work, our corporate sessions. During 2020, we supported over 40 organizations with online sessions for their employees and this has now moved to in-person sessions.

Breathwork Africa now has an international footprint with a reach into more than 50 countries. In terms of our training, over 500 people have gone through our foundation training, and 130 people through have gone through our advanced training. Our Breathing Buddies initiative focuses on teenagers and children. This is a passion project. We fundamentally believe that if conscious breathing is taught in classrooms, universities, on the playground, sports field, and in the home a new generation will arise that is more conscious, intuitive, and world changing. We offer one-on-one sessions, school programs, and training for people who engage with children. Breathwork Africa supports children, students, business leaders, entrepreneurs, NGO's, creatives, activists, educators, and athletes—anyone who is committed to physical and mental health, personal growth, and greater self-awareness.

About the Founder

Breathwork Africa was founded by Dr. Ela Manga when she saw the potential of conscious breathing as a fundamental pillar in the practice of integrative medicine. Ela had experienced her first conscious connected breathwork session in 2011 with Dan Brulé when he visited South Africa. Ela then realized the power of the breath and began working with it in her medical practice. Ela felt inspired to share this tool with every person who was open to tapping into their most powerful free and available inner resource and natural technology, so she began facilitating monthly group sessions. This practice then grew into basic training, advanced training, the start of Breathwork Africa, and then the birth of BreathCafe.

Since then, with the steadfast support of Marj Murray, Simon Kehagias, and a growing team of "Pneumanitarians," Breathwork Africa has grown in depth and breadth. It is manifesting its vision through the art and science of Pneumanity™ breathwork as a tool of self-empowerment, healing, and transformation. Through individual and group sessions, practitioner training, talks, and workshops, we are meeting a wide audience in Africa and globally.

Ela is an integrative medical doctor committed to healing and bringing heart back into the art of medicine. Her medical training was a step toward her true vocation as a facilitator of health and a catalyst for change. Ela's healing philosophy is based on the partnership between doctor and patient, who (as she believes) are co-creators in the journey of health. Ela has a special interest in the art and science of conscious breathing as a medicine and tool for growth and change. Her first book *Breathe: Strategising Energy in the Age of Burnout* (Manga 2019) brings all these principles together in an easy-to-use guide to optimum energy and health.

Key Features

There are many breathwork schools around the world, but since we are the only certified one on the African continent, Breathwork Africa is committed to sharing the breath in a way that reflects our history, the science of breath, and the ancient wisdom of the continent that is often ignored. We call this the Pneumanity™ methodology.

Pneumanity™ is an approach to conscious breathing that is inspired by an ancient vision of the future that is held and shared by the Breathwork Africa community. It is an integrative and embodied approach to breathwork that honors each individual as a unique expression of their history, character, and spirit. It draws on the vast scope of practices that are guided by ancient wisdom and grounded in modern science. Pneumanity™ is adaptable, simple, safe, and most importantly, accessible to all people regardless of age, culture, nationality, race, gender identity or sexual orientation, religion, and life circumstances. It guides every person to their own resources held within their body and breath. It is borne from the words "Pneuma" and "Humanity," the essence of Ubuntu[1] and the universal life force that weaves through the heart of humankind.

The seven threads of Pneumanity are the guiding principles that support the integrity of our work as "Pneumanitarians," the practitioners and members of the Breathwork Africa Community. They are universal principles of breath and consciousness, many of which are found within the Indigenous Wisdom Traditions of Africa. These seven threads are woven through our training both in terms of philosophy and practical application. We commit to breathing and embodying these principles into our own life in order that we may hold them for others.

Sankofa

Breath is the thread between remembering and imagining. Sankofa is a word in the Twi language of Ghana that means "go back and fetch it." It is symbolized by a mythical bird with its feet firmly planted forward and its head looking back with the egg of possibilities held within her beak. The spirit of Sankofa reminds us that we all come from somewhere and that we are custodians of a legacy. It is a reminder that healing is an invitation to go back to our roots and gather the best of what our past can teach us, using the insights as energy to step into the future.

As custodians of the breath and in honoring the principle of Sankofa, "to go back" means to turn inward and to breathe into the inherited and acquired memories of the past held within our cells and nervous system. Through the breath, we can release and heal unintegrated trauma, but we are also able to access the gifts, talents, and resilience that reside within our ancestral lineage. As we assert, our breath is also rooted in a timeless wisdom that reaches even further back into the hundreds of microscopic mitochondria within every cell that holds a unique set of DNA that has been passed down through our maternal line from our common ancestor, "Mitochondrial Eve," who through genetic studies was traced back to the Kalahari about 200,000 years ago.[2]

We also see Sankofa within the universal principle and natural law of "feedback loops"—information that is received from one part to inform the functioning of the other to maintain homeostasis or balance. Within the body-mind, Sankofa employs the breath to inform the brain of what the body is experiencing and vice versa. As breathwork practitioners, we often observe the feedback loops in the body-mind system that reflect fear and keep the system in a fixed pattern which reinforces the stress response. Through conscious breathing, an environment is created that allows access to intergenerational information held in our cellular memory. Sankofa also reminds us to go back and fetch the breath that is rooted in timeless wisdom. From here, we can repattern the trauma of the past and co-create new feedback loops and neural pathways that express our most natural state reflected within the parameters of our natural Breath Intelligence.

Safety

Safety creates the environment that supports the natural healing process. The thread of safety is symbolized by the mighty African Baobab tree, a sacred symbol of many Southern African traditions. The baobab tree is regarded as the African Tree of Life. It is considered to serve as a source of protection, providing shelter, sustenance, and comfort to all those who sit around it. It is a symbol of life and positivity.

While Sankofa reminds us that that we belong to something that is greater than our individual self, the Baobab reminds us that with the experience of belonging comes the feeling of safety. Safety allows the ability to relax, activating the body's self-healing capacity. We also experience safety when we feel heard, seen, understood, and accepted by others. We also feel this profoundly when we share stories and realize our shared humanity. Our own personal practice also helps to cultivate and embody safety within our own being in order that we can hold the space with integrity for others.

Embodiment

> The body already is a pure intelligence and THE unspeakable beauty. Every cell in your body is in a profound harmony with the rest of the cosmos […] light, air, water, the green realm, female male collaboration, all tangible and intangible conditions.
>
> (Whitwell 2021, 1)

Breathwork is the art and science of experiencing the body as an expression of and vehicle for the Breath, Spirit, Life Force, Nöm, Chi, Prana, Umoya, and Ruach. Our approach to breathwork is, therefore, deeply embodied. Through our study of the human form, biomechanics, biodynamics, and biochemistry, we learn to appreciate the body's magnificent inner workings, intricacies, and wisdom. With this understanding, we feel more inspired to tend to our inner environment—to listen, respect and respond to its inner cues. We support the body to facilitate the flow of breath.

Through the body and breath, we slowly and gently reintegrate fragmented aspects of ourselves that may have been split off because of trauma and stress responses (i.e. numbing, suppression, avoiding, armoring, projecting, overworking, perfectionism, and spiritual and intellectual bypass). Through the breath, we also begin to befriend the body to understand and relate to physical symptoms. We support our clients to experience safety slowly and gently within their own body, through a range of embodied practices and techniques. We encourage clients to experience the full range of energy from intensity to deep relaxation and expanded states while staying present in their body without dissociating or splitting from it or defaulting to old patterns of trauma. We use the body to understand, dissolve, and integrate emotional experiences. We use breath awareness as the foundation of staying embodied and stay present to internal cues. We encourage all kinds of movement styles to shake up and release the breath, make space in the body, and keep energy flowing.

The Khoisan people of the Kalahari used a "shaking medicine," rhythmically shaking up the body to shake up the breath and life force (Keeney 2007). Many African traditions use drums and rhythmic beats to mark rites of passage, connect to the ancestors and the spirit of nature, and activate healing. The Yogis work with physical asanas to create space in the body through release of fascial lines and creating flow of energy through the energy lines that run through them. Physical Asana is the preparation for Pranayama. Martial arts practitioners move the body poetically and dance with and master life force with graceful flowing and powerful movement. Pneumanity practitioners encourage conscious embodied experience of breath through movement styles inspired by ancient practices and creative ways of working with the body.

Wholeness

A translation of Sanskrit Mantra states, "This is whole, that is whole. And when whole is taken from whole, all that remains is whole." The thread of wholeness is the feeling we have when we gaze up into the stars in the night sky. We are reminded that we are already whole and complete; this is our natural state, and there is nothing to fix or control. It takes us away from the idea of a pathology paradigm, where it is easy to become over identified with our perceived illness, diagnosis, history, habits, addictions, and patterns. While these are all important to name, acknowledge, and accept as part of our experience, conscious breathing brings us back to the experience of wholeness within and that we are a part of, providing us with the inspiration and tools to integrate them. We are reminded that even illness or the symptom is part of the natural process of moving toward wholeness and that nature has a perfect order that integrates dark and light, life, and death.

In some indigenous African cultures, when someone in the village experienced a transgression, the person concerned was brought into a circle with the elders and the community. Rather than being reprimanded, they were reminded of their wholeness through song, music, dance, and other forms of enactment. Our role as practitioners is to honor and own our wholeness, so we can reflect for the other. We use conscious breathing to invest in, feed, and deepen our relationship with our wholeness, and we use it to see and respect every person that we work with as already whole and complete. It is from this place that we can relate to pain, anxiety, trauma, and stresses. Through the breath, we also experience wholeness as an ever-expanding state that contributes to the whole.

Ubuntu

As Archbishop Emeritus Desmond Tutu said, "We think of ourselves far too frequently as individuals, separated from one another, whereas you are connected and what you do affects the whole world" (as quoted in Schnall 2021). Ubuntu is a universal principle held deeply within the wisdom traditions of Southern Africa. The common translation of "I am because we are," speaks to Ubuntu only in terms of its social construct; however, this powerful universal truth expands more deeply and widely, embracing the interconnectedness of all of life. It is the thread of interconnected intelligence between each cell, organ, dimensions of our being, each other, every plant, animal, insect, the elements, the cosmos, and our past and present that connects us to the whole. We see this web fractal in the macro to the micro—the spiders web, fascia, neural network, and mushroom mycelia.

Ubuntu reminds us that separateness is simply an illusion and that disharmony occurs when the threads of connection are broken or when we identify as separate. Breath is the thread that reweaves us back to our natural state and the heart of humanity of which we are an inextricable part. It is the bridge between the conscious and unconscious and all the conflicting polarities we experience within and around us. Breath is embodied Ubuntu.

Creativity

Breath gives us the form for the flow. From the embodied experience of wholeness and interconnectedness, we can appreciate that we are all unique and individual expressions of what is shaped by our ancestry, unique gifts, tendencies, and traumas. In appreciating each person as a unique expression of life force, we communicate with breath as a form of art—creatively and fluidly, using the form of technique to support the flow.

A.R.T. (as defined below) supports that each one of us are also emotionally, energetically, and biochemically different each day; therefore, it reminds us to listen deeply to the body and to sense what is ready to be expressed through breath. Thus, we cannot work with a formulaic approach. By being deeply present and embodied within ourselves, we can work intuitively and creatively. The Thread of Art and the San people of the Kalahari also remind us to approach our practice and sessions with lightness, playfulness, joy, and curiosity.

The Mystery

Breath is the thread between the known and the unknowable. Ultimately, the nature of existence is mysterious and magical. Breath is the surrender to the great mystery and the invitation to embrace uncertainty, impermanence, the unknown, the void, and the space of pure potential. It holds the seeds of love sown in the dark night of dreams, ready to come alive through our body. Through the exhale, the pause that follows, and the next breath that follows that, we are taught to relax in the void. True freedom resides in the ability to surrender to this space to the unknown, knowing that we are an eternal expression of the whole. Breath allows us to practice the feeling of what we may be beyond the body. From the mystery and the void, yesterday's dream is tomorrow's Sankofa.

Teaching Style

Breathwork Africa trains and facilitates according to the A.R.T. framework (as referred to in Creativity above), which is a way to access many breathing techniques. All breathing techniques ultimately serve breath intelligence—our body's way of returning to its natural state of breathing as a daily baseline which brings about overall mental and physical well-being. In the A.R.T. framework, the "A" stands for Awareness. The "R" stands for Regulation, and the "T" stands for Transformation. We master techniques to ultimately be free from technique, and we learn to breathe from the breath itself. The A.R.T. of breathing framework is the guide, the form for the flow of creative expression of breath. The body is a canvas in which the breath gets to play.

(1) Awareness: One of the first things we need to do to be optimal breathers is to practice "breath awareness." In other words, we need to cultivate the habit of tuning into our breathing at different times, during different activities, or when desiring to accomplish certain things or to be in certain states. Breath Awareness is the foundation for all breathing and mindfulness practices. It is simply watching the breath, physical sensations, thoughts, and emotions without any judgment—always returning to the breath. How do we breathe when we are feeling calm, peaceful, and content? How do we breathe when we are upset, angry, afraid or in pain? It is important to bring awareness to our breathing at those times because the way we breathe (either consciously or unconsciously) will either exacerbate or relieve the short and long-term effects of those states.

(2) Regulation: Under the "R" of the A.R.T. framework the category of Regulation is supported by techniques in the Energy, Balance, and Relaxation field. For example, a wonderful breathing technique which brings homeostasis and calm to the body and mind is that of "coherent breathing." This technique is simply breathing in through the nose for a count of five and out through the nose for a count of five. This technique can be used any time of the day or night. If we are looking to bring deep relaxation to the body, we would extend our exhale which activates the Vagus nerve, the main nerve sending messages form the body to the brain, telling the brain that we are safe in our bodies and shifting us into the parasympathetic state, a state of rest and digest (Cazden 2017). When we hit our afternoon slump, we can then change the channel through which we breathe, perhaps using our mouth for five quick inhales and exhales, consciously activating the sympathetic system—our fight and flight mode—and giving us a burst of energy.

(3) Transformation: In the "T" in the A.R.T. framework, we work with Transformative Techniques. While any breathing technique, even simple breath awareness can be transformative, the practice of connected or circular breathing creates a powerful state of alerted consciousness where deep healing and transformative work can be done.

Breathwork Africa Goals, Certification, and Contact

Our intention at Breathwork Africa is to share the power of the breath and how becoming conscious of how we breathe can be life-changing on every level. We want to make learning about the breath accessible to every community no matter social status, creed, color, financial disposition, sexual orientation, gender identification, or faith. Breath is, after all, our birth right.

We offer a one-year Certified Advanced Breathwork Practitioner Course which is globally recognized. For anyone who would like to receive this certification a prerequisite is our three-day Breathwork Foundation Course, which we run about four times a year. We do an annual intake for the Advanced course in January of each year. You can find all our training details on www.breathworkafrica.co.za and our events on www. breathcafe.com, and we are on all social media platforms. The central e-mail is info@breathworkafrica.co.za.

Notes

1. Ubuntu is a term used in several African languages that refers to the moral attribute of a person.
2. See Lemonick (1987) for an introduction to this concept.

Disclosure statement

No potential conflict of interest was reported by the author(s).

References

Benchetrit, Gila. 2000. "Breathing Pattern in Humans: Diversity and Individuality." *Respiration Physiology* 122 (2–3): 123–129. doi:10.1016/S0034–5687(00)00154-7.

Brulé, Dan. 2017. *Just Breathe: Mastering Breathwork for Success in Life, Love, Business, and Beyond.* New York: Atria/Enliven Book.

Cazden, Joanna. 2017. "Stalking the Calm Buzz: How the Polyvagal Theory Links Stage Presence, Mammal Evolution, and the Root of the Vocal Nerve." *Voice and Speech Review* 11 (2): 132–153. doi:10.1080/23268263.2017.1390036.

Keeney, Bradford. 2007. *Shaking Medicine: The Healing Power of Ecstatic Movement*. Merrimac, MA: Destiny Books.

Lemonick, MD. 1987. "Everyone's Genealogical Mother." *Time*, January 26. Accessed on 24 February 2022. https://web.archive.org/web/20080923010301/http://www.time.com/time/magazine/arti cle/0,9171,963320,00.html

Manga, Ela. 2019. *Breathe: Strategising Energy in the Age of Burnout*. Johannesburg, South Africa: Jacana Media.

Perez-Chada, Daniel, Santiago Perez-Lloret, Alejandro J. Videla, Daniel Cardinali, Miguel A. Bergna, Mariano Fernández-Acquier, Luis Larrateguy, Gustavo E. Zabert, and Christopher Drake. 2007. "Sleep Disordered Breathing and Daytime Sleepiness are Associated with Poor Academic Performance in Teenagers. A Study Using the Pediatric Daytime Sleepiness Scale (PDSS)." *Sleep* 30 (12): 1698–1703. doi:10.1093/sleep/30.12.1698.

Schnall, Marianne. 2021. "Wisdom Shared With Me By Desmond Tutu: 'We Are All Connected. What Unites Us Is Our Common Humanity.'" *Forbes*. December 26. Accessed on 24 February 2022. https://www.forbes.com/sites/marianneschnall/2021/12/26/wisdom-shared-with-me-by-desmond-tutu-we-are-all-connected-what-unites-us-is-our-common-humanity/?sh=7f39e9b83cc6

Whitwell, Mark, 2021. "You Only Need to Realise It One Time." *Medium*, December 1. Accessed on 24 February 2022. https://markwhitwell.medium.com/you-only-need-to-realise-it-one-time-d6d7c55157e4

Steiner Speech

Geoffrey Norris

ABSTRACT

Vocal Traditions is a series in the *Voice and Speech Review* that highlights historically important voice teachers and schools of thought in the world of vocal pedagogy. This essay explores the background of Steiner Speech, the philosophical overview, and the key features.

Introduction to the Training

The Art of Steiner Speech (*Sprachgestaltung*/ creative or ensouled speech) was developed by Rudolf Steiner and his actress wife Marie Steiner in the early part of the twentieth century at the Goetheanum in Dornach, Switzerland, and the training remains unique in its musical and gestural approach to voice production and movement.[1] A unique vocal technique, it requires an intense four-year, fulltime training program simply to reach the journeyman stage, and it is akin to musical training, but it follows the laws of language and of speech sound production.[2]

There are several key concepts: (a) the use and freeing of the breath and tone from a body bound state, (b) awareness of rhythm and pulse, and (c) the formative gestures and movements of the very sounds of speech themselves in vowels and consonants. These ideas form the basis of this approach and lead to a sound sense symbiosis—raising the word from its limited abstract and intellectual sense to a creative depth of action, emotion and artistic feeling for form, beauty, and wholeness. Speech itself is the teacher, and breathing is not learned or approached separately; rather, it acts as an integral part of vocalizing, and one learns to breathe through this very act (Kimbrough 2009).

The journey from graduation to mastery asks for a deepening of one's artistic sensibilities, a love and knowledge of poetry and language, an experiential awareness of gesture and movement, and an awakening of the underlying force of volition enabling us dancelike to overcome gravity and move with ease and grace in both body and sound gesture. We do not only speak with our larynx and neighboring speech organs, but with our entire living, moving, sounding body—becoming eloquently speaking bodies and shaping, moving voices. The technique, through an artistic approach, enlivens our experiential core.

All diplomas issued worldwide need be countersigned by the leadership of the Section for the Musical and Performing Arts which from its inception was and is based at the Goetheanum, Dornach, Switzerland.[3] This collegial body oversees the integrity of the work.

Philosophical Overview of Steiner Speech

Steiner Speech supports that the words of our languages are not mere haphazard groupings of sounds conveying abstract meanings; they are living creative forms whose colors, resonances, sound combinations, rhythms, and gestures speak experientially of their content. Indeed, within the spoken word "the living breath of creation" can be deeply experienced (Steiner 1986; Norris 2019). The creative singing dance of the "verbum," the "logos," the "word" is at the source of the creation myths of many varied folk cultures (Steiner 2002; Norris 2019). And it resonates at the heart of many of the worlds spiritual/ religious movements, such as the Gospel according to St. John:

> In the beginning was the Word, and the Word was with God, and the Word was God. All things were made by Him, and without Him was not anything made that was made.
>
> (John 1:1–3 NIV)

In Genesis, too, the world was spoken into being; And God said, "Let there be light, and there was light." The creative power of the logos was also at the heart of the ancient Greek Mystery Center of Ephesus, where the mystery of human speech was studied intimately. Upon entering the Mysteries, the pupil was met with the words "Speak O Man, and thou revealest through thee, the coming into being (the evolution) of worlds" (Steiner 1986). On leaving, he again was exhorted with the words, "The coming into being of worlds reveals itself through thee, O Man, when you speak." The pupil was thus led to experience how the act of speaking echoed in its process the creation of the world and all that is in it and could truly feel the truth of the adage "as above so below," experiencing the mighty presence of the divine within the microcosm, the created world.

This power of the Word is still preserved in varying chant and mantric traditions around the globe in both eastern and western cultures and religious practices. The "poetic charge" in the use of language by the world's great poets, dramatists, and writers also preserve the transformative power of the Word in the many, varied, rich, and distinct languages—each a unique window into the mystery of the logos, the archetypal speech of the cosmos, from whence we all descend and ascend.

Steiner Speech argues that ancient languages carry with them greater or lesser resonances of the "primal tongue"—a resonance that our materialistic, head bound age has all but squeezed out of our modern language consciousness. Even though words of languages seem to have lost their power to heal as they once did, the genius of language can still be rediscovered, and words—which have become a mere abstract means of intellectual and often mundane communication, or bearers of unbridled emotion—can rise again in full creative splendor, both in everyday life and on the stage and screen. This is particularly true in the performing arts where naturalistic, mumbled, shrunken, or emotive words predominately hold sway.

Key Features

Rudolf Steiner developed numerous and carefully developed sound/sense exercises to awaken the artist to the living creative source of all languages spoken on the earth (Anderson 2011). These exercises can lead the practitioner to be inspired by the "genius" of speech itself and to be filled with creative might. One learns to love speech and to feel it resonating through one's entire fiber. One learns to experience the creative force of language surging through one's blood, nerves, breath, muscle, bones, and to the kernel of the bodily instrument. This exploration also includes the shaping energies out of which this body was formed and, more importantly, the very core of one's being—as an artist, individual, and one who inhabits and creates artistically with and through their being. In the exercises, we do not only speak but are spoken, like surfers riding the waves; in this case, the waves are the word both written and improvised. "Not I not I but the wind that blows through me" as D.H. Lawrence ([1928] 1994) expressed it in "Song of a Man Who Has Come Through." Through these vocal exercises (including intense work on the pentathlon)[4] and through contact improvisation, numerous theatre games, and Eurythmy,[5] the student is led to overcome the resistances of the gravity bound physical body, and they begin to experience the world of grounded levity and freedom. Through the downright, we learn the upright.

We become aware of the external shaping consonantal world consisting of four main types:

(A) Those that give form: /b/, /p/, /m/, /n/, /d/, /t/, /g/, and /k/ "*Earth*" sounds, which can be seen in nature in all solid or physical forms.

(B) Those that flow /l/ (and in English perhaps also /w/) "*Water*" sounds, which are felt in the flowing movement of our legs and seen in plant life and in water including precipitation cloud formation and rainfall.

(C) Those that moves with a rotational dynamic /r/ "*Air*" sounds, which are felt in the freedom of our arms and in the power of the wind.

(D) And those that burn up substance /h/, /f/, /s/, /z/, /ʃ/, /tʃ/, dʒ/, and /v/ "*Fire*" sounds,

which are seen in the dance of the flames and in warmth both inner and outer. You hear their gesture but can see them imaginatively (Kimbrough 2009; Steiner 1986)

Of course, we also are aware of the normal speech parlance used: impact sounds, fricatives, sibilants, and others, but these elements are what we work *with*, and we also work with the creative archetypal gestures, which each sound specifically makes as seen in the art of Eurythmy, a visible speech and a visible music.

The different inner world of the vowels and their gestures and movements are then explored and contrasted to the instrument building and external consonantal world (Steiner 2002). These working in harmony as syllables, become the tools to free the moving tone—the voice. We acknowledge the reality that the breath and the sounds born and reborn in it first must be breathed in; they must be inspired from our surround. This fact lies at the very foundations of our work. You cannot give what you have not first received, and speech is a gift to be given freely.

With this palette, we start with simple yet focused articulation exercises, which connect the body through rhythmic step and exact timing to the freely formed flow of the voice in the outgoing stream of the breath. (And here I must ad that they are not just supported by the breath but embedded in the very life-giving substance of this breath energy). We learn to walk in the breath, to move it syllable by syllable. We come, then, to the shaping forces of recitation, declamation, and of conversation, each of which uses the breath differently and dynamically, giving rise to an awareness of the varying styles

VOCAL TRADITIONS

of poetry, narrative, and old and modern dramatic texts. The awareness and mastery of these different dynamic breath techniques lead to a freedom in the playful improvisational element required for both written and devised dialogue, much like the jazz musician who endlessly master's technique to enable skill in improvisation.

From these pillars, we move into the everchanging fluency exercises, bringing dynamism and playfulness to the fore, becoming gymnasts of voice and dancers in the breathtone substance. In all, we as the artist are the still point of the turning world, the balanced poised center of the creative moving periphery. Then we reenter the colorful atmospheric world of the vowels, experiencing their placements in the body and mouth and their gesture and mood, from the wonder and receptiveness of "ah" to the awake aware focus of "u." This mystery can be experienced in the "AOUM chant." Each vowel opens a unique inner experience, and its vocalizing is directly connected to our emotions, feelings within the breath, and the deeper experiential meaning of words.

The five "pure" vowels move from "ah" figuratively in the center of the chest to "ee" and "eye"(phonetically ay as in hay and ee as in see) figuratively in the head and nerve system. The "aw" (as in "ought") is figuratively in the diaphragm, and the "u" is figuratively in the base of the belly. We assert that these are tonally deeper and connected to the blood and metabolism. This vowel world, unlike the elemental consonantal world, is an inner world of feeling, music, and color. The best way to experience this inner world is through practice, not theory, and everyone, layman included, can in my experience achieve this awareness easily.

The "three-foldness" of the instrument is then further worked upon (Anderson 2011; Kimbrough 2009). This three-foldness is acknowledge in several aspects: head, heart, and limbs; thinking, feeling, and willing; stick, cloth, and ball; straight line, wave, and circle; and the lips, teeth/hard palate, and the soft palate. Imagistically within our system, the lips correspond in the body to the rhythmic system, heart, feeling, expression of self, lyricism, and the future. The crystalline teeth and hard palate correspond to the head, awake thinking, dramatic communication, and the present moment. The soft palate (back of the mouth) corresponds to the limbs and the metabolism, the will, sculptural forming force, the power of epic texts in both rhythmic and alliterative forms, and to past events and retelling.

There are also exercises to establish the qualities that skillful speaking requires: form, flow, fullness, and focused distinction freely released within the stream of the outgoing breath:

(A) clarity of articulation and incisiveness through the sounds /m/, /s/, and /n/
(B) freely flowing through the sound /l/
(C) wholeness of form and fullness through /b/
(D) punctuation and differentiation through /k/.

Ultimately, there are over 70 exercises given by Steiner for actors, reciters, storytellers, teachers, lecturers, priests, and interested laymen, plus many more exercises developed by colleagues working in healing and in pedagogy (Steiner 1986).

Detailed attention is also paid to the seven main vocal gestures: (1) informing and effective speech, (2) thoughtful and questioning, (3) hesitant and uncertain, (4) antipathetic, (5) sympathetic, (6) self-assertion, and (7) finally apathetic and giving up (Steiner 1986).

(1) The first of these is a pointing gesture, which gives the speech a focus, direction, firmness, clarity, and incisiveness. Too much of this, and you will push the listener to step back into self-assertion as a defense.

(2) The second is a rounded, warm fullness—much like the old echo voice of inner thought. Here the gesture is a holding onto oneself. Rodin's Thinker is an archetype of this. This calm clear voice invites the listener in to understand what is being spoken, and we consider it to be the ideal teaching voice if fully inhabited, but boring if empty. All soliloquys are written in this style though often they are turned into a direct communication with the audience, becoming an outer dialogue not an internal one artistically shared. In Shakespeare, the rhythm needs to be understood and mastered to avoid intellectualizing the language.

(3) The hesitant voice has a slight vibration and wobble to it, and this voice gives rise to annoyance on the part of the listener. It is arguably the worst voice a teacher or lecturer can have. Its outer gesture is a kind of feeling forward against hindrances, an outer and then inner movement

(4) The antipathetic voice is hard and explosive with fists or an aggressive, dismissive flinging out of a limb—like when the volcano erupts after it first steaming. The teacher can use this for pedagogic effect, so long as it is not real and as long as the teacher does not actually loss their temper. If this becomes the case, the teacher has lost.

(5) Sympathy is warm caressing and gentle voiced—the gesture is a full handed touching or soothing stroke.

(6) Self-assertion is an abrupt forming with the gesture of an open palmed defensive wall. Figuratively, the idea is "Enough is enough. You do; I won't, ok!"

(7) The seventh gesture, the inability to come to a decision, is a long slow and drawn-out voice with all gestures subsiding into heaviness, an apathetic slump, and defeat. In a way, this can also be seen as a nuance of gesture 2.

Conclusion

Many of these ideas exist in an oral tradition, so the best way of progressing is to work with someone trained in the method, who has developed mastery and an up-to-date sound/sense style appropriate for the times we live in. For further inquiry, e-mail Geoff Norris, or contact the performing arts section at the Goetheanum for additional resources and trainings

Notes

1. The website for the Goetheanum is https://goetheanum.ch/en
2. Ultimately, Rudolf Steiner is associated with many philosophical, metaphysical, and educational concepts including Waldorf education. Voice and speech training was only a part of his historic legacy (Petrash 2002).
3. See https://srmk.goetheanum.org/en/
4. An event from the Ancient Greek Olympics that includes running, jumping, wrestling, discus, and javelin.
5. Eurythmy is an expressive movement art originated by Rudolf Steiner.

Disclosure statement

No potential conflict of interest was reported by the author(s).

References

Anderson, Neil. 2011. "On Rudolf Steiner's Impact on the Training of the Actor." *Literature and Aesthetics* 21 (1): 158–174.

Kimbrough, Andrew. 2009. "A Practical Critique of Rudolf Steiner's Speech and Drama." *Voice and Speech Review* 6 (1): 86–94. doi:10.1080/23268263.2009.10761510.

Lawrence, D. H. [1928] 1994. *The Complete Poems of D. H. Lawrence*. London: Wordsworth Editions.

Norris, Geoff. 2019. "What Is Steiner Speech." *Speech and Drama Studio*, January 1. https://speechand dramastudio.com/what-is-steiner-speech/

Petrash, Jack. 2002. *Understanding Waldorf Education: Teaching from the inside Out*. Lewisville, NC: Gryphon House.

Steiner, Rudolf. 1986. *Speech and Drama*. New York: Anthroposophic Press.

Steiner, Rudolf. 2002. *What Is Anthroposophy?: Three Perspectives on Self-knowledge*. Edited by Christopher Bamford. Great Barrington, MA: Anthroposophic Press.

Seven Pillars Acting Technique

Sonya Cooke, Tiffany Gilly-Forrer, Cynthia Bassham, Victoria Myssik, Adam Thatcher and Thomas Varga

ABSTRACT
Vocal Traditions is a series in the *Voice and Speech Review* that highlights both historically important and contemporary voice teachers and schools of thought in the world of vocal pedagogy. This essay explores Seven Pillars Acting, a modern acting technique developed by Sonya Cooke, designed to equip actors with a comprehensive and practical system of crafting character. Inspired by and drawn from the defining techniques of the twentieth century, the Pillars aim to bring acting training into the present by fitting to the current demands of the industry and needs of acting students today. It breaks down an actor's creative and physical instrument into seven major components. By dissecting these aspects of the craft, the technique enables the actor to utilize each one to its full potential. Upon integrating all seven pillars into one's process, an actor is equipped to craft their character with authenticity, depth, specificity, and ease. This essay explores the background technique, the central features of system, and the scope of the organization.

Overview

Seven Pillars Acting is a comprehensive acting technique for actors to transform into character with ease and authenticity. Influenced by the methods of Konstantin Stanislavski, Sanford Meisner, Jerzy Grotowski, and Declan Donnellan, actor, teacher, and scholar Sonya Cooke developed the technique to synthesize these well-known methods into a modern, approachable, and rigorous process for acting. The Seven Pillars refer to the inter-related skills that are considered essential to compelling acting. These skills are:

(1) Contact
(2) Circumstance
(3) Meaning
(4) Emotional Life
(5) Objective
(6) Action
(7) Physical Life

The first four pillars are devoted to "living truthfully under imaginary circumstances," and the last three are focused on the "reality of doing," according to Sanford Meisner's famous maxims (Meisner and Longwell 1987).

Contact, the first and foundational pillar, is the exploration of connection to the actor's scene partner while simultaneously remaining connected to self. Many exercises from this chapter are influenced by the work of Sanford Meisner. *Circumstance*, the second pillar, investigates the past, present, and imagined future from the character's perspective. Exploring the Circumstance pillar never ceases—because what is happening *to* the character is limitless. These ongoing discoveries can make a world of difference in creating a believable performance.

Meaning, the third pillar, dives into the character's interpretation of the circumstances and encourages the actor to take an inventory of whether they connect to those meanings. *Emotional Life*, the fourth pillar, explores the actor's access to their own emotions and personalization of the various meanings for a character, especially those to which the actor struggles to connect.

Objective, the fifth pillar, examines what the character needs or wants, as well as the opposing forces of aversion and obstacle. *Action*, the sixth pillar, looks at the strategies or tactics used to achieve the objective. It is also the container and conduit for emotional life in the form of transitive verbs. *Physical Life*, the seventh and final pillar, encourages the actor to physicalize and vocalize while acting so that characters are believably and healthfully embodied. This pillar runs through all the others and simultaneously stands on its own, as it can be taught in a myriad of ways based on the teacher's movement and physical acting expertise.

Although the pillars are taught sequentially to organize and structure an actor's path to character, they are ultimately interchangeable. They engender confidence, ownership, and ease, three crucial elements in a performance, carving a clear path that leads to personal and artistic transformation. The easeful actor has tremendous presence; they belong in the world of the character because they are authentically living within the circumstances. The technique is taught at schools and colleges nationally; therefore, this article is penned by teachers of the technique who are implementing this work in their classrooms.

Introduction and History of Seven Pillars Acting Technique

Seven Pillars Acting came about from founder and author Sonya Cooke's exploration of the craft of acting, both through her professional work and academic training, as well as through experimentation in the classroom with her students. Throughout her career, she has been drawn to healthy, creative, and specific processes for crafting and exploring character, which led to the development and formation of the Seven Pillars.

The principal source material comes from Sanford Meisner, as that was Cooke's primary and most influential training. Other major contributors are Konstantin Stanislavski, Jerzy Grotowski, and Declan Donnellan, and Cooke's teachers, Richard Brestoff, Ken Washington, and Annie Loui provided additional inspiration. The Pillars first started to come together in the early years of Cooke's career. A young actor in New York, working in multiple mediums of performance, she struggled to understand how to synthesize and implement on-the-job all that she had learned at New York.

University's Tisch School of the Arts. Always a fierce advocate for the training she received during her undergraduate education, she was surprised to discover what she had been taught by her professors differed from the way she crafted a role. Cooke recorded her musings on acting technique in the form of an online blog, originally called "The Cooke Technique." She understood that education evolved, and she sought to document how the craft was manifesting through her work and her students.

This eventually led her to University of California at Irvine's (UCI) Master of Fine Arts acting program. While at UCI, Cooke trained with the exceptional faculty, including Robert Cohen (2013), author of *Acting Power* and numerous other books on acting. Richard Brestoff's exercises in Personalization helped cement Cooke's approach to circumstances and meanings, and it was the extensive training in movement and voice that compelled her to incorporate Physical Life as the seventh and final pillar. Cooke first introduced her curriculum for Seven Pillars Acting while she was a teaching assistant for an undergraduate acting class.

After completing her MFA in acting and relocating to Los Angeles, Cooke continued to develop and share Seven Pillars Acting. She took ownership of a small acting studio in Orange County, where she codified the curriculum and system of training, and soon after, she opened Seven Pillars Acting Studio in Los Angeles. During these years, Seven Pillars Acting reached thousands of professional and budding actors in the Southern California region. Cooke coached actors on set and in the classroom with the purpose of empowering them to craft character with authenticity, depth, specificity, and ease. Students of the technique have gone on to start professional acting careers in film, television, commercials, and theatre. Meanwhile, Cooke began training and certifying acting teachers in the technique to satisfy the demand for the training, which led to the development of an international and online teacher program for acting teachers to gain certification in Seven Pillars Acting.

The technique is now taught at institutions across the country as more and more institutions adopt the curriculum as its core acting training. UC-Irvine and Louisiana State University have implemented the technique. Numerous other institutions have used or are currently using Seven Pillars Acting, including University of South Dakota, Western Kentucky University, Ball State University, Loyola Marymount University, Hussian College Los Angeles, Cypress College, and the University of Lethbridge—Alberta, Canada.

About the Founder

Sonya Cooke recently relocated to Baton Rouge, Louisiana to join the faculty at Louisiana State University's (LSU) School of Theatre as Assistant Professor of Acting and Head of Undergraduate Performance. She has implemented the Seven Pillars Acting methodology as the core pedagogy at LSU. She trains both the Master of Fine Arts cohort and undergraduate actors and certifies the graduate students to teach the technique both at LSU and beyond. Her book, *Seven Pillars Acting*, is the textbook for students of the technique (Cooke 2017). A member of SAG-AFTRA, Cooke is represented for film, television, voiceover, commercials, and theatre. Originally from Texas, Sonya got her start in regional theatre. While in New York, she frequently worked on the development of new works, both plays and musicals, while also establishing her career in film and television. Most recently, she played the title role in *Gloria* by Brendan Jacobs-Jenkins at regional theatre Swine Palace in Baton Rouge. Other career highlights include *Louie* on FX, *Time Sensitive* at the Guthrie Theatre, and playing the title role in the feature film, *Lily Grace*. Cooke has worked with many institutions all over the country as a teacher, curriculum writer, and program developer, such as Hussian College Los Angeles, University of California at Irvine, the Guthrie Theatre, and more.

Key Features

The use of "pillars" as a central image and structure for the technique illustrates interconnected support. As opposed to seven steps or seven levels, Seven Pillars uses the metaphor of supporting structures that undergird an authentic and engaging performance. At times, the actor may lean more heavily on one pillar or another, but each is essential in building an effective approach to their work. Unique in its flow, the technique explores each pillar separately over the course of study through exercises, lectures, and scene application. While it is impossible to separate these interrelated concepts from each other, this technique breaks down the craft of acting into each individual part first.

Once students have an intimate understanding of each gear of the actor's engine, they begin their work by putting the pieces together into a cohesive practice they can use to approach any scene. The Seven Pillars Acting framework gives actors strong insights and effective vocabulary in diagnosing what might be going wrong with a scene, or what may need more fine-tuning. From there, they can effectively reinforce that particular pillar. The Circumstance pillar serves as the structure's central pillar around which the other pillars orient themselves. The actor's immersion in the details, events, and facts in the character's past, present, and future lays down the blueprint for how the subsequent pillars work will unfold. Getting more specific and thorough with these circumstances can help clarify where an actor might be struggling to move forward in their development of a character.

The application and adaptation of Sanford Meisner's work in Seven Pillars Acting is another key feature. Cooke draws on Meisner throughout the technique, as it is effective for actors that need to develop stronger skills in presence and connection when working with the text. In the Contact pillar, for example, students begin with standard Meisner observation/repetition exercises, prompting students to focus their attention externally on the thoughts and feelings of their partner on a moment-to-moment basis. They then encounter the text through exercises such as the Impulse Game and "Meisnerizing" the Text, both of which build on Meisner's work. These exercises allow students to transition into speaking scripted words on a page while prioritizing their impulses that emerge from contact with their partner. Instead of immediately jumping into making choices about how these new words on the page "should" be said, actors focus on "draping" the text over their impulses, in other words, allowing the text to take the shape of and ultimately serve their impulse, which will be further explained in the section below. Cooke also builds on Meisner-based tools, such as Emotional Preparation and Particularization, by creating practical and repeatable steps and activating the full use of the body and voice.

Exercises

Impulse Game

The goal of the Impulse Game is to help actors trust their impulses and let go of the "lifeboat of meaning." This is a term Cooke uses to describe the actor's struggle to surrender what the text seems to mean, which restricts them from being able to explore the character's use of the text more freely. The exercise attempts to shake away any preconceived idea of their script and allow the actor to react to their scene partner honestly and authentically. There are three phases to this game with a bonus challenge phase.

Phase 1

Two actors take the same scripted scene and work as partners. They each take a separate sheet of paper and cover their scripts:

- Actor A lowers the paper covering their script to see only their first line. They look at the first line, "grab it with their mind," make eye contact with their partner (Actor B), then simply say the line without acting it. Instead of thinking of this step as speaking it "by rote," Cooke emphasizes emptying the text of meaning and letting it rest on whatever contact exists between the two partners.
- Actor B maintains eye contact and responds to what was said with whatever their impulse is, not the next scripted line. What would they say in response? Then, Actor B lowers the paper covering their script to reveal the line of text, "grabs the line" with their memory, reestablishes eye contact with Actor A, and says the text in the same inflection and tone as how the impulse was said. That is what "draping the text" means; by releasing the scripted line of any meaning, they are able to infuse the text with the impulse.
- In turn, Actor A first responds with an impulse and then drapes the text so that it takes the shape of the impulse.

This back-and-forth continues throughout the entirety of the scene, taking note of where nuances, physicality, and discoveries are made on impulse and draping the text on those impulses. The draping of text is the most important concept of the exercise. In every phase, the actor must abandon assumptions of what the text means and surrender to whatever their impulse is. By doing this, actors learn to prioritize their contact with their partners over their ideas about character.

Phase 2

Maintaining the same structure and rules as phase one, the actors now verbalize their impulses as if the other person cannot hear them. In this way, they speak *about* them, not *to* them. Resembling Meisner repetition, the second phase emphasizes what Actor A sees in Actor B psychologically or emotionally. So, "She seems angry with me," can be an appropriate impulse here. Phase 2 is designed to recreate what happens in our heads; we talk to ourselves about what we are experiencing, which influences our reactions. In this same way, we want to "break the line," another term for draping, to whatever impression we are getting from our partner.

Phase 3

The actors may employ either Phase 1 or Phase 2 for their impulse, but while keeping their impulses *silent*. In this phase, it is important that the actor concentrate on hearing how they say the impulse in their head and allow it, as Cooke puts it in the Contact chapter, "to ricochet through their body" (Cooke 2017, 10). They then must recreate this physical impulse when they go to the text so that the text takes the shape of the impulse.

Bonus Phase

After practicing Impulse Game until it is more easeful, the actors may then move into a bonus phase where they match the timing of their impulses with the line, marrying the two in truly impulsive listening with their scene partner. Many actors prioritize text, but in this exercise, the text does not have meaning. The honest and authentic reaction of one human to another is what holds true meaning; this is the heart of great acting.

Circumstance Improvisations

The Circumstance pillar is the most challenging to learn because it frequently requires a reversal of how an actor is accustomed to navigating through text. Essentially, this pillar instructs the actor how to build a world of external stimuli that can motivate all action, behavior, and text in a scene. In studying Circumstance, actors apply their understanding of the chapter by performing Circumstance Improvisations. Inspired by exercises Cooke studied with Richard Brestoff and similar to Stanislavski's Action Analysis, Circumstance Improvisations are the primary exercise used not only in comprehending circumstances but also in activating them. Students first study what Cooke calls "sequence circumstances," or, in other words, the circumstances that elapse through time: global, past, previous, present, future, and potential circumstances. From there, students break down their assigned scene into "episodes," often referred to as "beats" in Stanislavski-based scoring. Once the episodes are identified, students write a few circumstances for each episode. In this way students scaffold the scene with choices for what their character experiences. By focusing on what their character sees, they will be compelled to respond accordingly. Making these selections, therefore, will set up cause and effect in the scene as opposed to obligation and dutiful adherence to the text.

Working in pairs, the students are directed to live out the previous circumstances of their character. Doing so envelops the actor in the world of the character, allowing the first episode of the scene to unfold with ease. The partners then improvise the first episode, inviting their selected circumstances and partners to guide them. For this to be a true improvisation, they need not adhere to the scene; instead, the teacher instructs them to work off of their partner to see if the circumstances they selected naturally happen in the course of the improvisation. Once they reach the end of the episode, they then collect their scripts and do the scene again with the text.

Afterward, the instructor and students discuss two key questions: (1) What was in the improvisation that was not in the script? And (2) what is in the script that was not in the improvisation? Answering these questions will illuminate circumstances that, once added to the scaffolding, will gently align the actor's improvs with the script. Possible follow-up questions to the exercise include: "What circumstances can you craft that will help you do what is in the script?" or "Where are you pushing or initiating action?" and "What lines are you forgetting, and what circumstances will help you remember them?" The goal is ultimately to improvise the scene while saying the text.

The purpose of this exercise is to build behavior that is caused by external stimuli, not self-stimulated by the actor, as such behavior is more authentic and physically easeful. By drilling this exercise, the actor mines the scene for deeper circumstances that connect them to the character's world. A helpful byproduct of the exercise is that actors often find

144 VOCAL TRADITIONS

themselves memorizing the work faster and in a more connected way, rather than memorizing words by rote. If an actor forgets a line, it is often because they have not clearly identified or are not connected to the circumstance of the character and must craft one to alleviate the lapse.

The Bomb/Banana Peel List

There is a myriad of reasons that cause people to feel and express strong emotions. Sometimes they are aware of these emotional shifts, and sometimes they are not; but these emotional peaks and valleys must be identified and honed by the actor. In Seven Pillars Acting, they are called "bombs" or "banana peels" due to their explosive nature or ability to make a person "slip" out of their homeostatic emotional state. In the Meaning pillar, the actor builds a list of bombs or banana peels to map the emotional arc of the character. But the bomb list (for short) has an additional function: to help the actor assess their degree of connection to their character's emotional life. The Meaning pillar emphasizes emotional honesty over all; it is better to be clear when one does not emotionally connect than to pretend one feels as the character does. To do this, the actor evaluates the circumstances of the character to determine a small list of meaningful circumstances that could cause them to have a big emotional slip or kaboom.

The bomb list is a four-step process. First, the actor isolates the circumstance that seems to elicit the emotional reaction from the character. Second, the actor identifies the meaning of that circumstance, which deepens the potency of the moment. Third, the actor specifies how the meaning makes the character feel. This is the heart of the bomb where the actor determines the emotional core of this part of the character's journey. Fourth, they assess their personal connection to the character's circumstance, meaning, and emotion. They ask themselves, "Does this bomb actually make me feel this way?" They respond with a simple "yes" or "no." Actors are often inclined to feel they must answer "yes," but at this early stage in the crafting process, there is no greater value in answering "yes" over "no." Connecting to a bomb does not make one a better actor. Nor are they a lesser actor if they do not genuinely and deeply connect to it. What matters is that the actor has crafted a specific emotional experience and has made an honest assessment of their connection. If the answer is "no," there is a Meisner-based exercise called Particularization that helps the actor connect to the emotional bomb in the Emotional Life pillar.

All in all, the bomb list is an essential step in the actor's process for carving out specific and deep emotional moments. Through the process, they can also evaluate their own truth and gauge what more imaginative and emotional work needs to be done to embody the character's story.

The Diamonologue

The Diamonologue is a quick and active way for actors to score a piece of monologic text. Certainly, much work can be done on script analysis, episodes, and relationships, but the Diamonologue synthesizes the actor's process into just three pillars: Circumstance, Objective, and Action. Essentially, the process tasks the actor, from their character's perspective, to focus on what the *other* person is saying, thinking, feeling, or doing on a moment-to-moment basis.

Step 1

Before each line in a monologue, the actor identifies what the imagined other character is saying, thinking, feeling, or doing. This will certainly stretch the imagination, as the piece does not call for an exchange of lines from the other person. However, one could argue that even in a monologue the speaker is responding to micro-communications, whether they are transmitted through voice, body, or even thought. By taking this step, the person to whom the character is speaking will come to life in the imagination of the actor.

Step 2

Next, the actor identifies what they *want* the other person to say, think, feel, or do. In other words, what is the character's objective? This step is directed and focused on the hoped-for outcomes with other person, which will keep the energy moving in an outward and active fashion.

Step 3

Lastly, what does one *do* to get that? What action does the actor take to see and experience the other person as they desire and need? The actor simply identifies a verb here that will allow them to achieve that goal. Actions can sometimes be cerebral or academic, but when they are done through the Diamonologue, they are necessary and achieve a clear end.

The purpose of this exercise is to focus the actor externally rather than internally, motivating each thought with the other person's behavior. The Diamonologue is meant to activate the actor's imagination and make their connection to the circumstances immediate, moment-to-moment, and alive.

Teaching Style

Seven Pillars Acting simultaneously emphasizes acute specificity in text work and score notation and playful abandon into structured improvisations. As described above, Circumstance Improvisation is an exercise used to mine a scene for circumstances. Such an exercise demonstrates an important aspect of the overall teaching style of Seven Pillars Acting: play first and pin it down later. In the weeks that ensue, students practice an adaptation of this exercise, called Objective Improvisations, which similarly encourages experimentation followed by scoring of the text. This pattern shows up many times throughout the curriculum.

Specificity is of the utmost importance when teaching how to write the actor's score. The actor inserts a "CMOA," which is an abbreviation of four pillars: Circumstance, Meaning, Objective, and Action, before every line. The score is structured in a similar progression as the technique itself, where the actor first builds the world of the character (Circumstance), makes personal connection to it (Meaning), which causes a want (Objective), that in turn generates an action (Action). A thorough and detailed score reveals the journey the character experiences within each episode, scene, act, and full script. Seven Pillars Acting instructors help actors break down each scene and unpack the details that help the actor craft a specific and compelling performance. Additionally, the

CMOA uncovers many things that the actor must daydream to intimately connect to the experience of their character.

Actors use daydreaming as a tool to explore the character as well as themselves. By engaging all their senses, they bring imagined or fictional circumstances to life. In this imaginative exploration, the actor learns how to open up and be more connected to their own emotions. The exercise Daydreaming As Self challenges the actor to activate their own palette of emotions through imagining potential near-future circumstances that could make them experience the emotion their character feels in any specific moment. It is an enhanced way of using Stanislavski's "Magic If," rather than employing the actor's past experiences for emotional recall. These potential, near-future daydream subjects, as Cooke calls them, can be just as potent as past experiences because they are rooted in reality, and they would have real world implications. But they are safer and more pliable than one's past since they are not limited by the actual outcome of past events. They are also easier on the actor's imagination and mental health insofar as the actor can always return to the present moment where the potential near-future circumstance is just a fiction. By emphasizing emotional boundaries, the actor is more likely to take risks and to go deep into the work.

It is not enough to simply imagine the circumstances before the actor enters a scene in a heightened emotional state. The actor is taught to achieve this heightened state authentically by using the entire body, fullness of breath, and voice. Emotional Preparation, a Meisner tool, is adapted for Seven Pillars Acting by emphasizing the full engagement of all five senses, the body, breath, and voice. Emotional Preparation includes a list of movements that the actor can perform to achieve truthful heightened emotion. It is also accompanied with music and faucet-breath (the rapid speaking of the character's circumstances under the breath). This combination of physical, vocal, and imaginative work thrusts the actor into an all-encompassing emotion and helps break down unnecessary tensions or inhibitions in the actor.

Sometimes emotional and imaginative work is wearisome and difficult. Thus, Seven Pillars Acting teachers also discuss ways to healthfully protect the mind, body, and spirit. The actor's emotional work should never jeopardize their mental health. As the actor carries their instrument wherever they go, unable to leave their art fully in the performance space, such exercises or rituals contribute to what Seven Pillars Acting calls the Healthy Actor.

Goals of the Organization

The mission of Seven Pillars Acting is to teach actors a process for crafting character that suits the demands of the industry today. Its goal is to meet actors' aptitudes, talents, and needs where they are in the twenty-first century and to advance and challenge outmoded ideas of technique. Seven Pillars Acting, purporting that "acting is acting is acting," seeks to streamline acting for film and theatre into a singular approach that suits both mediums. Professional actors must also be *competitive* actors to succeed, and therefore, their technique must be rigorous, thorough, practical, and healthy.

The goal of Seven Pillars Acting is to bring these ideas and processes to young actors in training and to empower them with an effective, practical, and modern approach to the craft. An inclusive and Anti-Racist training system, Seven Pillars Acting seeks to topple white supremacy in the arts by decentering the canon and lifting up voices from actors and acting teachers of Color. The future involves broadening its reach to teachers through its international and online certification program and building a greater global community of Seven Pillars actors. And yet, the hub must always center on the growth of the individual student; they are the goal of this work.

Teacher Certification Process

Seven Pillars Acting hosts an annual certification program for acting professors, teachers, and professional actors every summer in various locations. After several weeks of training as both an actor and a teacher, participants undergo a certification exam and assessment in order to be officially certified to teach the technique. Upon successful completion of the training and assessment, certified instructors may teach Seven Pillars Acting for four years, with flexible options for renewal in perpetuity. Certified instructors may go on to become master instructors, able to certify teachers themselves. Seven Pillars Acting hosts year-round educational events for their certified instructors as well as students of the technique through its social media outreach and community engagement efforts. Sonya Cooke mentors all teachers in the technique personally to help them in their teaching practices and goals.

Contact Information/Resources/How to Get Involved

Visit the website, www.sevenpillarsacting.com, to learn more about the training and to find ways to join a class or an upcoming certification program.

Sonya Cooke is available at sonya@sevenpillarsstudio.com, and all are welcome to interact with the team through social media. Find us at @sevenpillarsacting.

Disclosure statement

No potential conflict of interest was reported by the author(s).

References

Cohen, Robert. 2013. *Acting Power*. New York: Routledge.
Cooke, Sonya. 2017. *Seven Pillars Acting: A Comprehensive Technique for the Modern Actor*. Los Angeles, CA: Rare Bird Books.
Meisner, Sanford, and Dennis Longwell. 1987. *Sanford Meisner on Acting*. New York: Vintage.

Vibrant Voice Technique

Pamela Prather

ABSTRACT

Vocal Traditions is a series in the *Voice and Speech Review* that highlights historically important voice teachers and schools of thought in the world of vocal pedagogy. This article explores the history and use of Vibrant Voice Technique (VVT) and its creator, Professor David Ley, along with a discussion of how new instructors are incorporating VVT into their teaching and coaching. Representative instructors include those who teach actors, singers, executives, and yoga students. VVT is not a stand-alone method; rather, it serves as an enhancement and tool for voice teachers.

Introduction

Vibrant Voice Technique (VVT) was developed by David Ley who is a drama professor at the University of Alberta. VVT uses external vibration on the human body through vibrators and explores uncharted territory in voice and speech with direct application to voice training and other kinds of performing art pedagogy. The work was first presented formally in Washington, D.C. at the 2012 VASTA Conference when David gained the moniker "the Canadian professor with the vibrator." And, yes, by vibrator, I am referring to an electronic devise that vibrates, which is used for massage or sexual stimulation.

This article gives an outline of VVT and includes a discussion of the work's history and applications. As a VVT instructor, I have firsthand knowledge of the methodology, and I offer this overview of VVT through my impressions and though conversations I had with David and various VVT teachers who are quoted throughout the article. VVT and I hope that this essay and these conversations introduce the work to a wider audience. Since VVT is not a stand-alone method, we hope that voice professionals and teachers will look to VVT for continued development, as a new tool and resource in their work.

The History of VVT

The predecessor of today's vibrators was patented in the early 1880s by London physician, Dr. J. Mortimer Granville, and it predated the invention of the electric iron and the vacuum cleaner by more than a decade (Aitkenhead 2012). Maines (1999) offers the history

VOCAL TRADITIONS

of vibrators in *The Technology of Orgasm*, where she explores the early days of vibrators and the stigma attached to them. This text is one of the few that discusses the topic in a rigorous and academic way, and it highlights the complicated relationship popular culture and academia have both had with the device.

Given the historic stigma around vibrators, reactions to Professor Ley bringing a bag full of sex toys to the annual VASTA gathering of voice professionals ranged from intense curiosity to distaste for what was perceived by some as a gimmicky technique. Nevertheless, the workshop was packed, without enough vibrators to go around. David led participants through a series of exercises he developed at the University of Alberta, using personal massage devices designed to help release tension in the vocal apparatus and facilitate a more open channel for sound. This idea is a central concept of VVT. This early workshop was the beginning of a greater awareness to the work, and the workshop highlighted the ease with which VVT could integrate with and compliment other methods of teaching voice. Five years later, in August 2016, seven other international participants and I completed the first eight-month long VVT Instructor Training Program in New York City. This huge transition in just a few years shows the scope and development of VVT; what began as a unique workshop has become a technique with certified teachers.

The Impetus for VVT

David developed VVT in order to aid a friend in need. In our conversation about the work on January 2, 2017, David said he developed the technique "because VVT evolves, anything that I've ever done is evolved out of inspiration and [the] moment, to help somebody for whom the techniques I already learned weren't sufficient." The client was a professional actress who had two big projects planned and she was losing her voice. An otolaryngologist had determined there was nothing abnormal with her vocal folds; however, the actor seemed to have a lingering case of vocal fatigue and an inability to project or sustain her voice. After listening to her speak and observing her vocal patterns, David believed it was likely that her hoarseness could be attributed to muscular tension around the larynx. Actively researching voice production and external vibrational tools, David believed that if he could find a vibrational device in the right size, then he could probably help her. Conventional back massagers were far too large for laryngeal use. Brainstorming a solution, led the two to a sex shop in Alberta, Canada, searching for a small vibrator that could help release laryngeal tension. David remembers, "We took it home; we worked with it, and after one session, it released a lot of tension in her throat and really improved her voice quality" (Glover 2013).

David is very clear that in creating the work he had not created a "method" but rather a "technique." David clarified:

> A method is designed to go from square one, to be all things to all people, and to cover all the basic needs for training somebody's voice. I think it is really important for me to say I'm not that, and I don't want to be that. I can give you a variety of techniques, but it's up to you to create your own method ... Anything that I've ever done has evolved out of inspiration in the moment to help somebody for whom the techniques I had already learned weren't sufficient ... Ultimately these techniques are all trying to do the same thing, but we are looking at what is the deep structure underneath. What is the fundamental goal, and how can I best achieve that goal with the resources that I have?

About the Founder

David Ley was born in Vancouver and studied acting there. He has always had an interest in anatomy; this is where his passion and interest in voice comes from. David holds an MFA in performance from York University with a diploma in voice teaching. He is a professor in the Drama Department at the University of Alberta, where he teaches voice and speech, dialects, and acting. David has extensive experience in private practice, teaching vocal skills to a wide array of professional voice users from schoolteachers to politicians, and he has taught voice workshops in Canada and abroad. He spent 10 seasons as a voice coach at Canada's Stratford Festival and has been a regular instructor in Stratford's Birmingham Conservatory. He has been featured in numerous newspaper interviews commenting on dialects and vocal performance and has appeared in two CBC documentaries on Canadian speech. Media outlets around the world have covered his work on the VVT including: the Toronto Star, the Globe and Mail, The Guardian UK, the Huffington Post, Metro News International, and many others.

In 2017, he completed a two-year, 2200-hour certification in massage therapy and is currently working with Tom Meyers and Anatomy Trains. On November 16, 2017, David elaborated on this training:

> [In Anatomy Trains,] we talk about the whole idea of triangles and having an understanding of the myofascial connections throughout the body. I want to look at the laryngeal nerves, so that I can better understand how vibration points can be releasing stress on the nerves. And I think the work with Anatomy Trains will be a key for me to see how we can move the vibrator into different places that are more precisely affecting the breathing and the voice.

David's philosophy as a teaching artist appears to be an assimilation of deep curiosity and wild creativity. He looks at the body, voice, and human being and believes that by understanding the structure of the individual, he can then determine "how that structure works and how it can function more effectively." He sees his role as a voice professional as one of ongoing investigation.

Growing the Work

From the early days of his research, David was consistently finding that using external vibration was creating palpable results. The question became how could it move out of the Canadian classroom and into the larger vocal community. Meeting Elissa Weinzimmer, an MFA student in the University of Alberta vocal pedagogy program, led David into the broader vocal training arena. She had been drawn to extended training as a vocal professional because of some personal vocal challenges; she lost her voice at one point and was put on a month of vocal rest. She had suffered chronic muscle dysphonia and was on a personal quest to heal herself and others. David worked with her, and she was amazed with the results of the experience. In a conversation on December 22, 2016, Elissa remembered, "I'd never been able to fully untangle the muscle tension dysphonia issues and when I started working with the external vibration, it really started untangling it for me."

Elissa suggested that she and David present at the VASTA conference in Washington, DC, and from that conference (as mentioned above), VVT was born. As Elissa recalls, "There was a mutual interest and rapport in what he was doing. I really understood its value, and he felt that I was a good person to be shepherding it forward in some way which obviously developed over time."

> Without Elissa, VVT may have been limited to students who worked directly with David or happened discover it on the web. As David said:

> Had I not met Elissa, I probably would've made a series of videos and put them out on the web for free; I just would've given it all away.

Elissa graduated and stayed on as a mentee under David's tutelage for a time. Elissa worked with David to develop an instruction manual, a website, a blog, workshops, and the beginning of a video series. She subsequently served as Managing Director of VVT and continues to co-teach with David in the VVT Instructor Program.

Key Concepts

VVT grew from a hypothesis that external vibration applied in specific locations could amplify and enhance vocal effectiveness. David continued experimenting with his students and clients to refine and codify his technique. According the VVT Website (Ley 2017), there are four categories of exercises:

(1) Reducing muscle tension
(2) Stimulating vibration in and around the voice box (larynx)
(3) Enhancing resonance
(4) Energizing the articulators.

While laryngeal massage is something that many vocal professionals either practice on themselves or their students, David found that many of his students and clients were uncomfortable with laryngeal self-massage. The simple and clear exercises he created using the vibrator seemed to facilitate his clients' release of laryngeal muscles to an extent that (in David's experience) other vocal techniques had been unable to accomplish as quickly. He found the self-massage device could be used not only during times of vocal distress, but it could also be used as a tool to expand a healthy vocal instrument. VVT exercises include humming (or toning) on vowel sounds while using vibration on the skull, cheekbones, and muscles around the larynx. David theorizes:

> Like anything we do in voice it all exists on this supernormal [or] subnormal range. Our goal is working in the supernormal range ... With vocal athletes, we extend their capacity ... It's helped people who have vocal problems, but it has also really moved certain people along really quickly with aspects of vocal range, placement, and things like that...The thing that I found as this [VVT] started to evolve is that it worked really well and it got really fast results. A lot of people don't like that. The most vocal opponents of this are the people who are not willing to try it.

While a variety of vibrational tools are on the market, David asserts that the optimal vibrational device should have a frequency between 100 and 120 hertz since his is closest to the vibration of the human voice. David said in an interview with the University of Alberta:

> You can actually watch on a spectrograph how vocal energy grows. Even when you take the vibrator off, the frequencies are greater than when first applied ... I've done this with singers, schoolteachers and actors. It always works ... Some people simply say, "Wow! Not only did it free tension in the laryngeal muscles, but it seemed to stimulate vibrations in the vocal folds". (McMaster 2016)

VVT Instructors Experiences

One year after the inaugural Training Program was held in New York, I recorded conversations with four of the eight original VVT instructors. The goal was to explore the widest range of instructor experiences possible by choosing four diverse backgrounds. I interviewed a business coach, a singing teacher, a yoga teacher trainer, and an acting professor to explore how VVT was impacting a broad range of clients, students, and instructor needs. The following are summations and excerpts from the discussions.

Executive Coach

Jay Miller came to VVT training as a voice and speech coach with a private practice in Toronto, Canada. Although he had worked in academia and on film sets in the past, his primary clients are currently business professionals who wish to improve their speaking skills. In his conversation on *January 5, 2017*, Jay said he VVT him because it seemed to "assist people that had a significant amount of tension in their voices." He claims he has been able to integrate VVT into his work quite successfully. He has used the tool primarily for business clients with vocal strain or vocal fatigue; he works with people that spend much of their time talking: lawyers, teachers, ministers. Generally, he uses VVT with more advanced clients and finds it is extremely effective with finding vibration in their back bodies.

One of the most rewarding experiences for Jay was working with a police officer who was from a Muslim background, who received a measure of scrutiny from both his family and his work community. This individual, who "was from a community where people don't usually have a foothold," was selected to be part of an elite force. Jay explains:

> People couldn't hear [the officer] … It was undermining his professional image, not to mention the fact that his voice hurt. I was in the midst of my VVT training, and I just started him on it. Normally, I give people at least four lessons of basic training, addressing relaxation, breathing, resonance, and that sort of thing, but with him, I thought: let's just go for it; let's just start with it. And that was really wonderful for him because [VVT is] so physical; it's so tangible, and he was just thrilled with the results.… That was really, really satisfying to see him make some significant changes and end up in a different place with his voice.

As for the external vibration being a sex toy, Jay responded, "I don't mention what they are because 95% of people won't know what it is."

Singing Teacher

Claudia Friedlander is a New York City-based singing teacher whose clients are primarily classical singers. Claudia came to VVT as a curious skeptic with some encouragement from her spouse. She said in my discussion with her on *February 20,2017*, "Everybody was going ha-ha 'vibrators'; then my husband finally said, 'You know I actually think there's something to this you should look at it.'" Claudia is deeply interested in the mechanics of singing; she has found that consistently using external vibration not only created more awareness of the vocal instrument, but it also gives clients extra feedback that often unlocks muscular holding. After working with one of her clients who suffered from temporomandibular joint dysfunction (TMJ), Claudia claims that the client's "TMJ never came back." Claudia surmises that the vibrator helped the student isolate and separate her muscles. "I'll often have them use it [the vibrator] mostly on the masseter and then also on the temporalis, but then I'll actually have them vocalize … using it to release the tongue."

With her classical singers, she has found that "vocalizing with the vibrator on the thyroid cartilage can save months of work." Claudia has discovered that VVT helps optimize articulation, phonation, and resonance for singers, and they avoid compensations. She went on to enthusiastically say, "This tool enables us to optimize our instruments and faster … who wouldn't use it? …There's no method that you can teach that wouldn't benefit from teaching VVT."

Yoga Teacher Trainer

Eric Stewart is the originator of Simple Yoga. He teaches at Oberlin College, and he is a registered teacher trainer with Yoga Alliance. He is particularly interested in somatic and manual therapies; Eric has studied Alexander Technique and craniosacral therapy, and he trained at the School for Body–Mind Centering. He has been running a yoga teacher training program for the past 16 years, but in 2008 he found himself suffering vocal stress. He had been using his voice constantly for a month, and he became acutely aware of the importance of optimal vocal use and vocal health for yoga teachers. This experience began his exploration of voice training for yoga teachers. On January 12, 2017, Eric chatted about this journey.

> I was really burning out my voice, and I worked on that with other tools. When I came to Vibrant Voice it was more of a concentrated encapsulation of what I had learned and a furthering what I had learned previously.

Eric found that the breath work and the awareness of vibration (both internally and externally) aligns with his yoga teacher training philosophy.

Eric is also helping yoga teachers find their physical and metaphorical voices in his teacher training program. On the physical level, "I would say that most people can find some really useful things within the vocal tension release exercises." On the metaphorical level, Eric notices that introducing VVT as an integrative part of the yoga program "encourages an open perspective on something like breathing, but still provides a structure." VVT has become a technique that Eric not only employs in his teacher training program, but he also practices it himself. Though he is clear to point out that he is not trying to integrate every element of VVT into the yoga teacher training program, he asserts:

> I use [VVT] a lot within the framework of the teacher training. And then there is how I use it for myself. As a singer, I've found it really beneficial … I get less into situations where I feel like I am straining my voice, and if I get into that situation I have tools to get out of it.

VVT has become an efficient and effective tool to help Eric as a teacher and an individual. Voice work is "a practice. It's about learning more about myself … I sing for the joy of singing. And learning about my voice is as another extension of the yoga."

Theatre Professor

Stacey Cabaj is an assistant professor of voice at Louisiana State University, Baton Rouge. She knew David and Elissa by reputation and was familiar with some of the online content. In our conversation on January 3, 2017, Stacey recalls, "Of course, there was the novelty factor and the kind of salacious quality that's really intriguing, but the zeal with which the people talked about [VVT]. They are really onto something. And I have found that to be true." Stacey works with both BA and MFA students, in addition to professional clients. She came to the work because she was "interested in work that works ... and was hungry for a really efficient way to coach and help actors experience more freedom and also to rehabilitate more quickly."

With VVT, she has found that she is more prepared for the "grand scope of what it means to be a voice trainer in a way that I wasn't after graduate school." Stacey, like many, came to voice work through her own healing. When she was 18 she had reconstructive jaw surgery and learned to speak and sing again. "It was a long journey to learn how to use this new instrument that never felt like my own." She found VVT training deepened her own connection to her voice:

> I found myself discovering sensation in areas where I had severed nerves and my face was numb. In terms of rehab, it's been more than a dozen years, and yet for me the use of the device [the vibrator] is stimulating sensation where I've never felt anything before. So, it literally feels like it's freeing vibration and sensation in my face, which allows me to feel my sound more fully, which makes me feel more like myself ... I think part of the teaching is that I know it [VVT] works for me. I can teach through my own trauma, my own heart breakthrough, and my own curiosity.

Stacey openly shares her journey with her students, modeling self-discovery through freeing vibration and sound. She has found that the preliminary VVT sequences all work well in her daily warm-up, and she has also found that VVT works well in academia. She has students read waivers and sign consent forms, and the use of the vibrators is optional. "Some people need a little information and some people need a lot," she said.

Stacey is most inspired about how VVT assists in her holistic approach to voice training. She encourages exploration, and she regularly moves from the traditional VVT sequence to unique places of tension that may be causing vocal holding. Stacey also has found VVT to be particularly useful when she is teaching the vocal health components of training, as well in advanced extended voice work for her graduate students.

Goals of the Organization

VVT began with Professor David Ley's mission to serve individuals and solve vocal problems in Alberta, Canada. It has now expanded into a full online training course and an Instructor Training program with plans to run another course in 2018. David hopes that there will be opportunities for practitioners of VVT to continue growing the work:

> My desire would be that we, as trainers, would find an opportunity to get together again, when we get a quorum of people who practiced it. And then we can go meet for a week and teach each other, so we create a quorum of people who can come together and freely explore conceptually.

Each of the current Official Instructors (myself included) has seen successful application of the technique in vocal users from quite diverse backgrounds and with varied levels of vocal experience. In my own work, I have seen "ah-ha moments" with undergraduate BFA students, and VP-level executives. To me, this is a technique that quickly and efficiently offers benefits to a wide range of clients. David went on to say:

> Many of us are motivated primarily by the desire to help. I would've given this up ages ago if I didn't feel that there was potential in this approach to really help some people for whom many other things had not worked, so that's the thing that makes me continue to stay in it, pursue it.

David hopes that this work will continue growing and that more vocal professionals will be curious about how VVT can enhance various modalities of vocal training.

VVT Official Instructor Training and Online Course

For those interested in learning the VVT, there is a "Vibrant Voice Online Course" available at www.vibrantvoicetechnique.com.

Application to an advanced training course is also available to those with an existing voice teaching practice (e.g. singing teachers, voice and speech coaches, speech language pathologists). The VVT Instructor Program gives participants the tools necessary to teach VVT to their own students and clients. Upon successful completion of the Instructor Program, participants are given the title "Official Instructor of VVT" and listed on the website.

December 2016 marked the first VVT Official Instructor Training Program in New York City. Eight voice professionals from three countries convened for an intensive weekend of training followed by eight months of virtual meetings, papers, coaching, and individual training sessions with both David and Elissa.

David had been developing his work to make it accessible to a wide variety of vocal professionals. David is a curious, open-hearted professional of deep integrity who is interested in creating ongoing dialogue and discoveries in his own work and in community with other professionals. As he said:

> I've worked with speech pathologists; I've worked with opera teachers, singing teachers, and voice teachers … And that's an interesting range of people … I think there is beauty in that … Bringing those people together is much more interesting than saying we're going to teach you guys in your corner how you would use it.

Elissa's enthusiasm seemed to fuel David to move his work to a broader audience while still holding his ideal of not creating a "method." The VVT Instructor Training Program became a group with a mission to help vocal professionals in varied fields add tools (in this case vibrators) to help clients and students navigate their vocal growth and connections.

Contact Information and Resources

You may learn all of the exercises of VVT by visiting www.vibrantvoicetechnique.com and enrolling in "Learn Vibrant Voice, the online course." The VVT Instructor program also provides additional training for established voice practitioners who wish to become officially recognized to teach the technique. For more information, please send an email to info@vibrantvoicetechnique.com.

Disclosure statement

No potential conflict of interest was reported by the author.

References

Aitkenhead, Decca. 2012. "How the Vibrator Came to Be." *The Guardian*, September 7. https://www.theguardian.com/lifeandstyle/2012/sep/07/how-the-vibrator-caused-buzz.

Glover, Dominic. 2013. "Sex Toy Vibrators Used by Alberta Voice Coach David Ley." *International Business Times UK*, March 22. http://www.ibtimes.co.uk/sex-toys-music-canada-449398.

Ley, David. 2017. "About the Vibrant Voice Technique." *Vibrant Voice Technique*. https://www.vibrantvoicetechnique.com/pages/about-us

Maines, Rachel P. 1999. *The Technology of Orgasm: "Hysteria", the Vibrator, and Women's Sexual Satisfaction*. Baltimore, MD: Johns Hopkins University Press.

McMaster, Geoff. 2016. "Good, Good, Good Vocal Vibrations." *University of Alberta*, March 9. https://www.ualberta.ca/news-and-events/newsarticles/2013/march/good-good-good-vocal-vibrations.

Acting and Singing with Archetypes

Bill J. Adams and Christine Morris

ABSTRACT

Vocal Traditions is a series in the *Voice and Speech Review* that highlights historically important voice teachers and schools of thought in the world of vocal pedagogy. This essay will present a pedagogical method which is codified in the book, *Acting and Singing with Archetypes*, by Janet Rodgers and Frankie Armstrong. The concept of archetypes or universal forms is present in all cultures of the world, throughout their existence. Janet and Frankie created a series of explorations called "Journeys" using the ubiquitous and primordial archetypes of mother, lover, trickster, spiritual, temporal leader, devil, and others as starting points for character development in performance. Discovery during the journeys expands the participant connecting by experience to others and to different times and places. The practice sheds new light on possibilities using the voice, body, and psyche, and it opens pathways to access creativity for application in performance. After an overview of the work, including a brief history and information about the founders, the article gives a description of a Vocal Archetype session and details of the certification process.

Overview

Acting and Singing with Archetypes (often simply called Vocal Archetypes) is a training method for the development of performance choices in creative artists. Through a series of journeys using archetypes, the imagination, voice, and body are explored to expand artistic expression. The goals of working with archetypes include a starting point for character development in performance and a process of releasing and retrieving parts of our creativity that are perhaps unfamiliar. The training tools and pedagogical experiences were created by Frankie Armstrong and Janet Rodgers and codified in their book, *Acting and Singing with Archetypes*.

What are archetypes? The philosophy of archetypes as primordial forms dates back to Plato, but more recent research in the guise of collective unconscious is borrowed from Carl Jung's analytical psychology. Archetypes are universal forms common to all cultures throughout existence. Archetypes are figures and creatures that inhabit the pools of the world's mythology, folk tales, epics, and ballads (Rodgers and Armstrong 2009, xiii). Arguably, everyone recognizes the Mother, the Lover, the Trickster, the Spiritual and Temporal Leader, the Devil. These are not fully developed characters but are essences: images, forms, voices, bodies, and ancient psychological projections into the imaginative world (Rodgers and Armstrong, 2009, xiii). In the Vocal Archetypes work, a clear distinction is stressed between the "larger than an individual" archetype and the stereotype, which is "smaller than the individual." While an acting role is a fully fleshed out human being, actors may discover that an archetype or multiple archetypes are part of or an aspect of a particular role.

What does archetype work do for performers? Archetypes expands the sense of self as they connect performers to others and to other times and places. Through the journeys (exercises), performers can become aware of more possibilities within themselves, especially the voice (its range, power, volume, and potential), the body (range of movement, stamina, breath, posture), and the psyche. Performers discover a broader range of possibilities as tactics for achieving performance goals. The work provides a fundamental starting point for character development. Artists learn physical, vocal, and psychological triggers that will allow them to return to each archetype with ease and confidence (Rodgers and Armstrong, 2009, xv).

Brief History

In 1987 at the First International Workshop Festival created by Nigel Jamieson, John Wright asked the visually impaired Frankie to "sing the mask" as she was holding an archetypal mask. While singing a traditional British folk ballad, she was instructed to shift between various archetypes and the effect on Frankie's singing of each stanza of the song was profound (Rodgers and Armstrong, 2009, xv). Frankie worked with Nigel and John Wright using the masks for approximately eight years before their paths diverged. Frankie began working with internalizations, imaginative explorations, storytelling, and movement, but she had no masks on which to rely.

In 1999, Janet attended the Giving Voice Festival and enrolled in Frankie's workshop Voices of the Archetypes of Myths. Having agreed to play Lucifer in a production Marlowe's *Doctor Faustus*, Janet struggled with an approach to creating such a mythic character, but through Frankie's exploration of Lucifer during the workshop, Janet experienced the physical, vocal, and psychological shards of the archetypal Devil and found a starting place within her own body, voice, and psyche for her characterization (Rodgers and Armstrong, 2009, xvi).

Janet developed the method as an advanced seminar of Archetypes and the Voice for students at Virginia Commonwealth University, and the book, *Acting and Singing with Archetypes*, was published in 2009. Since then, primarily through several week-long intensive workshops, there are 12 individuals who have become certified in the instruction of this work.

About the Founders

Frankie Armstrong has been working as a professional singing artist since 1964 (Armstrong, n.d.) and has produced nine solo albums in addition to being featured on numerous shared and themed recordings. She has contributed chapters to 11 books, written an autobiography, and co-edited *Well Tuned Women: Growing Strong Through Voicework* with Jenny Pearson. In 2017, Frankie was made president of the Natural Voice Network which is an organization that grew out of the Natural Voice Practitioners Network of which she is an initiating member.

Frankie's passion for the traditional styles of singing in the British Isles and from around the world informed the development of voice and singing workshops which were also influenced by her background as a trainer in social and youth work. She had the good fortune to study, perform, and record with leading figures of the folk revival such as Louis Killen, Ewan MacColl, and Bert Lloyd. With Peggy Seeger and Sandra Kerr, Frankie researched and developed *The Female Frolic* for live performance and a recording, which began her particular interest in women's lives as illuminated through song. Frankie's repertoire consists of rural, industrial, music hall, and contemporary British songs as well as her own compositions and those of other songwriters such as Sandra Kerr, Leon Rosselson, and Bertolt Brecht.

Frankie represents the best in folk art, and in 2018, she was awarded the Gold Badge Award by the English Folk Dance and Song Society for her outstanding contributions to traditional British song. Frankie is also a Distinguished Member of the international organization Voice and Speech Trainers Association (VASTA).

Janet Rodgers is Professor Emerita of Theatre at Virginia Commonwealth University (VCU) where she taught for 25 years and created the first MFA with emphasis in voice and speech pedagogy in the United States, and for seven years, she was Head of Performance (Rodgers, 2015). Prior to VCU, she taught at the Boston Conservatory of Music and was a principal actress with The Boston Shakespeare Company and Boston's Lyric Stage, as well as performing Off Broadway at La Mama Theatre.

Janet has dialect coached well over 150 productions (most recently Cadence Theatre's *Sight Unseen* and the PBS series *Mercy Street*). A Fulbright Scholar to Romania, she directed American and Romanian students in a production of Caryl Churchill's play *Mad Forest*, which was performed at the Sibiu International Theatre Festival in 2004.

Recognized as Distinguished Member for her many years of leadership in VASTA, Janet also received the Distinguished Teaching Award from VCU's School of the Arts. Recently she completed writing an Epic Performance Poem, *Irena Gut: Only a Girl*, which tours to New York and Los Angeles in 2020.

Description of Vocal Archetypes Work Session

While all studio sessions for this work are unique, they typically share a common structure:

- general vocal and physical warmup
- vocal/physical preparation for the specific archetype
- the Archetypal Journey
- stepping out
- reflection and discussion.

The work is most effectively initiated and explored in a group setting. As the teacher/leader (henceforward called "the leader") begins working with a new group, rules of working are articulated regarding parameters of the space, safety (physical and vocal), use of a sound instrument (typically a rattle, drum, or bell) to stop and/or guide the activity, and the protocol for "step out." Stepping out, inspired by the work of Susana Bloch and Alba Emoting (Bloch, 2017), is a structured physicalized breath exercise. Two original elements were added to stepping out for Vocal Archetypes; Steven Barker created removing the mask, and Olisa Enrico developed sending the energy of the archetype upward for future retrieval. As an essential part of the in-role/de-role embodiment of the work, stepping out is taught at the very beginning before any archetypes are introduced.

Following the warmup and preparation period, which may last anywhere from 15 to 40 minutes and may consist of individual and/or group work, participants are instructed to take their place in the room. Sometimes a specific physical posture may be suggested as a starting point. With one exception (the archetype of the Sensuous Dancer, aka the Lover) most often work is done with eyes open, allowing a "real time" interaction with the environment and others.

Once participants are in place, the leader begins the Archetype Journey, a narrative that serves as the guide for the participant, who embodies the story simultaneously with its telling. It is in the early moments of the Journey that the archetype is named and described. While some leaders may introduce the name and characteristics of the archetype at the beginning of a session, experience has repeatedly shown that students tend to enjoy the "reveal," reporting that it allows them to experience the preparation more freely and to begin the Journey without expectation or judgment. It is this freedom from expectation that is a hallmark of the work, akin to what children may experience as they pretend and role-play in the yard, in their rooms, or on the playground.

Most of the Journey narratives developed thus far are contained in the book *Acting and Singing with Archetypes*. Originally conceived by Frankie Armstrong (who leads archetype journeys without the aid of notes or prompts), they were shaped and written in collaboration with Janet Rodgers. The narratives are read aloud or spoken from memory by the leader, who usually stays in one place in the room, often using a music stand as a convenient anchor for notes and prompts. Some leaders use recordings of curated music to support or feed the narrative, with ready access to controls for on/off and volume. The language of each journey is simple and direct, most frequently linear, and deliberately rather formal in the style of an ancient tale or legend.

During the Journey, participants are directed to move and to vocalize; sometimes they are given prompts to perform tasks, to enter the storytelling themselves. Depending on the details of the Journey, participants may interact with one another, or work alone and simultaneously with the group.

All of this happens simultaneously with the leader's narration and instruction. From time to time, the leader may use the rattle (or drum or bell) to pause, to side-coach, or to re-direct. Some journeys are quite vigorous, some quiet; the ending is guided by the leader and followed with a period (usually 1–2 minutes) of silence, usually with eyes closed.

At this point, the session may go in one of several directions. The leader may choose to initiate stepping out, allowing participants to shift immediately into "de-role" mode, then perhaps moving into a discussion of what just transpired in the Journey.

Often, it is useful to stay "in-role" for a while longer, especially if a tandem activity such as writing or drawing is to be part of the session. In that case, participants are instructed to get their notebooks/journals (or the leader may provide writing or drawing materials) and a period of writing/drawing ensues; 5 to 15 minutes seems to be the optimum amount of time for this. Participants may wish to record details of their experience, or they may wish to allow the relaxed creative state induced by the session to fuel their expression on paper in other ways, through poetry/prose or drawing. Students often share vivid and surprising writing samples and drawings produced during this period.

If writing/drawing is pursued, the stepping out will occur afterward. This may be done individually (as participants finish their writing/drawing) or as a group. After the step out, it is useful to have a group discussion about the session just completed. The group generally comes into a circle for this, sitting on the floor or in chairs.

Group discussions often benefit by beginning with the exercise "Popcorn" (from the work of Dr. Tawnya Pettiford-Wates' Conciliation Project) as participants are invited to toss a single descriptive word into the circle by speaking it aloud: ideas, images, or feelings sparked by the session that just occurred. Students are encouraged to fully share these words, really hear one another, and fully articulate themselves. This helps what may still be private—the experience of the Journey, which may be quite profound—become more public. After a period of "Popcorn," which may last for several minutes, single words begin to naturally give way to phrases, then sentences, and the discussion may continue freely for as long as the leader and group may wish. Depending upon the makeup of the group, the discussion may extend into questions of application, specific theatrical roles, or other areas.

Observers and participants alike often comment on the efficiency of the archetype work in accessing full vocal and physical expression without hesitation or fear. Participants tend to engage whole-heartedly, and old habits frequently are bypassed as full engagement in the work requires that one listen and act impulsively within the parameters of the Archetypal Journey. Performers at all levels are sometimes surprised by the energy and truth of expression that the exuberant freedom of the archetype work often allows. As one participant described the work "it has been a defibrillator for my creative spirit."

Goals of the Organization

The founders and certified teachers of Acting and Singing with Archetypes are designing a path forward for the continued development of this extremely efficient, highly effective performance pedagogy. Our goal is twofold: 1) increase the physical strengths, vocal abilities, and creative potential of performers through the training method presented in established archetypal journeys, and 2) grow the organization through an expanded web presence, fostered intra-organizational dialogue, and an ongoing exploration of "new" archetype journeys as complementing performance training tools.

Certification Process

A process of certification was created for Acting and Singing with Archetypes to assist in providing evidence of additional training and expertise particularly for university positions. This is offered to serve the profession and to continue the development and dissemination of this work.

To qualify for certification, one must have completed a one week Acting and Singing with Archetypes intensive taught by Janet, Frankie or a certified teacher. In some exceptions, comparable learning experience with the work may fulfill this requirement. Applicants must have had practice leading archetypal journeys based on the descriptions in the book, *Acting and Singing with Archetypes*.

Certification requires a teaching observation adjudicated by Janet, Frankie, or a certified instructor. During an observation of two or three journeys, a teacher will be evaluated on the successful creation of "structured freedom" in a safe environment by setting out the guidelines included in the book while encouraging free expression. The introduction will include a brief history of the work and answer the question "What is an archetype?" Teaching the "stepping out" process and taking the group into application using monologues, songs, or poems are also part of the observation.

Criteria necessary for achieving certification includes the ability to develop an atmosphere for participants which avoids judgment; right and wrong evaluations as well as good and bad comments are not conducive to the work. How the leader uses the voice with sufficient energy and variation to embrace the qualities of story-teller will be evaluated along with the ability to lead the group from beginning to end of the imaginative Journey. Effective pacing will be observed as leaders encourage participants to surrender to the event by allowing time for digestion, discussion, journaling, and stepping out as a methodology to remove the remnants of the archetypal explorations.

Guiding post-journey reflection and discussion as it relates to the artistic process as well as handling possible emotional reactions that might arise are additional skills required for certification. A leader's ability to connect the work through application to dramatic text and/or song as an actor's tool will be observed. An understanding of the multicultural basis for each archetype and a clear concept of the distinction between archetypes and stereotypes is essential; an awareness of the differences between archetypes of myths and legends and contemporary archetypes is also necessary for certification.

Contact Information

Visit the website www.actingandsingingwitharchetypes.org to learn more about this performance pedagogy and to find contact information for the founders and certified teachers.

Disclosure statement

No potential conflict of interest was reported by the authors.

References

Armstrong, Frankie. n.d. "Home Page." http://frankiearmstrong.com
Bloch, Susana. 2017. "About Page." https://www.albatechnique.com
Rodgers, Janet. 2015. "Home Page." http://janetrodgers.com/about/
Rodgers, Janet, and Frankie Armstrong. 2009. *Acting and Singing with Archetypes*. Milwaukee, WI: Limelight Editions.

Index

accents 54, 56–61, 82–86, 108
Acting and Singing with Archetypes 161;
    certification process 161–162; founders 158–159;
    goals 161; history 158; overview 157–158
acting teachers 89–90, 140, 147
actors 4–5, 7–11, 13–14, 16, 18, 20, 23–31, 54–61,
    82–85, 88–96, 106–112, 138–139, 141–147,
    149, 151
Aikin, W. A. 5–6
Alexander, F. Matthias 14
apprenticeship 75, 79, 95
archetypes 136, 157–162
Armstrong, Frankie 157–158, 160
articulation 6–7, 15, 19, 50, 57, 59, 135, 153
artistry 50, 64
attention blueprint 92–93, 96
awareness 18–19, 36–39, 46–47, 49, 54, 57, 59,
    123–124, 129, 132, 134–135, 149, 152–153

Berry, Cicely 4–5, 7–9, 11, 22, 35, 98; and central
    tradition 8; and RSC 9–11
bodymind 42, 45–49
body NRGs 48, 50
breath 5–7, 10, 14–19, 25, 34, 36–38, 47–48,
    90–93, 95, 97–104, 117, 123–130, 132, 134–135,
    146; awareness 48, 127, 129–130; cycle 102, 118;
    experiences 99, 101, 104; movement 98–103;
    spaces 101–102, 104; support 107, 118
breathing capacity 19
breathwork 123–125, 127
Breathwork Africa 2, 123–125, 129–130; birth of
    124–125; founder 125; goals, certification, and
    contact 130; key features 125–126; teaching
    style 129–130

center note 7
Central School Tradition 2, 4
certification process 39–40, 59–60, 66, 68, 78–79,
    95–96, 113, 121–122, 161–162
certification program 2, 40, 43, 61–62, 68
certified teachers 39, 41, 60, 149, 161
conscious breathing 123–126, 128
consonant NRG 46, 50

consultant 35, 108–109, 117
Cooke, Sonya 140–141, 147

diamonologue 144–145

embodiment 20, 55, 80, 99, 127
emotional life 95, 138–139, 144
emotional states 16, 48, 144
emotions 13–14, 16–17, 20, 25, 28–29, 37–38, 48,
    129, 132–133, 135, 139, 144, 146
E-motivated breathing 48
English-speaking teacher training 21
Estill, Josephine Antoinette Vadala 64–67
Estill Voice Model 65–66, 68
Estill Voice Training® (EVT): certification process
    68; history 65–66; key features 66–67; overview
    64–65

Fitzmaurice, Catherine 34–36, 55, 107
Fitzmaurice Voicework 34–36, 39–41, 55;
    applications of 38–39; destructuring
    36–37; goals 40; history 35; key features
    of 36; overview 34–35; presence work 38;
    restructuring 37–38; teacher certification 40;
    teaching style 39
flexible pitch range 7
Fogerty, Elsie 4–5, 35, 37
Friedlander, Claudia 152

gestures 73, 75, 99, 132–136
Granville, J. Mortimer 148

Hart, Roy 70, 72–76, 78, 107
Hartstein, Reuben see Hart, Roy

intelligibility 55, 58, 60
intercostal-diaphragmatic breathing 6

Janov, Arthur 71

Knight, Dudley 41, 54–56, 59–60, 62
Knight-Thompson Speechwork (KTS) 54–60,
    62; "accent" or "dialect 58–59, 61; certification

164 INDEX

process 59–60; certification program 61–62; developmental 56; experiencing accents 61; experiencing speech 60; history 54; overview 54; phonetics intensive 60–61; playful approach 57; primary guiding principle 56; rigorous and systematic understanding, human speech 57; skillful 58; sociolinguistically aware 57–58

Lessac, Arthur 42–43
Lessac-certified trainers 43–44, 51
Lessac Kinesensics (LK) 42–46, 49–52; as embodied pedagogy 45–46; founder of 42–43; overview 42; teaching style 46–47
Lessac master teacher 51
Lessac practitioners 44, 51
Lessac Training and Research Institute® 42–45, 50–51
Ley, David 148, 150
Linklater Voice Method 13–15; exercises 18–20; History of 13; key features 16–18; overview 15; process 15–16
LoVetri, Jeannette 114–116

Maines, Rachel P. 148
Manga, Ela 125
Middendorf, Ilse 97–99
Middendorf Breathwork 2, 97, 99, 104; breath cycle 102; breath spaces 101; exercises 103–104; foundational principle 100; history 98–99; overview 99–100; principles and key features 100; teaching/learning 102–103; training 104; voice pedagogy based 97–105
Miller Voice Method (MVM) 88–92, 94–95; active breath 92; athletic event, acting 93; attention blueprint 92–93; certification process 95–96; creation 90–91; goals 94–95; history and founder 89–90; key features 92; on-camera integration 94; overview 88–89; teaching style and philosophy, work 91; text analysis and memorization 94
Moore, Harry 8
mystery 80, 98, 129, 133, 135

nasal resonance 19
NRGs 46, 48, 50

Patsy Rodenburg Master Teacher Certification Program 30–31
phonetics 51, 55–56, 59–61, 82
physical awareness 18–19
pneumanity 125–126
posture 5, 59, 102, 111, 118, 120, 158, 160
primal scream 71
professional actors 8, 82, 146–147
pronunciation 57–59, 61, 85
prosody 16, 59

relaxer-energizers 46, 48–50
resonating ladder 19
rhoticity 85
rib-reserve breathing 6, 9
Rodenburg, Patsy 5, 22–28
Rodenburg method 22; connection and power 26–27; craft of voice 25–26; focus of work 30–31; key features 24–25; overview 22; Shakespeare and 29; teacher certification 31–32; teaching style 29–30; technical exercises 28–29; text work 27; troubleshoot for habits 26
Royal Central School of Speech and Drama 4, 11, 35, 82
Royal Shakespeare Company (RSC) 8–10
Roy Hart International Artistic Centre (CAIRH) 74–75, 77–79
Roy Hart theatre 70, 73–78
Roy Hart tradition 2, 70, 74–77, 80; apprenticeship 79; certification process 78; history and founders 71–72; key features 75; overview 70; teaching style 75–77

safety 29, 89, 91, 102–103, 112, 126–127, 159
Sankofa 126, 129
Seven Pillars Acting Technique 138–147; founder 140; goals 146–147; history of 139–140; key features 141; overview 138–139; teacher certification process 147; teaching style 145–146
shaking medicine 127
Sharpe/Haydn Method 82–86; foundation 84; groove 85; rhoticity 85; seeing, feeling, and hearing 83; styles 83; vowel shapes 85
singing 5, 10, 20, 38, 41, 43, 46, 65–66, 71, 115–122, 152–153, 157–158, 160–161
singing teachers 153
sinus resonance 19
skull resonance 19
Smith, D'Arcy 106, 108
Smith, W. Stephen 20
Somatic Voicework™ The LoVetri Method 114–122; certification process 121–122; exercises and teaching style 119–121; founder 116–117; goals 121; history 115–116; key features 117–119; terminology 119
"Sound & Movement" 20
speech 4–6, 11, 14–17, 20, 22, 24–26, 28–31, 35, 46, 54–59, 67, 89–90, 94, 108–109, 132–134; skills 55, 83; sounds 5, 58–59, 61; training 4, 17, 54–55, 57–58
Steiner, Rudolf 132–133
Steiner Speech 2, 132–133; key features 133–136; philosophical overview of 133; training 132
Stern, David Alan 84
Stewart, Eric 153
structural NRGs 46, 49–50

INDEX

teacher training 21, 95, 113, 153
teaching style 29–30, 39, 46–47, 75, 77, 91, 98, 110, 119, 129–130, 145–146
technical exercises 25, 28–29
text transfusion 94, 96
text work 7, 10, 20, 27, 77, 145
Thompson, Philip 54, 59
tonal NRG 46, 49
tone 5–7, 17, 49–50, 66–67, 84, 132, 142
training 4–6, 8–9, 14, 43–44, 54–55, 64, 67–68, 70–71, 75, 89–91, 94–96, 98–99, 104, 106, 108–112, 124, 139–140, 146–147, 149–150, 154–155
transparency 20, 91, 95
Tutu, Archbishop Emeritus Desmond 128

Ubuntu 128

Vibrant Voice Technique (VVT) 148–155; executive coach 152; exercises 151; founder 150; goals 154–155; history of 148–149; impetus for 149; instructors experiences 152; official instructor training and online course 155; singing teachers 152–153; theatre professor 153–154; work, growing 150–151; yoga teacher trainer 153
vocal archetypes 157, 159; vocal archetypes work session 159–161
Vocal Combat Technique (VCT) 2, 106–113; certification process 113; consent 110;

consultants 108–109; empowering performer 110–111; founder 108; goals 112; history 106–108; holistic approach 111; key features 109; multiple approaches 112; overview 106; pillars of 110; screams 111; target practice 109–110; teaching style 110
vocal communication 16, 99
vocal fitness 109–112
vocal folds 15, 37, 117–118, 149, 151
vocal mechanics/effects 109
vocal NRGs 46–47, 49
vocal training 2, 46, 67, 155
voice: effects 111; pedagogy 97, 99, 104, 106; qualities 64–68, 149; teachers 4–7, 11, 17, 23, 30–31, 34, 66, 83, 89, 95, 99, 104, 122; training 2, 8, 13, 16, 35, 109, 148, 153–154; work 9, 14–16, 18, 25, 67, 78, 94, 99, 107, 153–154; workshop 23–24, 122, 150

Warren, Iris 13, 16, 19
Wells, John C. 85
wholeness 97–99, 128, 132, 135
Wolfsohn, Alfred 70–72, 75, 78
word formation 7
workshops 11, 41, 44–45, 52, 55–56, 59–62, 74–75, 77–79, 107–110, 112, 115, 149, 151

Zadek, Peter 71